EMISSIONS TRADING SCHEMES UNDER INTERNATIONAL ECONOMIC LAW

INTERNATIONAL ECONOMIC LAW

Andrew D Mitchell is Professor at Melbourne Law School, The University of Melbourne

Tania Voon is Professor at Melbourne Law School, The University of Melbourne

The *International Economic Law* series, established by the late Professor John H Jackson, addresses a range of issues in international economic law, which includes international trade law, international investment law, and the global financial order. The Series aims to encourage interest in the broad contours of international economic law, heightening awareness of its significance across the globe as well as its continuous interactions with other areas. The Series Editors encourage quality submissions from a wide range of perspectives, including doctrinal, theoretical, empirical, and interdisciplinary. Novel and cutting edge research is particularly welcome, as are contributions from both emerging and established scholars from around the world.

ALSO PUBLISHED IN THIS SERIES

The Trade Policy Review Mechanism
A Critical Analysis
Mathias Kende

Mega-Regional Trade Agreements: CETA, TTIP, and TiSA
New Orientations for EU External Economic Relations
Edited by Stefan Griller, Walter Obwexer, and Erich Vranes

Small and Medium-Sized Enterprises in International Economic Law
Edited by Thilo Rensmann

Domestic Law in International Investment Arbitration
Jarrod Hepburn

Treaty Shopping in International Investment Law
Jorun Baumgartner

Good Faith and International Economic Law
Edited by Andrew D Mitchell, M Sornarajah, and Tania Voon

Development at the WTO
Sonia E Rolland

The BRIC States and Outward Foreign Direct Investment
David Collins

Emissions Trading Schemes under International Economic Law

JAMES MUNRO

OXFORD
UNIVERSITY PRESS

OXFORD
UNIVERSITY PRESS

Great Clarendon Street, Oxford, OX2 6DP,
United Kingdom

Oxford University Press is a department of the University of Oxford. It furthers the University's objective of excellence in research, scholarship, and education by publishing worldwide. Oxford is a registered trade mark of Oxford University Press in the UK and in certain other countries

First Edition published in 2018

Published in the United States of America by Oxford University Press
198 Madison Avenue, New York, NY 10016, United States of America

British Library Cataloguing in Publication Data
Data available

Library of Congress Control Number: 2018942482

ISBN 978–0–19–882870–9

Foreword

Emissions trading continues to develop rapidly at both the domestic and international levels.

Negotiations on the rules and framework for Article 6 of the Paris Agreement are ongoing and scheduled to conclude at the end of 2018. The draft negotiating texts prepared by the co-chairs (March 2018) reveal a number of areas of potential relevance to international economic law and, therefore, to this book.

On the one hand, some positions reflected in the draft texts appear to indicate a desire for compatibility with international economic law through proposed principles of 'Participating Parties to avoid unilateral measures that constitute a means of arbitrary or unjustifiable discrimination or a disguised restriction on international trade' and 'Participating Parties to avoid unilateral measures and discriminatory practices in such cooperative approaches'. These principles appear to be advocated most especially by the Arab Group, which argues for '[i]nclusive participation on a voluntary basis by all Parties to Paris Agreement and all types of NDCs, and *no discrimination* to activities', as well as Ecuador on behalf of the Like Minded Developing Countries Group ('facilitate access for the potential participation of small and medium projects and initiatives, in a voluntary and *non-discriminatory manner*'), and Brazil ('Mitigation outcomes transferred under 6.2 must, moreover, be *fully comparable and fungible* with emission reductions monitored, verified and certified under Article 6.4'). These concepts flow from Article 3.5 of the United Nations Framework Convention on Climate Change (UNFCCC), which provides that '[m]easures taken to combat climate change, including unilateral ones, should not constitute a means of arbitrary or unjustifiable discrimination or a disguised restriction on international trade'.

On the other hand, there are elements of the draft negotiating texts that would prove problematic for international economic law. For instance, there are proposals for a range of quantitative restrictions on trade in carbon units. These include quantitative restrictions on the amounts of carbon units sourced from other countries that a country may use for complying with its mitigation commitment under the Paris Agreement (covering both other countries' allowance units as well as offset units generated under Article 6.4 of the Paris Agreement). Such restrictions flow from the principle of supplementarity, according to which countries should not outsource emissions reductions to third countries. Rather, reductions should principally occur domestically, with the purchase of carbon units from other countries only 'supplemental' to that domestic action. Such rules could lead to import restrictions on, or discrimination against, international carbon units, as well as domestic content requirements in respect of domestic carbon units. Such measures would, of course, raise questions under international economic law. Proposed quantitative restrictions on the banking of carbon units and carry-over could also raise questions, albeit less obviously.

The negotiating texts also link the creation and trade of carbon units to concepts of human rights, sustainable development, and price stability. Other proposals would prohibit secondary trading of carbon units through financial products such as derivatives, futures, or options. It is not difficult to conceive of such proposals leading to restrictions on international trade in carbon units unrelated to the primary goal of reducing emissions.

The concept of an 'exchange rate' or 'discount rate' as between different countries' emissions trading schemes—whereby the units of some countries would be subject to certain deductions or discounts—would likely lead to direct forms of discrimination against adversely affected units. The Environmental Integrity Group (comprising Liechtenstein, Mexico, Monaco, and Switzerland) advocates such a concept to account for alleged differences in the environmental 'worth' of different countries' carbon units. Thailand argues against such a concept, instead contending that minimum agreed international standards should suffice to demonstrate the environmental worth of all carbon units. New Zealand accepts there should be international minimum standards, but argues that discrimination should be permitted on the basis of higher environmental standards that individual countries choose to apply.

It remains to be seen which—if any—of these concepts and proposals survive the process of negotiations. The requirement for consensus in the UNFCCC system would suggest that the more extreme or prescriptive ideas would be tempered or discarded. Even if agreed to by consensus in the UNFCCC system, these kinds of rules and principles in the international climate regime would not be exempt from international economic law. The fact that they reflect internationally agreed standards would serve, at most, as evidence that they pursue legitimate objectives and are not necessarily unjustified or arbitrary, thus justified under an exception under international economic law. They would not provide a legal defence in any direct sense for a measure that otherwise violates international economic law.

Series Editors' Preface

The first preamble to the *United Nations Framework Convention on Climate Change* aptly describes climate change as a 'common concern of humankind'. Since that Convention was concluded in 1992, the significance of this global environmental problem has only intensified, along with the need for well-tailored policy solutions to lower greenhouse gas emissions. Market-based mechanisms, which seek to achieve environmental outcomes in the most cost- and resource-efficient manner, have become increasingly important in the effort to mitigate climate change.

Just a few years ago, emissions trading schemes ('ETSs') may have seemed out of favour as a tool of climate policy, with Australia scrapping its carbon-pricing scheme after only three years in operation, and the European Union ('EU') scheme experiencing a significant collapse in the price of units. However, as James Munro notes in this book, ETSs are back at the forefront of the international effort to address climate change. China announced in 2017 that it will join its various existing carbon pricing schemes into one national market, and over 80 countries have stated that they will use international carbon markets as part of their efforts to fulfil their commitments under the 2015 *Paris Agreement*. In light of these recent developments, Munro's systematic evaluation of the ways in which international economic law directly governs ETSs is particularly timely and relevant.

Munro provides a nuanced analysis of different forms of ETS and relevant disciplines of international economic law, including rules relating to trade in goods, services, financial services, and the protection of foreign investments. After concluding that a number of these disciplines could apply to certain models of ETS, Munro analyses the design of several existing schemes and finds many features that potentially violate core rules of international economic law, such as non-discrimination obligations or prohibitions on local content requirements. This volume reflects both Munro's expertise, which includes working for the World Trade Organization ('WTO') and advising the Australian government on matters of international economic law, and his practical, doctrinal approach to scholarship. The insights offered are of value to both practitioners and scholars of international economic law, as well as policy-makers designing and implementing ETSs and other market-based mechanisms to address environmental issues.

Often, scholarship considering how international economic law relates to the environment or influences environmental regulation responds to prominent disputes or conflicts that have already arisen in practice. To date, no dispute has been brought to the WTO or before an investment treaty tribunal regarding an ETS, although challenges to the inclusion of emissions from international aviation within the EU ETS were threatened (but ultimately abandoned when the EU decided to limit the scheme to flights within Europe). However, the potential for such disputes is real, given the current and potential future value of investment in carbon markets, and the fact that units are likely to be increasingly traded across international borders.

A recent avalanche of investment treaty disputes relates to the renewable energy sector, particularly against Spain, Italy, and other European countries for modifications to promised feed-in tariffs or other incentives for investment, while several WTO disputes concern alleged subsidies for renewables technology. These cases demonstrate the importance of certainty and predictability in market regulation, as well as the willingness of states and private entities to make use of mechanisms under international economic law to raise disputes regarding climate-related measures. If policy-makers heed Munro's prescient advice in this book to develop or adapt their ETSs to comply with the rules of international economic law, they will minimise the likelihood of successful future challenges in the WTO dispute settlement system or under an international investment agreement.

Andrew D Mitchell
Tania Voon
June 2018

Acknowledgements

I am extremely grateful for the wisdom, guidance, and patience of the two supervisors of this thesis that led to this book, Prof Andrew Mitchell and Assoc Prof Margaret Young. The comments and feedback of Prof Tania Voon have also been especially valuable. And particular gratitude to Rachel and Chloe for sanity-maintenance, and the support of my parents throughout this project.

Table of Contents

1
Introduction

This book addresses whether and how emissions trading schemes to mitigate climate change are subject to the network of treaties comprising the international trade and investment regime, collectively referred to as international economic law.

Emissions trading schemes are the future of climate mitigation policy. The announcement by China that it will implement a nationwide emissions trading scheme in the coming years confirms the status of this instrument as the pre-eminent policy choice for mitigating climate change. China will join the existing sixty-seven national and subnational carbon pricing schemes, whose markets the World Bank valued at US$52 billion in 2017,[1] as well as the 111 countries involved in generating and selling carbon units into those schemes.[2] China's announcement places setbacks such as the price collapse in the European Union's scheme, the repeal of Australia's scheme, and the failure of the United States to legislate for a national scheme firmly in the past.

The core activity of these schemes is *trade* and *investment* in carbon units. These units represent the right to emit one tonne of greenhouse gas. And yet, there is no clarity as to whether or how trade and investment in carbon units is subject to international economic law. Not only have past analyses tended to be cursory,[3] but they also rest on flawed assumptions, such as that only tangible items may qualify as 'goods', or that carbon units are purely domestic regulatory creations.

The question of whether and how emissions trading schemes are covered by international economic law is particularly acute at the present juncture for three reasons. First, carbon units—the object of trade and investment in these schemes—have evolved into objects of *international* trade and investment. This is through the development in recent years of ad hoc linking arrangements to facilitate the trade and use of units between the emissions trading schemes of two or more jurisdictions, as well

[1] World Bank, Ecofys, and Vivid Economics, *State and Trends of Carbon Pricing 2017* (World Bank 2017) 24–26. The World Bank classifies 24 of these as emissions trading schemes: see n 43.

[2] This includes the number of developing countries engaged in the Clean Development Mechanism. The figure may be higher, taking into account domestic offset programmes. See Executive Board of the Clean Development Mechanism, 'Annual report of the Executive Board of the clean development mechanism to the Conference of the Parties serving as the meeting of the Parties to the Kyoto Protocol' (19 October 2017) FCCC/KP/CMP/2017/5, [9].

[3] More substantive analyses include Felicity Deane, *Emissions Trading and WTO Law* (Edward Elgar Publishing 2015) and Erich Vranes, 'Climate Change and the WTO: EU Emission Trading and the WTO Disciplines on Trade in Goods, Services and Investment Protection' (2009) 43 *Journal of World Trade* 707. These analyses are engaged where relevant in subsequent sections.

as through the rapidly evolving architecture for international emissions trading originally provided for in the Kyoto Protocol and, more recently, the Paris Agreement.[4] Thus, carbon units cannot simply be viewed as regulatory instruments tied to a particular domestic scheme. Rather, through these developments, they are transforming into objects of international trade and investment. That notwithstanding, there is no consensus as to whether they have concomitantly transformed into objects that fall within the purview of international economic law.

Secondly, a real and growing commercial interest has developed in policies concerning climate mitigation, and with it, interstate and investor-state litigation over domestic climate measures has rapidly increased. Investors and governments have, in recent years, shown a distinct willingness to litigate the climate measures of other governments, and there is no reason to assume that emissions trading schemes—with huge and growing markets—will be immune.[5] Thus, the question of whether emissions trading schemes are actually covered by international economic law is a key threshold issue.

Finally, and relatedly, most emissions trading schemes restrict trade and investment in carbon units in qualitative and quantitative terms, and impose local content requirements concerning their use. Such aspects of emissions trading schemes curtail market access for carbon units originating in other countries, while potentially harming investments. These aspects are, on their face, contrary to the basic tenets of the international economic regime, such as non-discriminatory market access and the free flows of goods, services, and capital across borders. Thus, the prospect of interstate and investor-state litigation over emissions trading schemes is real. Understanding how international economic law applies to emissions trading schemes, and the circumstances in which prima facie violations could be justified and defended, is important to providing certainty to market participants and policymakers as they both design emissions trading schemes, as well as seek market access and investment opportunities for their own carbon units.

The confluence of these factors—the evolution of carbon units into objects of international trade and investment; the emergence of interstate and investor-state litigation over climate measures; and the propensity of emissions trading schemes to violate norms of international economic law—demonstrates the importance of resolving whether and how emissions trading schemes are subject to the disciplines of international economic law. This is underscored by the fact that emissions trading

[4] See Kyoto Protocol to the United Nations Framework Convention on Climate Change (opened for signature 11 December 1997, entered into force 16 February 2005) 2303 UNTS 148 art 17; Paris Agreement (opened for signature 22 April 2016, entered into force 4 November 2016) arts 6.2 and 6.3. The extent to which links between different emissions trading schemes will be facilitated or administered by specialized infrastructure and modalities under the Paris Agreement remains to be seen.

[5] As recent examples see *Eiser Infrastructure Limited and Energía Solar Luxembourg S.à r.l. v Kingdom of Spain (Final Award)* (ICSID Arbitral Tribunal, Case No ARB/13/36, 4 May 2017); *Windstream Energy LLC v Government of Canada (Award)* (Permanent Court of Arbitration, UNCITRAL Rules, 27 September 2016); Appellate Body Reports, *Canada—Renewable Energy/Canada—Feed-in Tariff Program; India—Solar Cells.*

schemes will soon be operational in jurisdictions covering almost half the world's economy, and that the US$52 billion value of existing markets is set to grow rapidly.[6]

The question addressed by this book is whether and how emissions trading schemes are subject to international economic law. In particular, it considers the *direct* engagement between emissions trading schemes and international economic law, namely the extent to which international economic law governs the actual objects traded within emissions trading schemes and the global carbon market: 'carbon units' (also known as emissions permits, carbon credits, and emissions allowances).[7] As mentioned above, these units represent the right to emit one tonne of greenhouse gas.

In broad terms, international economic law applies to four categories: (i) 'goods'/'products' under the General Agreement on Tariffs and Trade 1994 (GATT 1994)[8] and free trade agreements covering goods; (ii) 'services' under the General Agreement on Trade in Services (GATS)[9] and free trade agreements covering services; (iii) 'financial services' under the GATS Annex on Financial Services and free trade agreements covering financial services;[10] and (iv) 'investments' under international investment agreements (IIAs).[11] Therefore, the first step is to assess whether carbon units fall within any of these categories. This step is important not only in determining whether trade and investment in carbon units are governed by international economic law, but also in identifying which norms of international economic law apply. This is because the norms applicable to these four categories (ie 'goods'/'products', 'services', 'financial services', and 'investments') are contained in different instruments and are not necessarily uniform. The second step is to evaluate the particular attributes of emissions trading schemes that are inconsistent with these norms, and to identify possible exceptions or defences that might justify such inconsistencies.

The approach taken in this analysis is therefore twofold. It involves an initial process of treaty interpretation to determine the scope and content of relevant aspects of international economic law. This is followed by a subsequent process of applying the resulting interpretations to carbon units and the aspects of emissions trading

[6] World Bank, Ecofys, and Vivid Economics, (n 1) 24–32 (this figure includes carbon taxes, some of which are operated through the mandatory purchase and surrender of carbon units).

[7] See further Javier de Cendra de Larragan, 'Emissions trading schemes and WTO law: a typology of interactions' in Geert Van Calster and Denise Prevost (eds), *Research Handbook on Environment, Health and the WTO* (Edward Elgar Publishing 2013) 636, 638, and 647; Harro van Asselt, *The Fragmentation of Global Climate Governance* (Edward Elgar Publishing 2014) 167–70.

[8] Marrakesh Agreement Establishing the World Trade Organization (opened for signature 15 April 1994, entered into force 1 January 1995) 1867 UNTS 3 annex IA (General Agreement on Tariffs and Trade) (GATT 1994). Other instruments in annex 1A of the WTO Agreement cover 'goods'/'products', such as the TBT Agreement and SPS Agreement—these are, however, largely outside the purview of this book, which instead focuses on the principal instrument governing trade in goods. These other instruments are, in large part, elaborations or extensions on the disciplines contained in GATT 1994.

[9] Marrakesh Agreement Establishing the World Trade Organization (n 8) annex IB (General Agreement on Trade in Services) (GATS).

[10] The Annex on Financial Services is attached to GATS (n 9).

[11] For the purposes of this analysis, IIAs cover bilateral and plurilateral investment treaties, as well as bilateral and plurilateral free trade agreements containing an investment chapter.

schemes that affect their trade and investment in ways which attract the scrutiny of international economic law. The first facet of this approach requires a careful understanding of the rules and principles of treaty interpretation under international law. The second facet of this approach calls for a comprehensive appreciation of the nature of carbon units and the emissions trading schemes in which they are traded and invested. These aspects are addressed and elaborated upon in Part I, covering Chapters 2 and 3.

Part II, covering Chapters 4–7, then seeks to ascertain whether carbon units are subject to international economic law by evaluating whether they qualify as 'goods'/'products', 'services', 'financial services', and 'investments'. A key aspect in this regard, which is described in detail in Chapter 3, is the distinction between 'allowance' units and 'offset' units. These form the two principal categories of carbon units. Whereas allowance units are generated and distributed to the carbon market by the government or regulator administering an emissions trading scheme, offset units are largely generated and sold by private actors for commercial gain.

In respect of 'goods'/'products', Chapter 4 concludes that a strong argument can be made that 'carbon units' do qualify as 'products' and 'goods', although the lack of obvious 'production' involved in *allowance* units introduces some degree of uncertainty in that regard.

In respect of 'services', Chapter 5 concludes that, although measures affecting trade in *offset* units will likely be covered by GATS, measures affecting trade in *allowance* units would be unlikely to be covered—again, due to the lack of obvious economic activity involved in their production.

In respect of 'financial services', Chapter 6 finds that, although carbon units are unlikely to constitute 'negotiable instruments', 'transferable securities', or 'derivative products', they are nonetheless likely to be covered as either 'financial assets' or 'any service of a financial nature', thus subjecting the trade and supply of carbon units to GATS and its Annex on Financial Services.

In respect of 'investments', Chapter 7 concludes that carbon units are *capable* of constituting 'investments' where all parties to an IIA define the units as 'property' under their municipal law and where an investor acquired and owns the units with a requisite degree of durability and permanence related to some other economic activity in the host state. However, they would be less likely to qualify where one or more parties to an IIA confers no proprietary status on carbon units, or where the units are not acquired in the context of a meaningful economic activity in the host state.

Having determined that carbon units are, to varying extents, subject to international economic law, Part III assesses the consistency of emissions trading schemes and their rules affecting carbon units with that body of law. In particular, Chapter 8 identifies numerous prima facie breaches of international economic law embedded in the rules of most emissions trading schemes, including various qualitative and quantitative restrictions and local content requirements. Chapter 9 then considers the purported justifications for these prima facie breaches and assesses whether, if at all, such justifications could ground a defence using a policy-based exception, such as relating to the environment or prudential regulation.

The significance of carbon units being subject to the disciplines of international economic law should not be understated, particularly since the ability of governments to regulate trade and investment in carbon units would be materially diminished. Governments would be prevented from discriminating in favour of their own domestic carbon units or those of particular countries, their ability to impose export bans or import quotas would be constrained, there may be restrictions or prohibitions on the kinds of subsidies they could use, measures adversely affecting the value of carbon units might be impugned, and governments would be required to observe a series of other obligations, including on freedom of transit, fees and formalities, procedural fairness, the legitimate expectations of investors, and transparency.

Further, the potential for a government or investor to challenge a measure infringing these kinds of obligations under international economic law is by no means hypothetical. As mentioned, many countries and investors have a direct commercial interest in ensuring that their carbon units are afforded non-discriminatory market access and protection in other jurisdictions, and have argued for such treatment in United Nations climate negotiations and other fora.[12] Indeed, some offset programmes to generate carbon units, such as from forestry or land-related projects to reduce or remove emissions, have been premised on the assumption that those units would be able to be traded internationally into other countries' carbon markets.[13] It is thus a pertinent juncture for a comprehensive assessment of whether and how emissions trading schemes are regulated directly by international economic law.

[12] See eg UNFCCC Secretariat, 'Proposal from Papua New Guinea for amendments to the Kyoto Protocol' (17 June 2009) FCCC/KP/CMP/2009/13, 5 (New Article 21bis.5) (proposal to enshrine 'full access to global carbon markets' in a new forestry offsets mechanism); UNFCCC Secretariat, 'Ideas and proposals on the elements contained in paragraph 1 of the Bali Action Plan Submissions from Parties Addendum' (7 April 2009) FCCC/AWGLCA/2009/MISC.1/Add.4, 6 (proposal of 16 countries that forestry offsets 'be guaranteed direct market access, be fully fungible [with allowance units]', reconfirmed in their 2013 negotiation position in UNFCCC Secretariat, 'Views on a framework for various approaches' (7 May 2013) FCCC/SBSTA/2013/MISC.11, 6–8; Department of Climate Change and Energy Efficiency (DCCEE), *Carbon Farming Initiative Handbook* (Commonwealth of Australia 2012) 2 (Australian Government cultivating export markets for its offset units); UNFCCC Secretariat, 'Report on the workshop on the new market-based mechanism' (30 October 2013) FCCC/SBSTA/2013/INF.13, [23] (certain countries arguing for non-discriminatory treatment for offset units under a new UN mechanism); Emissions Trading Scheme Review Panel, *Doing New Zealand's Fair Share. Emissions Trading Scheme Review 2011: Final Report* (Ministry for the Environment 2011) [65]; UNFCCC Secretariat, 'Views on issues relating to modalities and procedures for applying the concept of additionality' (14 October 2013) FCCC/SBSTA/2013/MISC.19, 4–5 (China arguing that forestry offsets should be 'fully fungible in the carbon market under the Kyoto Protocol').

[13] See eg DCCEE (n 12) 2; UNFCCC Secretariat, 'Financing options for the full implementation of results based actions relating to the activities referred to in decision 1/CP.16, paragraph 70, including related modalities and procedures: Technical Paper' (26 July 2012) FCCC/TP/2012/3 [18]; Emissions Trading Scheme Review Panel (n 12) [65].

PART I

CONCEPTUAL FOUNDATIONS

2

Applying International Economic Law to Emissions Trading Schemes

Treaty Interpretation and the Paris Agreement

The process of treaty interpretation is a key aspect of the analysis undertaken in this book. The question of whether carbon units—and hence emissions trading schemes—are governed by international economic law depends principally on the proper interpretation of the terms 'goods'/'products', 'services', 'financial services', and 'investment' in the applicable instruments of international economic law, and whether such an interpretation is capable of extending to carbon units. Of particular salience in the context of climate change and carbon units is the extent to which the rights and obligations subsisting as part of the international climate regime may have a bearing on the process of interpretation in the international economic regime. This is because over eighty countries plan to engage in the international carbon market in fulfilment of their commitments under the Paris Agreement.[1]

Having set out in this chapter the process of treaty interpretation deployed in this book, Chapter 3 then addresses the nature and properties of carbon units and emissions trading schemes.

[1] World Bank, Ecofys, and Vivid Economics, *State and Trends of Carbon Pricing 2017* (World Bank 2017) 22.

A Vienna Convention on the Law of Treaties and Regime Interaction

At least at a high level of abstraction, the principles applicable to the interpretation of treaties are well settled in international law. They are chiefly reflected in Articles 31–33 of *the Vienna Convention on the Law of Treaties (Vienna Convention).*[2] At first instance, they call for a process of interpretation 'in accordance with the ordinary meaning to be given to the terms of the treaty in their context and in the light of its object and purpose'.[3] The following subsections give an overview of what is meant by the constituent elements of this process, namely, the 'ordinary meaning', the 'context', and the 'object and purpose'. As an initial matter, however, it is useful to note that the precise interaction between, and emphasis on, each of these constituent elements is less settled. For instance, some jurists emphasize teleological approaches that give primacy to the object and purpose of a treaty, whereas others take a strictly textual approach that focuses on the words used.[4] In this book, primacy is given to the approaches developed and deployed by the applicable adjudicatory bodies in the international economic regime, namely the Appellate Body of the World Trade Organization (WTO) in respect of the international trade regime, and investment tribunals in respect of the international investment regime.[5]

Before describing the nuances of the 'ordinary meaning', 'context', and 'object and purpose' in treaty interpretation, it is important to recognize that the objects evaluated by this book—carbon units—are, in fact, creatures of another regime in international law. In particular, they exist to enable the operation of emissions trading schemes, and are thus used as a tool to mitigate climate change.[6] Emissions trading schemes are adopted to attend to a matter that is the primary concern of the

[2] Ian Brownlie, *Principles of Public International Law* (6th edn, OUP 2003) 602–607; Isabelle Van Damme, *Treaty Interpretation by the WTO Appellate Body* (OUP 2009) 49–52.

[3] Vienna Convention on the Law of Treaties (opened for signature 23 May 1969, entered into force 27 January 1980) 1155 UNTS 331 art 31.1.

[4] See eg Brownlie (n 2) 602–07.

[5] While the international trade regime could be said to have developed a more coherent and consistent approach to treaty interpretation through harmonization by the Appellate Body (see Van Damme (n 2) 379–83), the approach to treaty interpretation in the international investment regime is, for various reasons, less harmonized and consistent. See eg J Romesh Weeramantry, *Treaty Interpretation in Investment Arbitration* (OUP 2012) 205–06; Michael Waibel, 'International Investment Law and Treaty Interpretation' in Rainer Hoffman and Christian J Tams (eds), *International Investment Law and General International Law: From Clinical Isolation to Systemic Integration?* (Nomos 2011) 29; Gabrielle Kaufmann-Kohler, 'Interpretation of Treaties: How Do Arbitral Tribunals Interpret Dispute Settlement Provisions Embodied in Investment Treaties?' in Loukas Mistelis and Julian Lew (eds), *Pervasive Problems in International Arbitration* (Kluwer 2006) 274–75. The divergent approaches in the international investment regime—for instance, as they relate to the interpretation of 'property' under international law—are canvassed at relevant stages in this book, where appropriate.

[6] Stefan E Weishaar, *Emissions Trading Design* (Edward Elgar Publishing 2014) 24–25, 41–42; Olivier Godard, *Domestic Transferable Permits for Environmental Management: Design and Implementation* (OECD 2001) 23–29; Theodore Panayotou, *Economic Instruments for Environmental Management and Sustainable Development* (Environmental Economics Series Paper No 16, United Nations Environment Program 1994) 13–15.

international climate regime. That regime is grounded in international law through the United Nations Framework Convention on Climate Change (UNFCCC),[7] the Kyoto Protocol,[8] and the Paris Agreement.[9] One of the key purposes of enacting emissions trading schemes, and thus stimulating trade and investment in carbon units, is to fulfil obligations to reduce or limit greenhouse gas emissions under those instruments.[10] The pertinence of the international climate regime to trade and investment in carbon units is underscored by the fact that a substantial proportion of the present trade in carbon units occurs through infrastructure set up and administered pursuant to the Kyoto Protocol, and much of the investment in certain kinds of carbon units is subject to approval by entities of the Kyoto Protocol.[11] It is currently envisaged that the Paris Agreement will administer and facilitate similar kinds of investment in carbon units, which may then be transacted between private actors or governments.[12]

This gives rise to an immediate question of regime interaction.[13] International regimes are 'sets of norms, decision-making procedures and organisations coalescing around functional issue-areas and dominated by particular modes of behavior, assumption and biases'.[14] The interaction between international regimes can involve synergies, such as shared principles and concepts,[15] or conflict, which the International Law Commission has described 'as a situation where two rules and principles suggest different ways of dealing with a problem'.[16] While the analysis in this book evaluates carbon units primarily through the lens of international economic law, the role of carbon units in fulfilling commitments made under another regime in international law calls for an understanding of the norms and principles of

[7] United Nations Framework Convention on Climate Change (UNFCCC) (opened for signature 9 May 1992, entered into force 21 March 1994) 1771 UNTS 107.

[8] Kyoto Protocol to the United Nations Framework Convention on Climate Change (opened for signature 11 December 1997, entered into force 16 February 2005) 2303 UNTS 148.

[9] Paris Agreement (opened for signature 22 April 2016, entered into force 4 November 2016).

[10] World Bank (n 1) 22. See eg *Climate Change Response Act 2002* (NZ) s 3.1; Directive 2003/87/EC of the European Parliament and of the Council of 13 October 2003 establishing a scheme for greenhouse gas emission allowance trading within the Community and amending Council Directive 96/61/EC [2003] OJ L275/32, recitals 3–5; Environment Quality Act (Quebec) s 46.6.4.

[11] That said, the market for offset units generated under the Kyoto Protocol is currently in a state of collapse (see Executive Board of the Clean Development Mechanism, 'Annual report of the Executive Board of the clean development mechanism to the Conference of the Parties serving as the meeting of the Parties to the Kyoto Protocol' (12 November 2015) FCCC/KP/CMP/2015/5, [7]–[13]; Joint Implementation Supervisory Committee, 'Annual report of the Joint Implementation Supervisory Committee to the Conference of the Parties serving as the meeting of the Parties to the Kyoto Protocol' (16 October 2015) FCCC/KP/CMP/2015/4, [8]–[10]).

[12] Paris Agreement (n 9) art 6.

[13] Harro van Asselt, *The Fragmentation of Global Climate Governance* (Edward Elgar Publishing 2014) 167–69.

[14] Margaret A Young, 'Introduction: The Productive Friction Between Regimes' in Margaret A Young (ed), *Regime Interaction in International Law: Facing Fragmentation* (CUP 2012) 11.

[15] Van Asselt (n 13) 55–57.

[16] ILC, 'Report of the International Law Commission on its Fifty-eighth Session (Fragmentation of International Law: Difficulties Arising from the Diversification and Expansion of International Law)' (13 April 2006) UN Doc A/CN.4/L.682, [25].

that regime. This is because the synergies or conflicts between the two regimes could potentially affect the process of interpreting whether carbon units constitute objects under international economic law and, equally, whether measures affecting their trade and investment constitute violations of international economic law.

The question of regime interaction is particularly pertinent to treaty interpretation in international economic law given the absence of tools in the WTO Agreement and many international investment agreements (IIAs) for managing conflicts with other regimes. For instance, there is a noticeable absence of conflict clauses or rules articulating a role for *lex specialis* or *lex posterior*.[17] Although some free trade agreements contain conflict clauses, these are often varied, ambiguous, and uncertain in application.[18] In any event, the notion of 'conflict' in WTO jurisprudence itself remains unsettled.

Thus, before assessing the ordinary tools of treaty interpretation that will be applied by the analysis undertaken in this book, the structure and norms of the international climate regime are evaluated, particularly insofar as that regime might, in turn, affect the interpretation of the instruments of international economic law.

B Overview of the International Climate Regime

As mentioned above, the international climate regime comprises three instruments under international law: the UNFCCC, the Kyoto Protocol, and the Paris Agreement. In broad terms, the international climate regime addresses both the *cause* of climate change through commitments on reducing or limiting greenhouse gas emissions,[19] and the *effects* of climate change through commitments on adaptation.[20] Commitments on the transfer of technology and provision of finance imbue both of these aspects.[21]

[17] See eg Appellate Body Report, *Peru—Agricultural Products*, [5.110]–[5.113] and fn 295. See also van Asselt (n 13) 64–71, 191–93; Graham Cook, *A Digest of WTO Jurisprudence on Public International Law Concepts and Principles* (CUP 2015) 60–61; Joost Pauwelyn, *Conflict of Norms in Public International Law: How WTO Law Relates to Other Rules of International Law* (CUP 2003) 315–23, 335–36, 343–45.

[18] See Andrew Mitchell and James Munro, 'State–State Dispute Settlement under the Trans-Pacific Partnership Agreement' in Tania Voon (ed), *Trade Liberalisation and International Co-operation: A Legal Analysis of the Trans-Pacific Partnership Agreement* (Edward Elgar Publishing 2014) 156, 159–65. It should be noted that some free trade agreements do address the international climate regime explicitly; see James Munro, 'Climate Change in the Trans-Pacific Partnership and Transatlantic Trade and Investment Partnership' in Panos Delimitas (ed), *Research Handbook on International Trade and Climate Change* (Routledge 2017) 394, 397–407. As the most prescriptive end of the spectrum, some free trade agreements bind their parties to the implementation of international climate obligations. Even such explicit provisions, however, do not shed light on the interpretative questions addressed in this book. As set out in section B, the international climate regime is far too general and non-prescriptive in terms of the manner of implementation to produce meaningful interventions in the characterization of carbon units for the purposes of international economic law.

[19] UNFCCC (n 7) arts 4.1 and 4.2; Kyoto Protocol (n 8) art 3.1; Paris Agreement (n 9) art 2.1(a) and 4.

[20] UNFCCC (n 7) art 4.1(b); Kyoto Protocol (n 8) art 10; Paris Agreement (n 9) art 2.1(b) and 7.

[21] UNFCCC (n 7) arts 4.4, 4.5, 4.7, 11; Kyoto Protocol (n 8) arts 10 and 11; Paris Agreement (n 9) arts 2.1(c), 9, 10, and 11.

Importantly, however, the commitments contained in the various instruments differ, and impose diverging norms and obligations on different sets of parties.

The UNFCCC is the foundational instrument of the international climate regime, setting out its core principles and objectives.[22] The 'ultimate' objective is to achieve the stabilization of greenhouse gas concentrations in the atmosphere at a level that would prevent dangerous anthropogenic interference with the climate system.[23] The principle of equity permeates the commitments it incorporates in order to achieve this objective.[24] This principle involves apportioning the burden and cost for mitigating and adapting to climate change based on the degree to which countries have caused the problem (measured both on an aggregate and a per capita basis),[25] the technical and financial capacity for countries to act to address the problem, the degree to which countries are affected by the problem, and the degree to which countries are capable of taking action while nonetheless being able to pursue economic development in a sustainable way.[26]

Equity is articulated in the text of the UNFCCC in a variety of ways. The norm of 'common but differentiated responsibilities' indicates that all countries have a responsibility to act in fulfilment of the ultimate objective of the UNFCCC, but the degree of responsibility varies for different countries or groups of countries.[27] The reference to 'respective capabilities and ... social and economic conditions' means that the degree of obligation to act depends on each country's individual circumstances, and the references to the 'largest share of historical and current global emissions' and differing levels of 'per capita emissions' reflect notions of historical responsibility for causing the problem.[28] The UNFCCC elaborates on various forms of differentiation, for instance the 'special difficulties' of countries that are 'particularly dependent on fossil fuel production, use and exportation', the 'special situations of the least developed countries', and 'that economic and social development and poverty eradication are the first and overriding priorities of the developing country Parties'.[29]

Equity is operationalized in the UNFCCC by categorizing countries into two principal subsets: Annex I countries, and non-Annex I countries.[30] Countries included in Annex I are the countries that, when the UNFCCC was negotiated in the early 1990s, represented the world's industrialized countries and those that had the highest historical and contemporaneous levels of emissions.[31] Thus, Annex

22 Farhana Yamin and Joanna Depledge, *The International Climate Change Regime: A Guide to Rules, Institutions and Procedures* (CUP 2004) 60–73.

23 UNFCCC (n 7) art 2.

24 Friedrich Soltau, *Fairness in International Climate Change Law and Policy* (CUP 2011) 190–93; Yamin and Depledge (n 22) 69–70; Tomilola Akanle Eni-Ibukun, *International Environmental Law and Distributive Justice: The Equitable Distribution of CDM Projects under the Kyoto Protocol* (Routledge 2013) 17–23.

25 See UNFCCC (n 7) preambular recital 3.

26 UNFCCC (n 7) arts 3 and 4.7.

27 See eg UNFCCC (n 7) arts 4.1, 4.2, and 4.7.

28 Soltau (n 24) 190–93.

29 See eg UNFCCC (n 7) arts 4.7 and 4.8.

30 Simone Schiele, *Evolution of International Environmental Regimes: The Case of Climate Change* (CUP 2014) 225.

31 Daniel Bodansky, 'The United Nations Framework Convention on Climate Change: A Commentary' (1993) 18 *Yale Journal of International Law* 451, 457, 505.

I countries are subject to more stringent obligations under the UNFCCC.[32] While non-Annex I countries are—like Annex I countries—required to '[f]ormulate, implement, publish and regularly update ... measures to mitigate climate change', the UNFCCC sets out less onerous reporting requirements and no specific targets in that regard, specifying that '[t]he extent to which developing country Parties will effectively implement their commitments under the Convention will depend on the effective implementation by developed country Parties of their commitments under the Convention related to financial resources and transfer of technology'.[33]

The manner in which equity is operationalized in the UNFCCC can aptly be characterized as a pragmatic compromise. Proposals to achieve common per capita levels of emissions and to include quantitative targets and timetables of emissions reductions by individual developed countries failed,[34] as did proposals for more specific commitments to be taken by developing countries.[35] Proposals for different or more nuanced ways of differentiating countries and the respective stringencies of obligations, such as through a category of 'newly industrializing countries', also failed, notwithstanding that it was generally understood that developing countries would become the main source of emissions.[36] Further, a proposal to subject the implementation of commitments, and the application of the precautionary principle, to the principle of 'cost-effectiveness' failed.[37] However, the principle of 'joint implementation'—which allows groups of countries to collectively reduce emissions by targeting the most cost effective sources of abatement within those groups—succeeded, notwithstanding the objection that this would be unethical by enabling developed countries to make reductions abroad instead of taking reducing emissions domestically.[38] Thus, while the text of the UNFCCC introduced certain indicative targets and gradations between particular sets of countries, it left unresolved how the burden for implementing its 'ultimate objective' should specifically be shared, over time, between particular countries. In other words, it left unresolved how the concept of 'equity' was to be applied, in practical terms, in the international climate regime.[39]

The Kyoto Protocol is different from the UNFCCC in a number of respects. In light of the apparent failure of the UNFCCC to stimulate meaningful action on climate change, the Kyoto Protocol took a more prescriptive approach that enshrines legally binding quantified targets and timetables for emissions reductions.[40] It additionally includes stringent accounting and reporting rules to monitor compliance with those targets and timetables.[41] Importantly, however, these quantified targets and timetables apply exclusively to Annex I countries. The Kyoto Protocol explicitly excludes additional commitments for non-Annex I countries.[42]

[32] UNFCCC (n 7) art 4.2. [33] UNFCCC (n 7) arts 4.1 and 4.7.

[34] See 'Negotiating text submitted by the Co-Chairmen of Working Group I on Principles' (18 September 1991) A/AC.237/WG.I/CRP.1/Rev.1; Bodansky (n 31) 498.

[35] Bodansky (n 31) 505–06. [36] ibid 506–07. [37] ibid 503–04.

[38] ibid 520–23. [39] ibid 508–09 and 512–14.

[40] Yamin and Depledge (n 22) 24; Lavanya Rajamani, 'The changing fortunes of differential treatment in the evolution of international environmental law' (2012) 88 *International Affairs* 605, 611–12.

[41] See Kyoto Protocol (n 8) arts 5, 7, and 8. [42] ibid art 10.

The principal mechanism for quantifying targets and measuring compliance under the Kyoto Protocol is to assign Annex I countries a specific amount of units, each corresponding to one tonne of greenhouse gas, which comprise the aggregate amount of greenhouse gas that each country may emit during the particular timetable.[43] By defining commitments in terms of divisible and quantifiable amounts, the Kyoto Protocol enables emissions trading between countries, such that Annex I countries can trade units amongst themselves in order to meet their obligations.[44]

Further, the Kyoto Protocol created a mechanism, the 'Clean Development Mechanism' (CDM), for non-Annex I countries to participate. In particular, so-called 'project activities' in non-Annex I countries resulting in certified reductions of greenhouse gas could be traded as divisible units, each representing one tonne of greenhouse gas, with Annex I countries.[45] These units can then be used by Annex I countries for compliance with their quantified targets under the Kyoto Protocol.[46]

While the ability for Annex I countries to acquire units from other Annex I and non-Annex I countries in order to source the most cost-effective means of abatement reflects the principle of 'joint implementation' in the UNFCCC, this principle is circumscribed in the Kyoto Protocol. In particular, it is subject to the rule that acquiring units from other countries 'shall be supplemental to domestic actions for the purpose of meeting quantified emission limitation and reduction commitments'.[47] In practical terms, this means that the primary source of emissions reductions by Annex I countries must be domestic.[48] However, the precise meaning of 'supplemental'—or what degree of emissions reductions must occur domestically—is not defined in quantitative terms under the Kyoto Protocol.[49]

The Kyoto Protocol furthers the equity-based distinction between Annex I and non-Annex I countries set out in the UNFCCC. However, the failure of the United States (US) to ratify the Kyoto Protocol, together with the subsequent withdrawal by Canada, and the refusal of Japan, Russia, and New Zealand to take on new commitments in 2013 after the expiry of the first commitment period, have left this distinction largely inutile. The relatively small group of Annex I countries persisting with a second round of commitments under the Kyoto Protocol through to 2020 account for less than 12 per cent of global emissions, rendering its norms and principles largely redundant.

Instead, a new architecture has formed under the Paris Agreement. This new architecture operationalizes the principle of equity articulated in the UNFCCC in a very different manner. The Paris Agreement reorients the international climate regime to the principle that all countries must adopt verifiable measures to mitigate climate change.[50] In practical terms, the differentiation between countries in the

[43] ibid art 3. [44] ibid arts 6, 12, and 17. [45] ibid art 12.

[46] As discussed in ch 3C, they may also be used by private entities—for instance, for compliance with liabilities under *domestic* emissions trading schemes.

[47] Kyoto Protocol (n 8) arts 6.1(d), 17. [48] Yamin and Depledge (n 22) 145–46.

[49] Froukje Maria Platjouw, 'Reducing Greenhouse Gas Emissions at Home or Abroad? The Implications of Kyoto's Supplementarity Requirement for the Present and Future Climate Change Regime' (2009) 18 *Review of European Community and International Environmental Law* 245. See also Yamin and Depledge (n 22) 145–46.

[50] Paris Agreement (n 9) art 3.

commitments they undertake is no longer defined according to Annex I or non-Annex I.[51] Rather, countries self-select the stringency of their commitments, albeit in a transparent and accountable manner, and subject to the principle that those commitments become increasingly stringent over time.[52] The architecture of the Paris Agreement means that countries' commitments are 'nationally determined' and taken by all, in contrast to the internationally determined commitments of the Kyoto Protocol taken only by Annex I countries. Like the Kyoto Protocol, it appears that Article 6 of the Paris Agreement will permit a kind of 'joint implementation' between countries, whereby countries' commitments may voluntarily be expressed in divisible and quantifiable amounts—ie in terms of carbon units—and traded between countries. Article 6 also foreshadows an offset mechanism conceptually similar to the CDM whereby offset units could be generated and traded amongst countries. However, negotiations on how to operationalize these somewhat vague provisions are slow and uncertain, and the final outcome and contours of Article 6 remain to be seen.[53]

In many ways, the demise of the Kyoto Protocol and the emergence of the Paris Agreement are indicative of an unresolved impasse over the implementation of equity in the international climate regime and over practical application of its attendant norms, such as common but differentiated responsibilities, historical responsibilities, and taking account of national capabilities and circumstances.[54] The 'nationally determined' structure of the Paris Agreement is, in reality, a consequence of the failure to reach multilateral consensus on how to apportion the burden of achieving the ultimate objective of the UNFCCC amongst individual countries—or, in other words, the failure to reach consensus on the meaning of equity.[55] Many have attributed the impasse over the operationalization of equity to the remarkable economic growth of certain developing countries and the concomitant growth in their greenhouse gas emissions, such that they are now responsible for the majority of the world's year-on-year emissions.[56]

Thus, in the absence of agreement on what it means to share the burden of addressing climate change equitably in the international climate regime, the Paris

[51] With the limited exception being found in art 4.4, which distinguishes between the types of mitigation commitments expected of developed and developing countries.

[52] Paris Agreement (n 9) arts 4.2, 4.3, 4.8, and 4.9.

[53] World Bank (n 1) 38–39.

[54] See further Rajamani (n 40) 615–20; Thomas Deleuil, 'The Common but Differentiated Responsibilities Principle: Changes in Continuity after the Durban Conference of the Parties' (2012) 21 *Review of European Community and International Environmental Law* 271, 273–81; Steffen Kallbekken, 'Observations from the climate negotiations in Durban, South Africa' in Todd L Cherry, Jon Hovi, and David M McEvoy (eds), *Towards a New Climate Agreement: Conflict, Resolution and Governance* (Routledge 2014) 3, 5–9.

[55] See eg 'Summary of the round tables under workstream 1 ADP 2 part 2' (Note by the Co-Chairs) (25 July 2013) ADP.2013.10.InformalSummary [7]–[31].

[56] See eg Kallbekken (n 54) 5–6; Rajamani (n 40) 615–16; Thomas Deleuil, 'The Common but Differentiated Responsibilities Principle: Changes in Continuity after the Durban Conference of the Parties' (2012) 21 *Review of European Community and International Environmental Law* 271, 278–80; Joost Pauwelyn, 'The End of Differential Treatment for Developing Countries? Lessons from the Trade and Climate Change Regimes' (2013) 22 *Review of European Community and International Environmental Law* 29, 30, and 33–35.

Agreement pursues an approach whereby countries set their own levels of ambition but are simultaneously required to demonstrate how that level of ambition is justifiable under the principles of the UNFCCC.[57] It also requires countries to review their level of ambition in light of other countries' levels of ambition and the aggregate contribution of all countries' commitments to the ultimate objective of the UNFCCC.[58] Further, whereas all countries must communicate and implement nationally determined mitigation commitments with increasing stringency over time under the Paris Agreement, those commitments are not per se legally binding under international law.[59]

The corollary is that, whereas the principle of equity in the international climate regime is expressed through norms such as common but differentiated responsibilities, historical responsibilities, and taking account of national circumstances and capabilities, the actual content of these norms is contested and unsettled. The lack of consensus over their meaning is foundational in the negotiation and structure of the Paris Agreement, which has replaced the Kyoto Protocol as the prevailing architecture of the international climate regime. This has two important consequences in terms of the interaction between the international climate and economic regimes. First, with the exception of the partially redundant Kyoto Protocol, emissions trading schemes are not adopted—and carbon units are not created—in pursuance of substantive legally binding *levels of ambition* under the international climate regime. Rather, they exist as part of obligations that are more procedural in character, namely, to communicate and implement climate mitigation policies. Therefore, countries are not *bound* by their respective levels of ambition in addressing climate change on the international legal plane, and therefore such levels of ambition do not subsist within the same broader legal framework as international economic law. Second, the norms for apportioning the burden of addressing the ultimate objective of the UNFCCC are, in practical terms, undefined.[60] This limits their potential to 'interact' in any meaningful sense with the norms of international economic law.

It is important to note, however, that the international climate regime includes other norms relevant to its interaction with the international economic regime. In particular, the UNFCCC includes the principle in Article 3.5 that:

> The Parties should cooperate to promote a supportive and open international economic system that would lead to sustainable economic growth and development in all Parties, particularly developing country Parties, thus enabling them better to address the problems of climate change. Measures taken to combat climate change, including unilateral ones, should not constitute a means of arbitrary or unjustifiable discrimination or a disguised restriction on international trade.

[57] Adoption of the Paris Agreement, Decision 1/CP.21, 21st sess (12 December 2015) FCCC/CP/2015/L.9/Rev.1 [27].

[58] Paris Agreement arts 4.9 and 14.

[59] ibid art 4.2. Parties are obliged to 'pursue domestic mitigation measures, with the aim of achieving the objectives of such contributions', rather than actually meet their set level of ambition.

[60] Rajamani (n 40) 616–19.

This language is—deliberately—a reproduction of Article XX of General Agreement on Tariffs and Trade 1994 (GATT 1994)[61] and Article XIV of the General Agreement on Trade in Services (GATS);[62] the UNFCCC was negotiated concurrently with the both the Rio Declaration on Environment and Development (Rio Declaration) and the Marrakesh Agreement Establishing the World Trade Organization (WTO Agreement).[63] The Rio Declaration incorporated the principle that:

> States should cooperate to promote a supportive and open international economic system that would lead to economic growth and sustainable development in all countries, to better address the problems of environmental degradation. Trade policy measures for environmental purposes should not constitute a means of arbitrary or unjustifiable discrimination or a disguised restriction on international trade.[64]

The desire for the international climate regime to be mutually supportive with the international economic regime is evinced through the inclusion of Article 3.5 in the UNFCCC. For its part, the WTO Agreement included a preambular recital stating:

> Recognizing that their relations in the field of trade and economic endeavour should be conducted with a view to raising standards of living, ensuring full employment and a large and steadily growing volume of real income and effective demand, and expanding the production of and trade in goods and services, *while allowing for the optimal use of the world's resources in accordance with the objective of sustainable development, seeking both to protect and preserve the environment and to enhance the means for doing so* in a manner consistent with their respective needs and concerns at different levels of economic development . . .[65]

This recital posits the means for protecting and preserving the environment as a function of allowing for the optimal use of the world's resources, and consistent with the goals of the disciplines of the WTO Agreement, such as full employment and expanding international trade. As Eckersley points out, these respective aspects of international trade and climate treaties share a number of important features.[66] They endorse sustainable development and an open economic system. Sustainable economic growth is posited as a normal good that can assist in protecting and preserving the environment and combating climate change. Thus, sustainable economic

[61] Marrakesh Agreement Establishing the World Trade Organization (opened for signature 15 April 1994, entered into force 1 January 1995) 1867 UNTS 3 annex IA (General Agreement on Tariffs and Trade) (GATT 1994).

[62] Marrakesh Agreement Establishing the World Trade Organization (n 61) annex IB (General Agreement on Trade in Services) (GATS).

[63] Bodansky (n 31) 505; Bradly J Condon and Tapen Sinha, *The Role of Climate Change in Global Economic Governance* (OUP 2013) 22–23. The subsequent Kyoto Protocol does not recapitulate art 3.5 of the UNFCCC, but rather, it states in art 2.3 that: 'The Parties included in Annex I shall strive to implement policies and measures under this Article in such a way as to minimize adverse effects, including . . . effects on international trade . . .'.

[64] United Nations Conference on Environment and Development, 'Rio Declaration on Environment and Development' (Annex I) (1992) A/CONF.151/26 (Vol. I) principle 12.

[65] Marrakesh Agreement Establishing the World Trade Organization (n 61) (Agreement Establishing the World Trade Organization) (WTO Agreement) premabular recital 1 (emphasis added).

[66] Robyn Eckersley, 'Understanding the Interplay between the Climate and Trade Regimes' in Benjamin Simmons, Harro van Asselt, and Fariborz Zelli (eds), *Climate and Trade Policies in a Post-2012 World* (UNEP 2009) 1, 12.

growth through an open economic system on the one hand, and environmental and climate protection on the other hand, are presumed to be mutually supportive, akin to Principle 12 of the Rio Declaration.

Only one WTO case has thus far approached the interaction between the international climate and economic regimes in any substantive manner. In *India—Solar Cells*, India sought to justify its otherwise prohibited use of domestic content requirements to support its solar manufacturing industry by invoking Article XX(d) of GATT 1994. India contended that these requirements were 'necessary to secure compliance with laws or regulations which are not inconsistent with the provisions of [GATT]', including the UNFCCC and domestic laws enshrining certain climate change obligations.[67] In respect of the UNFCCC, the WTO Appellate Body found that it did not have direct effect as an instrument in India's domestic legal system, and thus did not qualify as a 'law or regulation' within the meaning of Article XX(d).[68] In respect of India's domestic climate laws, the Appellate Body found that they did not set out a *rule* 'to ensure ecologically sustainable growth while addressing India's energy security challenge, and ensuring compliance with its obligations relating to climate change', contrary to India's characterization of these laws.[69] The Appellate Body considered the relevant instruments to be more hortatory and aspirational in character, as opposed to reflecting a *rule*.[70] In view of these findings, the Appellate Body was thus not required to assess *how* the international climate regime might affect the case before it. Interestingly, India did not invoke the instruments of the international climate regime in the *interpretation* of the provisions of WTO law at issue—rather, India tacitly sought to introduce those instruments as themselves quasi-applicable law through Article XX(d).

C Ordinary Meaning

In applying the principle that treaties be interpreted 'in accordance with the ordinary meaning to be given to the terms of the treaty in their context and in the light of its object and purpose', the Appellate Body has stressed that this represents 'an integrated operation' and a 'holistic exercise'[71] that should not be 'mechanically subdivided into rigid components'.[72] That notwithstanding, the Appellate Body has—along with many investment tribunals—recognized that the task of interpreting a treaty must begin with its specific words and text.[73] This is because the specific terms used by parties to a treaty are understood to provide the most reliable indication

[67] Appellate Body Report, *India—Solar Cells* [5.92]. [68] ibid [5.149].

[69] ibid [5.137]. [70] ibid [5.133].

[71] Appellate Body Report, *US—Continued Zeroing* [268].

[72] Appellate Body Report, *EC—Chicken Cuts* [175]–[176]. See also Rudolf Dolzer and Christoph Schreuer, *Principles of International Investment Law* (OUP 2012) 30.

[73] Appellate Body Report, *Japan—Alcoholic Beverages II* 12; Appellate Body Report, *India—Patents (US)* [45]; Appellate Body Report, *US—Shrimp* [114]. See also Weeramantry (n 5) 51–52; Andrew Newcombe and Lluís Paradell, *Law and Practice of Investment Treaties* (Kluwer 2009) 109–12; Cook (n 17) 277.

of their common intention. Along the same lines, it is generally presumed that the parties to a treaty were deliberate in the specific terms they used, and therefore the interpretation of a treaty should only consider words *actually* used in a treaty, as opposed to imputing into a treaty 'words that are not there',[74] 'concepts that were not intended',[75] nor 'words that the interpreter may feel should have been used'.[76]

While not necessarily dispositive[77] and often limited in their ability to resolve complex questions of interpretation,[78] dictionaries have been recognized as a useful starting point in shedding light on the ordinary meaning of a term.[79] They provide, at least to some degree, an objective touchstone for the ordinary meaning of a term. In many cases, however, a term will have multiple dictionary definitions that offer a spectrum of particular meanings. In such cases, the context surrounding the term, and the object and purpose of the treaty, can play a pivotal role in distilling the correct ordinary meaning of the term for the purposes of treaty interpretation, as discussed below.[80] In practical terms, as Van Damme states, this results in the selection of the dictionary definition that seems most apt to the particular context of the provision under consideration.[81]

Importantly, in light of the interaction between the international climate and economic regimes in the process of treaty interpretation undertaken in this book, other international instruments can also play a role in distilling the ordinary meaning of a term. As the panel stated in *EC—Approval and Marketing of Biotech Products*:

> [I]n addition to dictionaries, other relevant rules of international law may in some cases aid a treaty interpreter in establishing, or confirming, the ordinary meaning of treaty terms in the specific context in which they are used. Such rules would not be considered because they are legal rules, but rather because they may provide evidence of the ordinary meaning of terms in the same way that dictionaries do.[82]

For instance, the Appellate Body in *US—Shrimp* used Article 56 of the United Nations Convention on the Law of the Sea[83] as evidence that the ordinary meaning of 'natural resources' in Article XX(g) of GATT 1994 could refer to both living and non-living resources.[84] The international investment regime has analogous examples.[85]

[74] Appellate Body Report, *India—Patents (US)* [45].
[75] ibid.
[76] Appellate Body Report, *EC—Hormones* [181].
[77] Appellate Body Report, *US—Offset Act (Byrd Amendment)* [248]. See also Zachary Douglas, *The International Law of Investment Claims* (CUP 2009) 82.
[78] Appellate Body Report, *US—Gambling* [164] n 191.
[79] Appellate Body Report, *EC—Chicken Cuts* [175]–[176]. See also Weeramantry (n 5) 54–55; Cook (n 17) 278.
[80] Appellate Body Report, *Peru—Agricultural Products* [5.94]. See also Weeramantry (n 5) 56.
[81] Van Damme (n 2) 221.
[82] Panel Reports, *EC—Approval and Marketing of Biotech Products* [7.92]–[7.93].
[83] United Nations Convention on the Law of the Sea (opened for signature 10 December 1982, entered into force 16 November 1994) 1833 UNTS 3.
[84] Appellate Body Report, *US—Shrimp* [130]–[132].
[85] See eg *Veteran Petroleum Limited (Cyprus) v Russian Federation (Final Award)* (PCA Case No AA 228, UNCITRAL Rules, 18 July 2014) [765]; *Southern Pacific Properties (Middle East) Limited v Egypt (Award)* (ICSID Arbitral Tribunal, Case No ARB/84/3, 20 May 1992) [78], [154], [191]; *Chemtura Corporation v Canada (Award)* (Ad hoc arbitration, UNCITRAL Rules, 2 August 2010) [135]–[136].

Thus, the instruments of the international climate regime could potentially inform the ordinary meaning of terms in international economic law. For instance, they could inform whether the ordinary meaning of terms such as 'goods'/'products', 'services', 'financial services', and 'investments' are capable of covering carbon units. They could also inform how the ordinary meaning of 'likeness' applies to differing sets of carbon units, and whether differential treatment between certain types carbon units falls within the ordinary meaning of terms such as 'arbitrary' or 'unjustifiable'.

Nevertheless, the use of other instruments of international law in this manner is somewhat rare in international economic law.[86] Further, in the process of treaty *interpretation*, other instruments of international law cannot be used tacitly to *amend* or *modify* the ordinary meaning of the treaty's terms.[87] The norms of other international instruments do not *apply* to the ordinary meaning of a treaty's terms. Thus, while they might shed light on the ordinary meaning of a term, they cannot displace or operate as a defence to what would otherwise constitute its ordinary meaning in the process of treaty interpretation.

In any event, a strong inference can be drawn from the above overview of the international climate regime that measures pertaining to climate change—including measures affecting trade and investment in carbon units—are not intended to be exempted from the international economic regime; nor should such measures be permitted as derogations where they violate international economic law. Rather, the UNFCCC expressly incorporates the principle from the international economic regime that '[m]easures taken to combat climate change, including unilateral ones, should not constitute a means of arbitrary or unjustifiable discrimination or a disguised restriction on international trade',[88] and the Kyoto Protocol calls on parties to implement their obligations 'in such a way as to minimize adverse effects . . . on international trade'.[89] In this connection, it is worth noting that the Rio Declaration—whose Principle 12 reflects both of these concepts—has been used in past WTO disputes as evidence of the 'ordinary meaning' of terms.[90]

See generally Saverio Di Benedetto, *International Investment Law and the Environment* (Edward Elgar Publishing 2013) 90–93, 140–49.

[86] See eg Cook (n 17) 82–85; Moshe Hirsch, 'Investment Tribunals and Human Rights: Divergent Paths' in Pierre-Marie Dupuy, Ernst-Ulrich Petersmann, and Francesco Francioni (eds), *Human Rights in International Investment Law and Arbitration* (OUP 2009) 97, 100–109; Newcombe and Paradell (n 73) 107–08.

[87] Appellate Body Report, *Peru—Agricultural Products* [5.94]–[5.97].

[88] UNFCCC (n 7) art 3.5.

[89] Kyoto Protocol (n 8) art 2.3.

[90] Appellate Body Report, *US—Shrimp* [154]–[156], [168]. See further Margaret A Young 'Principle 12: The Environment and Trade' in Jorge Vinuales (ed), *The Rio Declaration on Environment and Development* (OUP 2015) 325, 345.

D Context

Pursuant to the Vienna Convention, the plain or dictionary meaning of a term must be assessed 'in its context' in order to establish its correct interpretation.[91]

An assessment of the context of treaty terms involves the immediate context of a term and its surrounding provisions, as well as the broader context of the text, preamble, and any relevant annexes or other instruments.[92] It requires a reading of each article in relation to other potentially relevant provisions and an analysis, where necessary, of any differences in terminology.[93] For instance, the use of different terms might indicate an intended difference in meaning.[94] Further, interpretations of particular terms that would render other terms or provisions void of meaning, or that would lead to a conflict with other aspects of the treaty, should be avoided.[95] This reflects the presumption that the provisions of a treaty are cumulative and complementary and should therefore be interpreted harmoniously. It would not make sense for drafters to include provisions that contradict one another, or to include some provisions that are effectively redundant owing to the practical application of other provisions.[96] Silence on a specific issue can also inform the context of a term and impart meaning on its scope.[97] For example, the absence of any qualifications may suggest a broad construction of a term.[98]

Further, against the background of the interaction between the international economic and climate regimes evoked in this book, Article 31.3(c) of the Vienna Convention is of particular relevance to the role of 'context' in treaty interpretation. It provides that '[t]here shall be taken into account, together with the context . . . any relevant rules of international law applicable in the relations between the parties'. The International Law Commission has posited this principle as a key tool in achieving systematic integration across different regimes in international law.[99] From that perspective, Article 31.3(c) provides an avenue for taking into account the norms and disciplines of the international climate regime in the interpretation of international economic law.

The role that Article 31.3(c) *should* play in treaty interpretation in international economic law has been the subject of significant academic commentary.[100] Of greater relevance to this book, however, is the role that it *does* play, in practical terms, as applied by adjudicators in international economic law. As will be shown, two factors have led to its role being heavily circumscribed, and, consequently, it is unlikely to facilitate any meaningful role for norms arising from the international climate regime in the process of treaty interpretation in international economic law.

[91] Van Damme (n 2) 223; Weeramantry (n 5) 51–52; Douglas (n 77) 82.
[92] Panel Report, *Canada—Pharmaceutical Patents* [7.14]. See also Douglas (n 77) 82.
[93] Panel Report, *India—Autos* [7.222].
[94] Cook (n 17) 283; Weeramantry (n 5) 143–45.
[95] Cook (n 17) 282; Weeramantry (n 5) 145.
[96] Van Damme (n 2) 285–87; Weeramantry (n 5) 66–70.
[97] Appellate Body Report, *US—Carbon Steel* [65].
[98] ibid [104].
[99] ILC (n 16) 244.
[100] See Cook (n 17) 59–60.

The first factor concerns which rules of international law are 'relevant' under Article 31.3(c). Adjudicators in international economic law have tended to take a particularly narrow view in this regard. For instance, the Appellate Body has stated that, in order to be 'relevant', other rules of international law must concern the same subject matter of the treaty terms being interpreted. In terms of practical application, by 'same subject matter', the Appellate Body meant that the other treaty must specifically bear upon the interpretation of the particular term at issue in order to be considered 'relevant'.[101] Investment tribunals have been similarly reticent to posit other rules of international law as 'relevant' to the process of treaty interpretation by virtue of Article 31.3(c), emphasizing both the limited jurisdiction of such tribunals as well as concerns over using other rules of international law to erode or obscure the applicable rights and obligations in the IIA at issue.[102]

Even if, however, a rule of international law—for instance, stemming from the international climate regime—can be considered 'relevant' to the interpretation of a term under international economic law, a second factor might frustrate its role in the interpretive process. In particular, Article 31.3(c) is limited to rules of international law that are 'applicable in the relations between the parties' to the treaty under consideration. This requirement has been interpreted in international economic law to mean that the relevant rule of international law must bind all of the parties to the treaty under consideration.[103] This presents an obstacle to the consideration of the UNFCCC and the Kyoto Protocol through Article 31.3(c) because, although they are two of the most widely ratified treaties in existence, Canada, the US, and Taiwan are not party to the Kyoto Protocol,[104] and nor is Taiwan a party to the UNFCCC or Paris Agreement,[105] whereas they all are Members of the WTO. Further, the US has signalled its intention to withdraw from the Paris Agreement. Thus, not all WTO Members may necessarily be bound—or in the case of Taiwan, be capable of being bound[106]—by its terms.

[101] See Appellate Body Reports, *EC and certain member States—Large Civil Aircraft* [851]; *Peru—Agricultural Products* [5.101]–[5.103].

[102] Weeramantry (n 5) 89–95; Saverio Di Benedetto, *International Investment Law and the Environment* (2013) 135–57; *Grand River v United States (Award)* (NAFTA Tribunal, UNCITRAL Rules, 12 January 2011) [69]; *RosInvestCo v Russian Federation (Jurisdiction)* (Stockholm Chamber of Commerce, Case No 079/2005, 5 October 2007) [39]–[40]. Cf *Tulip Real Estate and Development Netherlands BV v Republic of Turkey (Annulment)* (ICSID Arbitral Tribunal, Case No ARB/11/28, 30 December 2015) [86]–[92].

[103] Appellate Body Report, *Peru—Agricultural Products* [5.106] (although ostensibly not determining the issue conclusively (see [5.105]), the Appellate Body nonetheless considered that an extraneous instrument would need to establish the '*common* intention of WTO Members' in respect of a provision of WTO law in order to be capable of being 'applicable between the parties' in the sense of art 31.3(c)). See also Appellate Body Report, *EC and certain member States—Large Civil Aircraft* [844]–[845].

[104] UNFCCC Secretariat, 'Status of Ratification of the Kyoto Protocol' http://unfccc.int/kyoto_protocol/status_of_ratification/items/2613.php (last accessed 29 November 2015).

[105] UNFCCC Secretariat, 'Status of Ratification of the Convention' http://unfccc.int/essential_background/convention/status_of_ratification/items/2631.php (last accessed 29 November 2015).

[106] Paris Agreement (n 9) art 20.1. Taiwan could, of course, unilaterally declare its intention to be bound by the norms of a treaty to which it could not accede—such as the Paris Agreement—or otherwise indicate its consent that such a treaty may qualify as relevant rules of international law for the interpretation of the WTO Agreement even though it is not a party to such treaty.

This second factor may have less salience for free trade agreements and IIAs, which typically involve significantly smaller subsets of parties, and are thus more likely to involve a situation whereby all parties are bound by one or more of the principal instruments of the international climate regime.

E Object and Purpose

The object and purpose of the instruments of international economic law may also shed light on the scope of their terms. Recourse is typically had to the object and purpose in international economic law where an assessment of the ordinary meaning of a treaty's terms in their context leaves them unclear, or where multiple plausible meanings nonetheless remain.[107] The starting point for ascertaining the object and purpose of a treaty is the treaty itself, in its entirety.[108] Its object and purpose may be deduced from the its preamble,[109] as well as from its particular provisions if doing so assists the interpreter in determining the object and purpose of the treaty on the whole.[110]

The main interpretive function of the object and purpose is to ensure that an interpretation is chosen that is consistent with the treaty's object and purpose, and that an interpretation that might undermine its object and purpose—such as one which could permit the circumvention of a treaty's disciplines—is rejected.[111] However, an interpreter should not attach undue importance to arguments concerning the object and purpose of a treaty where the treaty contains no express statement of its object and purpose, or where the ordinary meaning of a term is clear on its face.[112]

In view of the potential relevance of the international climate regime to the task of treaty interpretation at hand, it is worth recalling at this juncture that the preamble to the WTO Agreement includes the following in the description of its objectives:[113]

> while allowing for the optimal use of the world's resources in accordance with the objective of sustainable development, seeking both to protect and preserve the environment and to enhance the means for doing so in a manner consistent with their respective needs and concerns at different levels of economic development.

The international climate regime is relevant to the terms of this aspect of the object and purpose of the WTO Agreement—and hence to the interpretation of the terms of the WTO Agreement—in two ways. First, the use of the term 'sustainable development' in this preambular recital creates an opening to the norms of the international climate regime, since addressing climate change is a key part of

[107] See Appellate Body Report, *Peru—Agricultural Products* [5.94]. See also Weeramantry (n 5) 67–68.
[108] Appellate Body Report, *EC—Chicken Cuts* [238].
[109] Panel Report, *EC—Chicken Cuts (Brazil)* [7.318]. See also Weeramantry (n 5) 71–72.
[110] Appellate Body Report, *EC—Chicken Cuts* [238]–[239].
[111] Appellate Body Report, *US—Softwood Lumber IV* [64]. See also Weeramantry (n 5) 76.
[112] Panel Report, *Canada—Aircraft* [9.119].
[113] WTO Agreement (n 65) preamble recitals 1 and 4.

sustainable development as defined by the UNFCCC, the Kyoto Protocol, and the Paris Agreement.[114] Secondly, this preambular recital posits environmental protection, including 'enhancing the means for doing so', as within the scope of the trade and economic relations of WTO Members that it governs. This, in turn, suggests that market-based approaches to environmental protection that commodify pollution for international trading could be potentially covered by the WTO Agreement. This recital evokes Principle 12 of the Rio Declaration, discussed above, and presupposes that the international economic and climate regimes are mutually supportive, rather than mutually exclusive.

IIAs do not typically include similar language on sustainable development or the environment in their preambles or statements of object and purpose. However, of relevance to the question at hand, a small number of IIAs contain references to climate change or the environment. For instance, the 2004 Canada Model IIA lists the 'promotion of sustainable development' as one of its objectives,[115] the 2012 US Model IIA desires to achieve its objectives 'in a manner consistent with the protection of... the environment',[116] and the Energy Charter Treaty 'recall[s]' the United Nations Framework Convention on Climate Change'.[117] These kinds of elements of object and purpose could—as with the WTO Agreement—provide an avenue the norms of the international climate regime to play a role in the process of treaty interpretation.

F Summary: Treaty Interpretation

The foregoing sets out, in general terms, the approach that will be used in this book for engaging in the process of interpreting the instruments of the international economic regime. Additional and specialized principles of treaty interpretation—such as relating to the role of different authentic language versions of treaties, the role of the negotiating history of treaties, and the role of municipal law in treaty interpretation—are addressed in the particular areas of this book where they arise.

It is important to emphasize that, given the current and likely future approach of the WTO Appellate Body, the norms of the international climate regime cannot be invoked as a defence or otherwise apply beyond the manner described in the foregoing sections. The international climate regime does not represent applicable law in the international economic regime, and its norms and disciplines will not apply directly as waivers, amendments, or inter se modifications to the instruments comprising the international economic regime, nor as a form of *lex posterior* that

[114] UNFCCC (n 7) art 3.4; Kyoto Protocol (n 8) arts 2 and 10; Paris Agreement (n 9) preambular recital 8 and art 2.1.

[115] 2004 Canada Model IIA, preambular recital 1 italaw.com/documents/Canadian2004-FIPA-model-en. pdf (last accessed 29 November 2015).

[116] 2012 US Model IIA, preambular recital 5 www.state.gov/e/eb/ifd/bit/index.htm (last accessed 29 November 2015).

[117] Energy Charter Treaty (signed 17 December 1994, entered into force 16 April 1998) 2080 UNTS 95, preambular recital 14.

displaces its disciplines.[118] The same holds true in respect of international investment tribunals.[119]

That notwithstanding, is it worth recalling that a key function of carbon units is to facilitate one of the pre-eminent means by which countries seek to fulfil their commitments under the international climate regime. Thus, to the extent that the international climate regime imbues the very nature of carbon units, it will have salience to addressing the questions raised by the analysis in this book.

[118] See Appellate Body Report, *Peru—Agricultural Products* [5.110]–[5.114]. Although this represents the prevailing view in the jurisprudence, contrary views have been expressed in the scholarship. See eg Pauwelyn (n 17) 323–24 and 466.

[119] See generally Andrew Mitchell and James Munro, 'Someone Else's Deal: Interpreting International Investment Agreements in the Light of Third-Party Agreements' (2017) 28 *European Journal of International Law* 3. Arbitrators are limited to applying the laws consented to by the disputing parties, and further, the applicable law comprises in IIAs includes only the protections contained therein (including any umbrella clause and associated domestic law). In light of that, unless the disputing parties otherwise agree, there would not ordinarily be any basis for a tribunal to *apply* external norms (as distinct from how such norms may be considered as part of the interpretive process described above).

3

Carbon Units and Emissions Trading Schemes

Before being able to classify carbon units correctly under international economic law—and hence ascertain the extent to which emissions trading schemes are thereby regulated—their inherent qualities and characteristics need to be understood. This calls for a factual inquiry, which will provide the evidence necessary to determine their proper legal classification.

As part of this factual inquiry, the historical and policy origins of carbon units, as well as their key attributes and nature, are assessed in this chapter. This includes how they are created, what they represent, how they may be used, and the source of their value. The legal classification of carbon units under municipal law is also surveyed, since this can potentially inform their proper construction under international economic law.

A Policy Origins of Carbon Units and Emissions Trading Schemes

Carbon units are the direct outcome of a particular policy prescription on how to manage a resource (ie the atmosphere) used by many individuals in common.[1] This

[1] Daniel Cole, 'Origins of Emissions Trading in Theory and Early Practice' in Stefan Weishaar (ed), *Research Handbook on Emissions Trading* (Edward Elgar Publishing 2016) 9–26; Ted Gayer and John K Horowitz, 'Market-based Approaches to Environmental Regulation' (2006) 1(4) *Foundations and Trends in Microeconomics* 201, 204–06; Olivier Godard, *Domestic Transferable Permits for Environmental Management: Design and Implementation* (OECD 2001) 11.

policy prescription is the creation of a transferable permit scheme to remedy the so-called 'tragedy of the commons'.[2] In basic terms, the 'tragedy of the commons' is where otherwise 'rational' individuals produce outcomes that are not 'rational' with respect to the use of a resource that is used or owned in common.[3] For example, individuals may overexploit a common resource to the extent that it disappears and is no longer able to be exploited. In a market system, irrational behaviour in respect of a common resource manifests itself as a market imperfection, where the damage or harm done by the unsustainable use of a common resource is not reflected in the price of a given transaction.[4] In effect, the cost of the harm or damage inflicted is externalized and borne by others, such as the community as a whole—or, in the case of climate change, by future generations—rather than being incurred by those causing the damage or harm.[5]

Since the unsustainable use of a common resource stems from the unrestricted access to its use, the logical policy response is to impose restrictions on its access.[6] In broad terms, there are two approaches to imposing such restrictions: command-and-control policies, and market-based policies.[7] The essential difference between these approaches lies in the allocation of decision-making responsibility in relation to who may access a resource, and the terms under which it may be accessed. Under the command-and-control approach, a government prescribes who may access a resource (eg who has the right to emit greenhouse gas) as well as the terms of access (eg how much greenhouse gas an entity may emit, or certain technology standards that must be used in order to reduce emissions). However, this approach has been criticized as inefficient or unnecessarily expensive.[8]

By contrast, under the market-based approach, governmental decision-making is generally limited to setting broad parameters on the use of a resource, such as a quantitative limit, quota or cap that ensures its sustainable subsistence. Once scarcity is imposed on access to the resource, it is then for private actors to determine who and how it may be accessed on the basis of market forces. As Weishaar explains, market-based approaches 'provide greater flexibility (taking into account each polluter's individual opportunity for optimal pollution abatement) and ... provide optimal incentives towards environmental technological innovation rather than simply

[2] Matthieu Wemaere, Charlotte Streck, and Thiago Chagas, 'Legal Ownership and Nature of Kyoto Units and EU Allowances' in David Freestone and Charlotte Streck (eds), *Legal Aspects of Carbon Trading: Kyoto, Copenhagen and beyond* (OUP 2009) 37–43.

[3] See eg Theodore Panayotou, *Economic Instruments for Environmental Management and Sustainable Development* (Environmental Economics Series Paper No 16, United Nations Environment Programme 1994) 3, 7–12; J H Dales (1968) 1 *Canadian Journal of Economics* 791, 795–96; Daniel Cole, 'Clearing the Air: Four Propositions about Property Rights and Environmental Protection' (1999) 10(13) *Duke Environmental Law & Policy Forum* 103, 106.

[4] Gayer and Horowitz (n 1) 204–05.

[5] ibid 205. See also Terry Anderson and Bishop Grewell, 'Property Rights Solutions for the Global Commons: Bottom-up or Top-down?' (1999) 10(13) *Duke Environmental Law & Policy Forum* 73, 75.

[6] Cole, 'Clearing the Air' (n 3) 106.

[7] ibid.

[8] See eg Dales (n 3) 800–01; Gayer and Horowitz (n 1) 214–15; Godard, *Domestic Transferable Permits for Environmental Management* (n 1) 13–17; Panayotou (n 3) 2, 46; Cole, 'Clearing the Air' (n 3) 110.

striving for compliance with a regulatory standard'.[9] Transferable permit schemes facilitate this by converting the common resource, or access to its use, into divisible private rights that can be traded amongst those seeking to use it.[10] By requiring those seeking to use the resource to own a right to its use, and by imposing scarcity on the number of rights available, the cost of using the resource—including any harm or damage caused by that use—is borne by the individual user, which is subsequently passed on in the cost of a relevant commercial transaction.

As such, this approach is said to correct the market failure implicit in a 'tragedy of the commons' by internalizing the cost of using a resource and giving a price signal to the market on its use.[11] Its key advantage lies in allowing the market to discover the most economically and technologically efficient means of sustainably managing the resource.[12] This policy tool has been deployed in a wide variety of contexts where common resources might be susceptible to mismanagement, such as in air pollution control, fisheries regulation, water pollution and unsustainable water use, municipal waste management, and renewable energy development.[13] Despite the diversity of subject matter that may be governed by a transferable permit scheme, all have two core elements.[14] First, a quantified physical constraint is imposed on the use of a resource in the form of rights or permits that are allocated to certain target groups, who are usually the primary users of the resource.[15] This quantitative constraint usually applies over a given time period, for example only a given number of fish may be caught or only a given amount of pollution may be released over a particular twelve-month period. Secondly, these target groups are allowed to trade these rights or permits amongst one another.[16] This means that those using the resource (rather than the regulator that has set the constraint) are able to choose the most economically and technologically efficient means of operating within the quantitative constraint.[17]

A further important element of transferable permits is the characteristic of private ownership or property.[18] This characteristic facilitates trade and investment in permits by private actors, which is the core function of a transferable permit scheme. Further, in relation to climate change in particular, the kinds of long-term investment-backed decisions required to transition to a low-carbon economy are contingent on a degree of predictability and stability in the operation of the market

[9] Stefan E Weishaar, *Emissions Trading Design* (Edward Elgar Publishing 2014) 11, 13–14. See also Dales (n 3) 800–801; Panayotou (n 3) 5.

[10] Godard, *Domestic Transferable Permits for Environmental Management* (n 1) 9–11; Olivier Godard, 'Domestic Transferable Permits: Summary of Lessons Learned' in *Implementing Domestic Tradeable Permits: Recent Developments and Future Challenges* (OECD 2002) 11–12; Panayotou (n 3) 7–8.

[11] Panayotou (n 3) 8. [12] Gayer and Horowitz (n 1) 210–12.

[13] Godard, *Domestic Transferable Permits for Environmental Management* (n 1) 7–8.

[14] ibid. [15] ibid. [16] ibid. [17] Gayer and Horowitz (n 1) 210–12.

[18] Cole, 'Origins of Emissions Trading in Theory and Early Practice' (n 1) 9, 16–17; Godard, *Domestic Transferable Permits for Environmental Management* (n 1) 28–29; M J Mace, 'The Legal Nature of Emission Reductions and EU Allowances: Issues Addressed in an International Workshop' (2005) 2 *Journal of European Environmental and Planning Law* 123, 124–25; Karoliina Anttonen, Michael Mehling, and Karl Upston-Hooper, 'Breathing Life into the Carbon Market' (2007) 16 *European Environmental Law Review* 96, 97–99.

and its fundamentals relating to the price of carbon units, such as supply and demand, which is enabled and strengthened through the conferral of proprietary status.[19] However, as will be elaborated upon later in this chapter, some jurisdictions have been reluctant to confer proprietary status on their carbon units. This is to retain flexibility for future governmental intervention in view of both the *artificial* nature of the carbon market created by emissions trading schemes (whereby demand is legally mandated and supply set by government), as well as the risks and uncertainties pertaining to the nature of the climate mitigation objective itself.[20]

As described in Chapter 2, the Kyoto Protocol does—and it is expected that the Paris Agreement will—facilitate international emissions trading in carbon units between countries by both governments and private actors. Additionally, the World Bank counted twenty-four regional, national, and subnational emissions trading schemes in 2017, with most of these comprising cap-and-trade schemes whereby the physical quantitative restraint on emissions takes the form of a single aggregate amount of greenhouse gas emissions that may be emitted in the jurisdiction by the facilities or companies covered by the scheme.[21] This is, for instance, how the schemes in the European Union (EU), California, Quebec, Switzerland, Korea, Norway, and New Zealand function. The now-repealed Australian emissions trading scheme also took this form.

It is important to note, however, that some schemes set quantitative caps at the level of individual covered facilities as opposed to an aggregate amount of greenhouse gas that may be emitted cumulatively by all covered facilities. Such schemes are known as 'baseline-and-credit' or 'credit-and-trade' schemes. In basic terms, such schemes permit a covered facility that emits *less* than its individual target to sell its 'surplus' emissions in the form of carbon units to a covered facility whose emissions *exceed* its individual target.[22]

Australia is currently implementing a variant of such a scheme, whereby covered facilities are set a baseline initially by reference to their highest annual emissions in the period 2009–2013.[23] Covered facilities that emit less than their baseline (ie outperform it) may be issued certain carbon units if they meet certain additional requirements typical of offsetting mechanisms (discussed in section B), and such units may then be sold to facilities that exceed their baseline. It is also envisaged that covered facilities exceeding their baseline will be able to source carbon units from

[19] Godard, *Domestic Transferable Permits for Environmental Management* (n 1) 67; Panayotou (n 3) 52; Ross Garnaut, *The Garnaut Climate Change Review* (CUP 2008) 322–323; Weishaar, *Emissions Trading Design* (n 9) 24.

[20] Daniel W Bromley, *Environment and Economy: Property Rights and Public Policy* (Blackwell 1991) 95–96; Simon Grant and John Quiggin, 'Climate Change and the Precautionary Principle' in John Quiggin and others (eds), *Carbon Pricing: Early Experiences and Future Prospects* (Edward Elgar Publishing 2014) 167, 170–74; Julia Black, 'The Role of Risk in Regulatory Processes' in Robert Baldwin, Martin Cave, and Martin Lodge (eds), *The Oxford Handbook of Regulation* (OUP 2010) 301, 317–23.

[21] World Bank, Ecofys, and Vivid Economics, *State and Trends of Carbon Pricing 2017* (World Bank 2017) 43.

[22] Weishaar, *Emissions Trading Design* (n 9) 55–56.

[23] National Greenhouse and Energy Reporting (Safeguard Mechanism) Rule 2015 (Cth) ss 10–13. Calculations and projections are made for new entrants and for periodic adjustments to baselines.

international markets and from Australian offsetting projects to meet their shortfall in emissions.[24]

The International Civil Aviation Organization also established a form of baseline-and-credit scheme in 2016 (the 'Carbon Offsetting and Reduction Scheme for International Aviation', or 'CORSIA'), with the aim of limiting emissions from international aviation to a baseline of emissions in 2020.[25] Any shortfall of an aeroplane operator's emissions can be met by purchasing offset units that satisfy certain environmental criteria that are as yet undetermined, but are likely to include offset units generated under the Kyoto Protocol and Paris Agreement.[26]

Japan has also established a 'joint crediting mechanism' with seventeen partner countries, through which offset units are generated from offset projects (described further in section B) which have thus far included solar power projects in Mongolia and energy conservation in Indonesia, amongst others.[27] The Government of Japan intends to procure a portion of the offset units generated for the purposes of meeting its obligations under the Paris Agreement, with the remainder likely to be either traded on the international carbon market or retained by the partner country to satisfy their own international climate obligations.

It should also be noted that there exists a voluntary market for carbon units, whereby—unlike emissions trading schemes—demand is not driven by compliance with legal obligations. This is discussed further in section E.

B The Creation and Categories of Carbon Units: Allowance Units and Offset Units

While the exact nature of a given carbon unit will depend on the particular scheme in which it is created, traded, and used, the basic understanding of a carbon unit is largely uniform across different schemes. A carbon unit represents a right to emit one tonne of greenhouse gas, usually within a certain time period. Some schemes are explicit in defining their carbon units in this way. For example, the EU scheme defines its carbon units as 'an allowance to emit one tonne of carbon dioxide equivalent during a specified period',[28] the Californian scheme similarly defines its units as 'a limited tradeable authorization to emit up to one ton of carbon dioxide equivalent',[29] and the Swiss scheme defines its units as 'tradable rights to emit greenhouse

[24] National Greenhouse and Energy Reporting Act 2007 (Cth) ss 22XM and 22XN.

[25] Consolidated statement of continuing ICAO policies and practices related to environmental protection—Global Market-based Measure (MBM) scheme, ICAO Resolution 22/2 (7 October 2016) A39-WP/530, [3].

[26] ibid [20]–[23].

[27] Government of Japan, *Recent Development of The Joint Crediting Mechanism (JCM)* (January 2017).

[28] Directive 2003/87/EC of the European Parliament and of the Council of 13 October 2003 establishing a scheme for greenhouse gas emission allowance trading within the Community and amending Council Directive 96/61/EC [2003] OJ L275/32, art 3(a).

[29] California Cap on Greenhouse Gas Emissions and Market-based Compliance Mechanisms 17 Cal Public Health Code § 95802(8).

gases'.[30] The Kyoto Protocol defines its units as 'equal to one metric tonne of carbon dioxide equivalent'.[31] The Quebecois scheme similarly defines its carbon units as being 'equal to one metric ton of greenhouse gas expressed in CO2 equivalents'.[32]

Other schemes are less direct in defining their units. The now-repealed Australian emissions trading scheme stated that if an applicable person 'does not surrender one eligible emissions unit for each tonne of carbon dioxide equivalence of the gas [it emits], the person is liable to pay a unit shortfall charge'.[33] In other words, a person must possess and surrender a carbon unit in order to avoid a fine or penalty for emitting one tonne of greenhouse gas. The New Zealand scheme takes the same approach.[34] In practical terms, the ability to avoid a fine for emitting one tonne of greenhouse gas by owning a carbon unit represents a right to emit that greenhouse gas, even if not expressly stated.

Across all schemes, carbon units take the form of a unique serial number.[35] This number contains a string of component numbers that provide information on the unit, such as its year of creation, and the scheme in which it originated, or the offset project from which it was generated. This makes each individual unit unique and capable of identification.

Carbon units can be 'created' in one of two ways, and the difference in how they are created forms the basis of the two major categories of carbon units.[36] These two categories are 'allowance units' and 'offset units'.

Allowance units are created by the government or regulator operating an emissions trading scheme and are distributed to participants in the scheme through auctioning, selling, or freely allocating the units.[37] The maximum number of allowance units created and distributed by a government will usually equate to the quantitative limit it has set for greenhouse gas emissions in a given period. By allocating only a limited number of allowance units, a government effectively controls the amount of greenhouse gas that may be emitted.[38] Once distributed to private actors, carbon units may be freely traded in an open market. Thus, two key attributes of allowances units are: (i) they are created by governments or regulators; and (ii) their creation and release to the market is pursuant to, and circumscribed by, the statutory regime

[30] Federal Act on the Reduction of CO_2 Emissions (Switzerland) art 2.3.

[31] Modalities, rules and guidelines for emissions trading under Article 17 of the Kyoto Protocol, Decision 11/CMP.1, 1st sess (30 March 2006) FCCC/KP/CMP/2005/8/Add.2, annex [1].

[32] Environment Quality Act (Quebec) s 46(6).

[33] Clean Energy Act 2011 (Cth) s 4.

[34] Climate Change Response Act 2002 (NZ) ss 63–65, s 134.

[35] Partnership for Market Readiness and Forest Carbon Partnership Facility (PMR), *Emissions Trading Registries: Guidance on Regulation, Development, and Administration* (World Bank 2016) 4, 56–57. See eg Clean Energy Act (n 33) s 95; Climate Response Act (n 34) s 15; Modalities for the accounting of assigned amounts under Article 7, paragraph 4, of the Kyoto Protocol, Decision 13/CMP.1, 1st sess (30 March 2006) FCCC/KP/CMP/2005/8/Add.2, 23; Commission Regulation (EU) No 920/2010 of 7 October 2010 for a standardised and secured system of registries pursuant to Directive 2003/87/EC of the European Parliament and of the Council and Decision No 280/2004/EC of the European Parliament and of the Council [2010] OJ L270/1 art 39; California Market-based Mechanism (n 29) § 95802(285).

[36] Wemaere, Streck, and Chagas (n 2) 41–45.

[37] Godard, *Domestic Transferable Permits for Environmental Management* (n 1) 34–37, 69–75; Wemaere, Streck, and Chagas (n 2) 41–42.

[38] Godard, *Domestic Transferable Permits for Environmental Management* (n 1) 13, 91.

that supports the emissions trading scheme. Beyond generating the requisite quantity of unique serial numbers and releasing these to the market, there is no activity or effort involved in the creation of allowance units.[39]

By contrast, offset units are ordinarily[40] brought into existence by private actors.[41] In basic terms, they represent the reduction of greenhouse gas emissions outside of an emissions trading scheme. This reduction is usually the outcome of a project that either *removes* greenhouse gas from the atmosphere, for example through planting trees, or *avoids* emissions of greenhouse gas that would otherwise occur in the absence of the project, for example by installing cleaner technology in a factory leading to lower emissions.

In order to receive offset units for removing greenhouse gas from the atmosphere or for avoiding its emission, these projects must demonstrably lead to real, permanent, additional, and verified outcomes that achieve a net decrease and/or avoidance of greenhouse gas emissions.[42] Reductions in greenhouse gas that would have occurred in any case—for instance, through the use of less emissions-intensive technology because it is cheaper than higher emissions-intensive equivalents—would not meet the standard of generating 'real' and 'additional' greenhouse gas reductions. Removals of greenhouse gas from the atmosphere that are capable of being reversed at a later time—for instance, planted trees that are subsequently felled or cleared for urban or agricultural use—would not meet the standard of 'permanent' emissions removals. In practical terms, this means that such projects must be solely for the purpose of generating offset units that are then sold into domestic and international carbon markets.[43]

In that context, the presence of regulatory oversight in the generation of offset units is critical. While private actors undertake the project that reduces greenhouse gas emissions, regulatory agencies retain authority for issuing the offset units corresponding to those reductions. Accordingly, such regulatory agencies take responsibility for approving, monitoring, and verifying the projects and their resulting reductions of greenhouse gas.[44] Only once it has been independently verified that

[39] See PMR (n 35) 4, 57–61.

[40] It is also possible that a government might itself manage or investment in the generation of offset units, such as appears to be the case with Japan's Joint Crediting Mechanism.

[41] Wemaere, Streck, and Chagas (n 2) 43–44; Martijn Wilder, 'Nature of an Allowance' in Paul Q Watchman (ed), *Climate Change—A Guide to Carbon Law and Practice* (Global Business Publishing 2008) 93, 94–95.

[42] See eg UNFCCC Secretariat, 'Framework for various approaches: Technical Paper' (25 November 2014) FCCC/TP/2014/9, [25]–[26].

[43] See eg Executive Board of the Clean Development Mechanism, 'Sixty-Second Meeting Report' (15 July 2011) CDM-EB-62, annex 13 [6]. This stems from the principle of 'additionality' in the generation of offset units, which is embedded in all offset schemes: see eg Carbon Credits (Carbon Farming Initiative) Act 2011 (Cth) s 41 (CFI Act); California Market-based Mechanism (n 29) § 95972(a)(9); Modalities and procedures for a clean development mechanism, Decision 3/CMP.1, 1st sess (30 March 2006) FCCC/KP/CMP/2005/8/Add.1, annex [43] (CMP Decision 3). This includes both compliance markets established by emissions trading schemes, as well as voluntary carbon markets.

[44] Wilder (n 41) 93, 94. See eg CMP Decision 3 (n 43) annex parts H, I, and J; CFI Act (n 43) s 11(2), 16–18; California Air Resources Board, 'Chapter 6: What are the requirements for offset credits and how are they issued?' in *Cap-and-Trade Regulation Instructional Guidance* (California Air Resources Board 2012) [6.1]. http://www.arb.ca.gov/cc/capandtrade/guidance/guidance.htm (last accessed 15 January 2013).

emissions reductions have occurred can offset units be issued to the private actor undertaking the activity and then be sold into an emissions trading scheme, whereupon those units become fungible with allowance units. In essence, offset units allow companies and facilities covered by an emissions trading scheme to outsource the need to reduce their own emissions.

Thus, in contrast to allowance units, offset units are: (i) primarily the outcome of activity and effort by private actors seeking commercial benefit; and (ii) not required to be generated by a statutory regime, but are issued pursuant to statutory regimes provided that projects meet the monitoring, reporting, and verification requirements of that regime.

C Market for Trade and Investment in Carbon Units

Each carbon unit exists in an electronic form as a record in an emissions trading scheme's 'registry'. Registries effectively function as a bank for carbon units, and private entities may open accounts in a scheme's registry in which they can hold carbon units.[45]

Once a private entity has an account in a registry, it may buy and sell carbon units with other account holders in the registry.[46] This ability to trade carbon units represents one of their key uses. While most transactions of carbon units occur on established exchanges, there is also an active 'primary' market in offset units, whereby those engaged in a project that produces emissions reductions and generates offset units sell these directly to participants in the carbon market.[47] Participants in the carbon market include companies that are covered by an emissions trading scheme and are therefore required to hold carbon units in order to emit greenhouse gas and avoid a fine, as well as financial traders, investment banks, carbon funds, and commodity traders who treat carbon units as just another kind of tradable asset.[48] The diversity of participants in the carbon market reflects the different ways in which carbon units may be used. For some, they are used to avoid a financial penalty

[45] See eg Clean Energy Act (n 33) ss 104–107; Climate Response Act (n 34) s 18A, 18C; CMP Decision 13 (n 35) 28; Directive 2003/87/EC (n 28) art 19; California Market-based Mechanism (n 29) § 95831, § 95921.

[46] See eg Clean Energy Act (n 33) ss 104–107; Climate Response Act (n 34) s 18A, 18C; CMP Decision 13 (n 35) 28; Directive 2003/87/EC (n 28) art 19; California Market-based Mechanism (n 29) § 95831, § 95921.

[47] Karan Capoor and Philippe Ambrosi, *State and Trends of the Carbon Market 2009* (World Bank 2009) 30–38.

[48] See eg Jolene Lin, 'Private Actors in International and Domestic Emissions Trading Schemes' in David Freestone and Charlotte Streck (eds), *Legal Aspects of Carbon Trading: Kyoto, Copenhagen and beyond* (OUP 2009) 138; Anju Sanehi, 'Market Contracts' in Paul Q Watchman (ed), *Climate Change: A Guide to Carbon Law and Practice* (Globe Law and Business 2008) 111, 112. See also Damien Lockie, 'Closing Pandora's Box: The Case for Carbon Market Integrity after the Global Financial Crisis—Conditioning Ownership of the Right to Emit Greenhouse Gases in an Australian Emissions Trading Scheme' (PhD Thesis, Bond University 2011) 38–50.

imposed by an emissions trading scheme on those who emit greenhouse gas without holding a carbon unit.[49] For others, their trade is speculative and profits are made as prices rise and fall over time.

Additionally, the generation of offset units may be treated by some as an investment project or a form of security[50] and can be used to borrow money at attractive rates in a process called 'inventory monetisation'.[51] Carbon units may also be purchased as an investment asset (in competition with other potential investment opportunities) to generate longer-term returns.[52] Equally, as an alternative to acquiring carbon units as an investment, it is also possible to purchase carbon units in order to voluntarily offset one's own emissions.[53] In other words, by voluntarily paying for a carbon unit and refraining from reselling it into the market (eg by cancelling the unit), the purchaser is effectively funding the reduction of greenhouse gas emissions elsewhere. This forms the basis of the 'voluntary' market in carbon units, whose main participants include businesses, non-governmental organizations, and governmental bodies in pursuit of Corporate Social Responsibility goals and reputational or green-marketing objectives. The voluntary market is elaborated upon further in section E.

These varied uses of carbon units inform their economic value. Their value arises not only from their ability to be used to avoid a fine under an emissions trading scheme, but also from their ability to be traded as financial products, investment assets, and environmental offsets for individuals and companies that are not otherwise subject to liabilities under emissions trading schemes. Through the subsistence of value in carbon units, greenhouse gases are effectively converted from a waste product with negative value into a tradable article of commerce.[54] Lockie describes this as a process of 'commodification' of carbon units, whereby they are endowed with value and uses extraneous to the discrete environmental objective pursued by an emissions trading scheme.[55] In this regard, the trading of carbon units exhibits some characteristics common to trade in commodities, whereby trades often occur in large volumes through dedicated exchanges, and although the price of units may be fluid across time, the price for a given unit at any particular time is largely uniform across the market.[56]

[49] Wilder (n 41) 93, 100; Lin (n 48) 136.

[50] Wilder (n 41) 93, 94; CFI Act (n 43) s 157A.

[51] Neil C Schofield, *Commodity Derivatives* (John Wiley & Sons 2008) 257.

[52] Garnaut (n 19) 319; Lockie (n 48) 39–42.

[53] Wilder (n 41) 93, 100.

[54] For a general discussion of the conversion of waste products into valuable commodities see Mirina Grosz, *Sustainable Waste Trade under WTO Law* (Brill 2011) 15, 18, 48–49.

[55] Lockie (n 48) 25–50, 95–123.

[56] ibid 25–50, 95–123; Robert Howse and Antonia Eliason, 'Domestic and international strategies to address climate change: an overview of the WTO legal issues' in Thomas Cottier, Olga Nartova, and Sadeq Bigdeli (eds), *International Trade Regulation and the Mitigation of Climate Change* (CUP 2010) 54; Nadim Ahmad and John Verrinder, *OECD/EUROSTAT Task Force on the Treatment of Emission Allowances and Emission Permits in the National Accounts: Final Report* (Joint OECD/EUROSTAT Publication 2010) 35; Lin (n 48) 136, 137; Wilder (n 41) 93, 100. See also *Armstrong v Winnington Networks* [2012] EWHC 10 (Ch) [48]–[49].

Trading in carbon units can occur either through spot transactions,[57] whereby units are purchased at current prices for immediate delivery, or as derivative products,[58] which tend to dominate the carbon market.[59] Derivative products are financial instruments whose value derives from an underlying asset (eg carbon units),[60] and in the carbon market they usually take the form of forwards, futures, and options contracts.[61] In basic terms, a forward contract fixes an agreed price for delivery of carbon units at a future date.[62] Futures contracts are essentially the same, but are traded in standardized forms over organized exchanges.[63] Options contracts provide the right—but impose no obligation—to purchase carbon units at some time in the future for an agreed price.[64] These products also offer different ways of structuring or determining the payment of carbon units at a future date, such as a fixed price per unit, a price to pegged to the prevailing market at the time of maturity of the contract, or the use of a floor or ceiling price.[65] They therefore present a means of managing the risk of spikes or collapses in the price of carbon units.

Where the registries of two or more schemes are linked to one another, private entities may also trade units across these different schemes.[66] This is a crucial feature of carbon units, because it leads to their exportation and importation across national borders, which converts them into an article of international commerce. The linking of different schemes also alters the nature of carbon units, because they are no longer simply an object inherently embedded in a particular domestic regulatory framework.[67] Instead, they become more autonomous objects that are capable of being used in different regulatory schemes, independent of the original regulatory framework in which they were created. In other words, they are capable of having a valuable existence outside their original emissions trading scheme.

The increasing establishment of domestic emissions trading schemes around the world has seen a recent increase in moves to link different schemes. For example, the EU and Switzerland have recently finalized of a linking arrangement, whereby each scheme recognizes the carbon units issued by the other.[68] The EU emissions trading

[57] Andrew Hedges, 'The Secondary Market for Emissions Trading' in David Freestone and Charlotte Streck (eds), *Legal Aspects of Carbon Trading: Kyoto, Copenhagen and beyond* (OUP 2009) 324–25; Scott Deatherage, *Carbon Trading Law and Practice* (OUP 2011) 257.

[58] See Capoor and Ambrosi (n 47) 64–65.

[59] Alexandre Kossoy and Pierre Guigon, *State and Trends of the Carbon Market Report 2012* (World Bank 2012) 10, 30; European Commission (EC), 'Review of the Markets in Financial Instruments Directive (MiFID) and Proposals for a Regulation on Market Abuse and for a Directive on Criminal Sanctions for Market Abuse: Frequently Asked Questions on Emission Allowances' (Memo/11/719, 20 October 2011).

[60] Wilder (n 41) 93, 106; Schofield (n 51) 1–4.

[61] Schofield (n 51) 255; EC (n 59) 1; Hedges (n 57) 324–25.

[62] Schofield (n 51) 2.

[63] ibid.

[64] ibid 4.

[65] Martijn Wilder and Louisa Fitz-Gerald, 'Carbon Contracting' in David Freestone and Charlotte Streck (eds), *Legal Aspects of Carbon Trading: Kyoto, Copenhagen and beyond* (OUP 2009) 296, 303.

[66] See eg Clean Energy Act (n 33) s 108; Climate Response Act (n 34) ss 23, 23A, 30E; Directive 2003/87/EC (n 28) art 25; California Market-based Mechanism (n 29) § 95920, § 95943.

[67] Javier de Cendra de Larragan, 'Emissions trading schemes and WTO law: a typology of interactions' in Geert Van Calster and Denise Prevost (eds), *Research Handbook on Environment, Health and the WTO* (Edward Elgar Publishing 2013) 636, 647.

[68] Agreement between the European Union and the Swiss Confederation on the linking of their greenhouse gas emissions trading systems (7 December 2017) OJ L322/9, art 4.

scheme is also designed to interlink with Norway's emissions trading scheme, thereby recognizing each other's carbon units.[69] Similarly, California and Quebec have finalized a linking arrangement, whereby each other's carbon units will be accepted for compliance under their emissions trading schemes.[70] Prior to its rescission, the original Australian emissions trading scheme was due to recognize the allowance units of the EU for compliance after 2015, and the EU emissions trading scheme was due to reciprocate after 2018.[71]

Other domestic schemes are de facto linked through their common acceptance of offset units generated under the Kyoto Protocol in their domestic schemes.[72] The rules of the Kyoto Protocol allow private actors to transact in its carbon units, and it establishes an infrastructure through which its units can be traded across borders and between domestic schemes.[73] It is possible that the Paris Agreement will set out a framework for further linking of domestic emissions trading schemes, including a basic set of common rules, elements, and standards, however the outcome of those negotiations remain uncertain.[74]

Aside from domestic emissions trading schemes that are linked, the Kyoto Protocol established an international emissions trading scheme for countries with emissions reduction obligations in that treaty. Under that scheme, governments can trade carbon units generated under the Kyoto Protocol amongst themselves in order to obtain sufficient units to comply with those obligations.[75] In effect, this involves a form of government procurement of carbon units under the Kyoto Protocol to satisfy a country's obligations under that treaty. It is also possible that the Paris Agreement will facilitate a framework for international emissions trading, albeit less centralized, through which governments (and, most likely, private actors) will be able to purchase carbon units to fulfil their obligations, including offset units generated under the offset mechanism established by the Paris Agreement.[76]

[69] European Commission, 'Emissions trading: Commission announces linkage EU ETS with Norway, Iceland and Liechtenstein' (Media Release, IP/07/1617, 26 October 2007).

[70] California Air Resources Board, 'Air Resources Board amends cap and trade program, enhances market security' (News Release, 12–27, 28 June 2012); Regulation respecting a cap and trade system for greenhouse gas emission allowances 2014 (Quebec) appendix B.1; California Market-based Mechanism (n 29) § 95943.

[71] Department of Climate Change and Energy Efficiency, 'International linking' http://www.cleanenergyfuture.gov.au/international-linking/ (last accessed 15 April 2013); European Commission, the Hon Greg Combet AM MP, 'Australia and European Commission Agree on Pathway Towards Fully Linking Emissions Trading Schemes' (Media Release, 28 August 2012).

[72] David Freestone and Charlotte Streck, 'Linking of Emissions Trading Schemes' in David Freestone and Charlotte Streck (eds), *Legal Aspects of Carbon Trading: Kyoto, Copenhagen and beyond* (OUP 2009) 112–15.

[73] CMP Decision 11 (n 31) annex [5]. This distinction was also recognized by the European Court of Justice: Case 556/14 P *Holcim (Romania) SA v European Commission* (ECJ 7 April 2016) [64].

[74] World Bank, Ecofys, and Vivid Economics (n 21) 38–39.

[75] See eg Alexandre Kossoy and others, *State and Trends of Carbon Pricing 2014* (World Bank 2014) 44.

[76] World Bank, Ecofys, and Vivid Economics (n 21) 38–39.

D Legal Classification under Municipal Law

While by no means determinative, the legal classification of carbon units under municipal law can serve as evidence as to the proper classification of carbon units under international economic law.[77] As such, it is useful to assess how different schemes classify carbon units under their municipal legal systems.

Under some schemes, carbon units are expressly designated as property rights. For example, the current Australian scheme expressly classifies its carbon units as private property,[78] as does New Zealand legislation to regulate securities and for accounting purposes.[79] Carbon units have also been held to constitute property under English common law.[80] Under Chinese rules, carbon units (particularly offset units) appear to be designated as public property owned by the government, but whose proceeds are shared jointly by the government and the private entities involved in their generation.[81]

In contrast, under the rules of the Kyoto Protocol, it is explicitly clarified that its carbon units do not 'create or bestow any right, title or entitlement to emissions of any kind'.[82] Similarly, the Californian scheme expressly states that carbon units are *not* property rights.[83] Nonetheless, the majority of a Californian appellate court held that this designation relates 'only to property rights as against the state, not rights as between private parties', finding instead that 'the whole point of the "trade" part of the cap-and-trade system [is] the free alienability of the allowances as between private parties [which] makes them property for due process purposes'.[84] The court of another municipal division of the United States, namely Louisiana, also rejected an argument that carbon units are not property under its legal system. Instead, it found that 'the right to report, transfer, or sell carbon credits is a part of the bundle of rights associated with property ownership'.[85]

The difference in how jurisdictions approach the issue of proprietary status can affect whether carbon units have a permanent and stable quality. For instance, in the New Zealand emissions trading scheme, the government may only cancel (ie destroy) carbon units without the consent of their owner where the owner has failed

[77] The precise function of municipal law in determining whether an object constitutes 'property' under international economic law is subject to continuing debate, and there are divergent approaches in the international trade and investment regimes. These differing approaches are discussed further in chs 4 and 7.

[78] CFI Act (n 43) s 150.

[79] Securities Markets Act 1988 (NZ) s 37(1); Income Tax Act 2007 (NZ) s YA 1 (Definitions).

[80] *Armstrong v Winnington Networks* [2012] EWHC 10 (Ch).

[81] Measures for Operation and Management of Clean Development Mechanism Projects in China (People's Republic of China) art 24 http://cdm.ccchina.gov.cn/english/NewsInfo.asp?NewsId=905 (last accessed 20 January 2015).

[82] Principles, nature and scope of the mechanisms pursuant to Articles 6, 12 and 17 of the Kyoto Protocol, Decision 2/CMP.1, 1st sess (30 March 2006) FCCC/KP/CMP/2005/8/Add.1, 4.

[83] California Market-based Mechanism (n 29) § 95820(c).

[84] *California Chamber of Commerce et al v State Air Resources Board et al*, Court of Appeal, Third District, California (6 April 2017).

[85] *Roseland Plantation v United States Fish and Wildlife Service*, 2006 U.S. Dist. LEXIS 29334, 2.

to comply with certain laws, or where the cancellation is necessary to comply with New Zealand's obligations under the Kyoto Protocol.[86] Under Australia's current emissions trading scheme, the government may only cancel carbon units without the consent of their owner where those units were issued on the basis of false or misleading information, where those units were issued for offset projects that are subsequently found not to permanently reduce greenhouse gas, or where fraud was involved in the issuance of the units.[87] Outside of these defined circumstances under the New Zealand and Australian schemes, the subsistence of carbon units in registry accounts is at the behest of their owners. Carbon units in such systems thus possess a degree of permanence and stability, since they continue to exist in a registry account and subsist from year to year until they are sold, cancelled or surrendered for compliance purposes.

This can be contrasted with the Californian and Quebecois schemes, under which the respective governments expressly reserve the right to cancel carbon units without the consent of their owners for any reason.[88] This could potentially lessen the perception by the owners of such units of their permanent or stable character.

Other jurisdictions are silent as to whether they confer proprietary status on carbon units. For instance, the European Court of Justice expressly avoided addressing whether carbon units qualify as property under Article 17(1) of the Charter of Fundamental Rights of the European Union in a recent case.[89] Uncertainty over the status of carbon units in the EU emissions trading scheme has been subject to criticism and calls for reform, such as clarifications on how they should be treated for tax and accounting purposes, how they should be dealt with in the insolvency of a registered holder, whether and to what extent they should be treated as subject to regulation as an investment, and whether they are capable of being stolen, or otherwise being the subject of property-based criminal activity.[90] Indeed, the European Court of Auditors unambiguously recommended in 2015 that carbon units be designated as property under EU law to enhance certainty and promote stability in the market.[91]

Carbon units are also regulated as financial products under some schemes. Under the Australian scheme, carbon units constitute 'financial products' under the Corporations Act 2001 (Cth) and the Australian Securities and Investments Commission Act 2001 (Cth), which means that the providers of financial services in relation to carbon units must hold a financial services licence.[92] Initially, EU rules

86 Climate Response Act (n 34) s 7(2). 87 CFI Act (n 43) s 175.

88 Environment Quality Act (Quebec) s 46(12); California Market-based Mechanism (n 29) § 95820(c). Note that these provisions apply to allowance units issued under those schemes, not to offset units.

89 Case T-317/12 *Holcim (Romania) SA v European Commission* (ECJ 18 September 2014) [161]–[170].

90 Bank of England, 'Legal assessment of lacunae in the legal framework of the European Emissions Trading Scheme and the case for legislative reform' (Issue 1116, Financial Markets Law Committee, October 2009) 5.

91 European Court of Auditors, 'The Integrity and Implementation of the EU ETS' (Special Report No 6, 2015) 47.

92 Corporations Act 2001 (Cth) s 764A(1)(kaa); Australian Securities and Investments Commission Act 2001 (Cth) s 12BAA(7)(ka).

only regulated the derivative products of carbon units (options, futures, and forwards) as financial products, with the units themselves not regulated in that way.[93] However, the EU has now moved additionally to classify the units themselves as financial products subject to financial market regulation.[94] This will likely bring a degree of certainty and harmonization to the classification of units across different EU Member States in financial markets, which have varied from expressly classifying units as financial instruments, such as in Sweden, to expressly exempting them from certain financial regulation, such as in Germany.[95]

Interestingly, Austria, the Czech Republic, Finland, France, Germany, Italy, Poland, Portugal, and Spain had treated carbon units as commodities for the purpose of financial regulation.[96] Kazakhstan also regulates its carbon units as commodities.[97] Commodities are tradable goods without qualitative differentiation across a given market, suggesting carbon units exhibit goods-like aspects.[98] By contrast, a non-binding EU rule that is almost universally applied by its Member States specifies that the transfer of carbon units is a taxable supply of services for the purposes of value-added taxation.[99] Similarly, under Australian law, buying and selling carbon units on behalf of another person is a 'designated service' for the purposes of the Anti-Money Laundering and Counter-Terrorism Financing Act 2006 (Cth).[100]

The question of how to classify carbon units for accounting purposes has similarly led to conceptual difficulties. The most recent System of National Accounts, which is the internationally agreed standard set of standards on how to account for economic activity, acknowledges that '[t]radable emission permits are a relatively new phenomenon, but they are gaining rapidly in importance', while nonetheless conceding that '[t]he full treatment of all types of permits is not explicitly described in the SNA, and in order to remove uncertainty, this shortcoming should be addressed as quickly as possible'.[101] The International Accounting Standards Board initially found that carbon units are 'intangible assets' to be recognized as such in financial statements, but subsequently withdrew this finding after controversy over their proper classification.[102]

In view of the foregoing, there appears to be a marked lack of consistency across different jurisdictions as to how carbon units are legally classified. This may, in part, be explained by the fact that legal characterizations are designed to serve specific purposes, such as protection from expropriation, ensuring accurate and consistent

[93] EC (n 59). [94] ibid.

[95] See Anttonen, Mehling, and Upston-Hooper (n 18) 98, 103.

[96] European Environment Agency (EEA), *Application of the Emissions Trading Directive by EU Member States—reporting year 2008* (Office for Official Publications of the European Communities 2008) 74–75.

[97] Carbon Limits and Thomas Reuters Point Carbon, 'The Domestic Emissions Trading Scheme in Kazakhstan' (Discussion Paper, European Bank for Reconstruction and Development 2013) 14.

[98] EEA (n 96) 74–75. [99] ibid.

[100] Anti-Money Laundering and Counter-Terrorism Financing Act *2006* (Cth) item 33 of the table in s 6(2).

[101] EC, IMF, OECD, UN and World Bank, *System of National Accounts 2008* (United Nations 2008) [A4.47].

[102] International Accounting Standards Board, 'IFRIC 3—Emission Rights (withdrawn)' http://www.iasplus.com/en/standards/ifric/ifric3 (last accessed 30 May 2015).

accounting standards, imposing fiduciary duties, and clarifying tax treatment.[103] These considerations will vary from jurisdiction to jurisdiction, and hence preferred designations will vary.

E Voluntary Market

The foregoing analysis applies to carbon units insofar as they are the units of exchange in government-mandated emissions trading schemes. There is, however, a voluntary market in carbon unit that caters for individuals, companies, and governments that seek voluntarily to reduce their carbon footprint by purchasing and cancelling carbon units. The voluntary market is significantly smaller than the 'compulsory' market serving emissions trading schemes, representing just US$191 million worth of transactions in 2016.[104]

The voluntary market can comprise trade in both allowance units and offset units. However, these different types of units perform subtly different functions in the voluntary market. In respect of allowance units, a consumer may voluntarily purchase and cancel an allowance unit for the purpose of reducing the permissible quantum of emissions in an emissions trading scheme. In effect, the purchase and cancellation of an allowance unit in the voluntary market means that the emission of one tonne of greenhouse gas in the context of an emissions trading scheme has been prevented. In respect of offset units, a consumer may purchase an offset unit because it represents the verified reduction or removal of one tonne of greenhouse gas from the atmosphere—there is no nexus to emissions trading schemes.

Carbon units thus possess some different attributes when used in the voluntary market vis-à-vis emissions trading schemes. First, they do not represent the right to emit one tonne of greenhouse gas, and there is no threat of a penalty for those emitters that do not hold carbon units. Instead, they represent a desire on the part of those consuming the carbon units to reduce the amount of greenhouse gas in the atmosphere. As such, their origins do not lie in a policy choice to convert a common resource into divisible private rights through a transferable permit scheme. Their origins are instead derived from consumer demand for emissions reduction.

Secondly, and relatedly, the economic value of carbon units in the context of the voluntary market is not derived from the possibility of a financial penalty or from speculative trading. Instead, it is derived from the altruistic motivations of the individuals consuming the units.

The avenues through which carbon units are traded in the voluntary market are diverse. For instance, the Clean Development Mechanism created a platform in 2015 for private consumers to purchase and cancel offset units generated by private actors under its auspices.[105] Consumers can select offset units by reference to their

[103] See Mace (n 18) 123; Anttonen, Mehling, and Upston-Hooper (n 18) 96.

[104] World Bank, Ecofys, and Vivid Economics, (n 21) 40–41; Kelley Hamrick and Melissa Gallant, *State and Trends of Voluntary Carbon Markets 2017* (Ecosystem Marketplace 2017) 15.

[105] See UNFCCC Secretariat, 'CDM Registry' https://cdm.unfccc.int/Registry/index.html (last accessed 8 January 2018).

project type, country of origin, or other criteria in line with their organizational or personal preferences. As another example, in 2016 the International Finance Corporation developed a 'Forests Bond' that aims to pay a coupon in the form of offset units to bondholders on the basis of a forest conservation offset project in Kenya.[106] The World Bank has also set up a 'Pilot Auction Facility' that sets a floor price for future offset units from projects reducing methane emissions at waste sites in the form of a tradable put option, which is competitively allocated via auction.[107] It is likely that the means and tools for trading carbon units in the voluntary market will continue to grow as the international carbon market matures over time.

In most other respects, the inherent characteristics of carbon units in voluntary markets are the same as discussed above.

[106] See International Finance Corporation, 'Forests Bonds' https://www.ifc.org/wps/wcm/connect/5299a595-721b-41ef-90fa-2cff3d50982c/FINAL+Forests+Bond+Investor+Presentation+10-5_pdf.pdf?MOD=AJPERES (last accessed 8 January 2018).

[107] See World Bank, 'Pilot Auction Facility for Methane and Climate Change Mitigation' http://www.worldbank.org/content/dam/Worldbank/document/Climate/climate2014-paf-brief-091214.pdf (last accessed 8 January 2018).

PART II

CHARACTERIZATION OF CARBON UNITS

4

International Trade in Carbon Units under GATT 1994 and Free Trade Agreements*

This chapter surveys whether carbon units constitute objects that fall within the meaning of the terms 'goods' or 'products' under international economic law and, more specifically, under the General Agreement on Tariffs and Trade 1994 (GATT 1994)[1] and free trade agreements covering trade in goods.

At the outset, it is useful to note that GATT 1994 contains no express definition of the terms 'products' and 'goods'.[2] Further, despite the absence any express definition of those terms, there have been exceptionally few examples of their scope being questioned and tested over the seven decades of their application through GATT 1994 (and its predecessor, GATT 1947).[3] As such, there has tended to be a very

* The content of this chapter revises, updates, and builds upon James Munro, 'Pushing the boundaries of "products" and "goods" under GATT 1994: An analysis of the coverage of new and unorthodox articles of commerce' (2013) 47 *Journal of World Trade* 1323.

[1] Marrakesh Agreement Establishing the World Trade Organization (opened for signature 15 April 1994, entered into force 1 January 1995) 1867 UNTS 3 annex IA (General Agreement on Tariffs and Trade) (GATT 1994).

[2] See GATT 1994 (n 1). The term 'products' is the principal term used in arts I, II, III, and XI. The term 'goods' is used in the preamble, art V, and in isolated instances elsewhere in the text.

[3] The few examples include: GATT Panel Report, *Canada—Measures Affecting the Sale of Gold Coins* (unadopted) (application of GATT 1947 to gold coins); Appellate Body Reports, *Canada—Renewable*

limited body of jurisprudence that directly informs the question of the precise content and scope of 'goods' and 'products' under GATT 1994.

Therefore, following the approach to treaty interpretation set out in Chapter 2, the analysis of this chapter begins with the ordinary meaning of the terms 'products' and 'goods', followed by an assessment of their context, as well as the object and purpose of GATT 1994 and the Agreement Establishing the World Trade Organization (WTO Agreement).[4] The limited body of relevant jurisprudence is then considered, including panel and Appellate Body reports in *Canada—Renewable Energy/Canada—Feed-in Tariff Program, China—Publications and Audiovisual Products, US—Softwood Lumber IV, US—Large Civil Aircraft (2nd Complaint)*, and *US—Large Civil Aircraft (2nd complaint) (Article 21.5—EU)*. Finally, a sample of free trade agreements is reviewed to assess the extent to which they might also cover carbon units as 'goods' or 'products'. This chapter concludes that it is more likely than not that carbon units would be considered to fall within the scope of those terms. Indeed, the main feature causing doubt is the absence of any clear 'production' involved in the creation of certain classes and kinds of carbon units.

Although a number of authors have grappled with the question of whether carbon units may be considered 'goods' or 'products' for the purposes of GATT 1994, it is argued that these analyses tend either to be obsolete due to subsequent developments, or premised on incorrect assumptions. For instance, some have asserted that 'goods' or 'products' must be 'tangible things' and therefore carbon units cannot fall within the scope of GATT 1994 owing to their intangible quality as an electronic record.[5] As will be shown, however, there is not a strong basis for a limitation relating to tangibility in either the ordinary meaning of these terms or in WTO jurisprudence.

Others have argued that carbon units are 'fundamentally government creations to facilitate compliance with international obligations' under climate treaties, and thus 'a form of "legal tender" or "means of payment" in satisfaction of sovereign obligations', which is not subject to GATT 1994.[6] It is true that some carbon units are used and purchased by governments for compliance with international

Energy/Canada—Feed-in Tariff Program (application of GATT 1994 to electricity); *Application of GATT to International Trade in Television Programmes: Report of the Working Party* (21 November 1961) GATT Doc L/1646 (application of GATT 1947 to television); Appellate Body Report, *China—Publications and Audiovisual Products* (application to physical media containing copyright content—although this was in relation to China's Accession Protocol, not GATT 1994); Appellate Body Report, *Canada—Periodicals* (application of GATT 1994 to periodicals).

[4] Marrakesh Agreement Establishing the World Trade Organization (n 1) (Agreement establishing the World Trade Organization) (WTO Agreement).

[5] Glenn M Wiser, 'The Clean Development Mechanism Versus the World Trade Organization: Can Free-Market Greenhouse Gas Emissions Abatement Survive Free Trade?' (1999) 11 *Georgetown International Environmental Law Review* 531, 558; Jacob Werksman, 'Greenhouse Gas Emissions Trading and the WTO' (1999) 8 *Review of European Community & International Environmental Law* 251, 255; Marisa Martin, 'Trade Law Implications for Restricting Participation in The European Union Emissions Trading Scheme' (2006) *Georgetown International Environmental Law Review* 437, 446–47; Felicity Deane, *Emissions Trading and WTO Law* (Edward Elgar Publishing 2015) 97.

[6] See Annie Petsonk, 'The Kyoto Protocol and the WTO: Integrating Greenhouse Gas Emissions Allowance Trading into the Global Marketplace' (1999) 10 *Duke Environmental Law and Policy Forum* 185, 199–201; Steve Charnovitz, 'Trade and Climate: Potential Conflicts and Synergies' in Pew Centre on Global Climate Change, *Beyond Kyoto: Advancing the International Effort Against Climate Change* (2003) 141. These views have since been cited on numerous occasions to justify an apparent general

obligations.[7] However, it does not follow that carbon units are therefore exempt from international economic law.[8] Nothing in the WTO Agreement suggests that trade by and between governments should be exempt, ipso facto, from its scope. On the contrary, the WTO Agreement contains express provisions concerning government procurement and concerning state trading enterprises.[9] In any case, trading by governments in carbon units to satisfy international obligations is nowadays a peripheral component of the international carbon market, which is instead dominated by private investors, financial traders, and large emitters with liabilities under domestic emissions trading schemes.[10]

In contrast, some have conceded the possibility that carbon units could potentially be considered 'goods' or 'products'—albeit without proceeding to conduct an in-depth study of the contours and outer limits of 'goods' and 'products', and whether carbon units may fall within their scope.[11] This chapter undertakes a fresh and comprehensive assessment of whether carbon units qualify as 'goods' and 'products'.

A Ordinary Meaning of 'Goods' and 'Products'

As mentioned above, the Appellate Body has recognized that the task of interpreting a treaty must begin with its specific words and text in order to ascertain their 'ordinary meaning'.[12]

However, the fact that GATT 1994 uses two different terms to refer to the objects that it covers, namely, 'products' and 'goods', presents an immediate difficulty of interpretation in determining their ordinary meaning: are these different terms

academic consensus on the issue. See eg James Windon, 'The Allocation of Free Emissions Units and the WTO Subsidies Agreement' (2010) 41 *Georgetown Journal of International Law* 189, 207; Jillian Button, 'Carbon: Commodity or Currency? The Case for an International Carbon Market Based on the Currency Model' (2008) 32 *Harvard Environmental Law Review* 571, 502; Javier de Cendra, 'Can Emissions Trading Schemes Be Coupled with Border Tax Adjustments? An Analysis vis-a-vis WTO Law' (2006) 15 *Review of European Community & International Environmental Law* 131, 137; Wen-chen Shih, *Legal Nature of the Traded Units under the Emissions Trading Systems and Its Implication to the Relationship between Emissions Trading and the WTO* (National Chengchi University 2011) 28–30.

[7] See eg Alexandre Kossoy and others, *State and Trends of Carbon Pricing 2014* (World Bank 2014) 44; Alexandre Kossoy and Philippe Ambrosi, *State and Trends of the Carbon Market Report 2011* (World Bank 2011) 6.

[8] See eg Christina Voigt, *Sustainable Development as a Principle of International Law* (Brill 2009) 208.

[9] See eg Marrakesh Agreement Establishing the World Trade Organization (n 1) annex IB (General Agreement on Trade in Services) (GATS) art XIII; GATT 1994 (n 1) arts III.8(a), XVII.

[10] See eg Kossoy and others (n 7) 44; Kossoy and Ambrosi (n 7) 61.

[11] Elias Leake Quinn, 'The Solitary Attempt: International Trade Law and the Insulation of Domestic Greenhouse Gas Trading Schemes from Foreign Emissions Credit Markets' (2009) 80 *University of Colorado Law Review* 201, 248; Christina Voigt, 'WTO Law and International Emissions Trading: Is There Potential for Conflict?' (2008) 1 *Carbon & Climate Law Review* 54, 55–56; Sikina Jinnah, 'Emissions trading under the Kyoto Protocol: NAFTA and WTO concerns' (2003) 15 *Georgetown International Environmental Law Review* 709, 721; Erich Vranes, 'Climate Change and the WTO: EU Emission Trading and the WTO Disciplines on Goods, Services and Investment Protection' (2009) 43 *Journal of World Trade* 707, 717–18.

[12] Appellate Body Reports, *Japan—Alcoholic Beverages II* 12; *India—Patents (US)* [45]; *US—Shrimp* [114].

intended to denote different scopes and meanings, or are they used interchangeably as synonyms? This is an important preliminary issue to resolve because, if they are intended to denote different meanings, two separate analyses will be required—one into the scope of the term 'goods', and one into the scope of term 'products'. Furthermore, their respective interpretations will likely affect one another and have an impact on each other's scope.

On the other hand, if they are interchangeable synonyms, one holistic inquiry will suffice that blends and harmonizes the ordinary meaning of the two terms. As will be shown, this analysis requires interpretive tools beyond those normally used at the 'ordinary meaning' stage of the interpretive process, including recourse to the French and Spanish language versions, as well as the negotiating history of GATT 1947. While this may, strictly speaking, extend beyond 'ordinary meaning', it is useful to address as a preliminary question because it informs subsequent stages of the analysis. Having addressed this issue, this section turns to a more orthodox assessment of the ordinary meaning.

1 'Goods' and 'products': synonyms or different terms?

An overview of the use of the terms 'goods' and 'products' in GATT 1994 paints a convoluted picture. Overall, the term 'products' appears significantly more frequently, with over 200 references compared to only about a dozen for 'goods'. Some provisions tend to use 'products' as the chief descriptor of the objects regulated,[13] while others tend to use 'goods'[14]—but even within particular provisions, there is a mixed use of terms.[15]

On one hand, the Appellate Body has repeatedly stressed the importance of the principle of effectiveness in treaty interpretation.[16] According to this principle, a treaty interpreter must read all provisions of a treaty in a way that gives meaning to *all* of them.[17] This means that a treaty interpreter must give meaning to a difference in wording,[18] and that the use of different terms should give rise to a presumption of an intended difference in scope.[19] If 'goods' and 'products' were simply treated as interchangeable synonyms, it would deprive the use of these different terms of any meaning or effect, contrary to the principle of effectiveness.

On the other hand, however, an analysis of the terms reveals that it is by no means obvious what reasonable difference could be ascribed to 'goods' and 'products' in GATT 1994. The use of 'goods' in the preamble of GATT 1994 and title of Annex 1A of the WTO Agreement (which contains GATT 1994) suggests that it should be the broader term, given the scene-setting function of preambles and titles. Further, the clarification in Ad Article XVI.2 that 'goods' in that specific paragraph is limited

[13] See eg GATT 1994 (n 1) arts I, II, III, and XI.

[14] See eg ibid, preamble and art V.

[15] See eg ibid, arts V.6, III.8(a), II.1(c), and ad art VI.1.

[16] See eg Appellate Body Reports, *Canada—Dairy* [133]; *US—Gasoline* 23; *US—Upland Cotton* [549].

[17] See eg Appellate Body Reports, *US—Gasoline* 23; *Argentina—Footwear (EC)* [81].

[18] Appellate Body Reports, *China—Raw Materials* [325].

[19] See eg Appellate Body Reports, *US—Gasoline* 23, [44]–[45]; *EC—Hormones* [164].

to '*products* as understood in commercial practice' suggests that 'goods' should ordinarily be understood as broader than 'products'.[20]

However, Article III.8(a) points to an opposite inference. It provides for a government procurement exception that applies to the procurement of '*products* purchased for government purposes and not ... with a view to use in the production of *goods* for commercial sale'.[21] Clearly, this suggests that 'products' can be an input material in the production of 'goods', which seems to be an end-use category. However, it can be inferred from other provisions both in Article III and elsewhere in GATT 1994 that 'products' can also refer to end-use items for commercial sale.[22] This suggests that 'products' is the overarching term, with 'goods' referring to something more akin to retail merchandize. The inference that 'products' should be interpreted as the overarching term is further strengthened by the significantly higher frequency of its use, as well as its use as the principal term in the core provisions.[23]

To add to the confusion, the French and Spanish language versions of GATT 1994 reveal a somewhat incoherent usage of terminology corresponding to 'products' and 'goods'.[24] As a general tendency, the term 'produits' is used in the French version and 'productos' in the Spanish version, where 'products' is used in the English version,[25] with 'marchandises' and 'mercancías' similarly used for 'goods'.[26] However, this is by no means consistent. On a number of occasions in GATT 1994, 'goods' appears as 'produits'/'productos',[27] and, similarly, 'products' appears as 'marchandises'.[28] This mix-and-match of terms in the different language versions suggests that, at least to some extent, 'products' and 'goods' could be viewed as interchangeable terms.

With these divergent strands of logic leaving the question of whether 'products' and 'goods' are synonyms or different terms 'ambiguous' and 'obscure', it is appropriate to consult the negotiating history of GATT 1994.[29] This too, however, reveals a fragmented picture.

On one hand, the negotiating history appears to demonstrate that the drafters were considered in their selection of the term 'products' vis-a-vis 'goods'. For example, on

[20] GATT 1994 (n 1) art XVII.2 (emphasis added).

[21] ibid art III.8(a) (emphasis added).

[22] For example, references to 'offering for sale' of products in GATT 1994 art III.1 and 'requirements affecting the internal sale' and 'purchase' of products in GATT 1994 art III.4, and generally provisions on anti-dumping in GATT 1994 art VI. See also Panel Report, *US—Cotton Yarn* n 203.

[23] See eg GATT 1994 (n 1) arts I, II, III, and XI.

[24] According to GATT 1994 (n 1) art 2(c)(i): 'The text of GATT 1994 shall be authentic in English, French and Spanish'. According to the Appellate Body, 'the terms of a treaty authenticated in more than one language—like the WTO Agreement—are presumed to have the same meaning in each authentic text. It follows that the treaty interpreter should seek the meaning that gives effect, simultaneously, to all the terms of the treaty, as they are used in each authentic language': Appellate Body Report, *US—Softwood Lumber IV* [59].

[25] See eg GATT 1994 (n 1) arts I.1, I.4, II.1(b), II.1(c), II.2, II.4, III.1, III.2, III.3, III.5, VI 1, VI.2, VI.3, VI.4, VI.5, IX.1, X.1, XI.1.

[26] See eg ibid, arts III.8(a), V, XII.3(c)(ii), XVII.2, and XVIII.10.

[27] See eg ibid, preamble recital 1 and art II.1(c).

[28] See eg ibid, arts VII.2 and XXXVII.3(a).

[29] This is permitted where the meaning remains ambiguous or obscure, as here: Vienna Convention on the Law of Treaties (opened for signature 23 May 1969, entered into force 27 January 1980) 1155 UNTS 331 art 33(a).

a number of occasions, it appears that the drafters were deliberate in their choice of terminology between 'products' and 'goods'.[30] On the other hand, the minutes of a discussion on proposals for the term 'product' versus 'class of goods' in a particular draft provision suggests that they were not considered to have materially different scopes; the negotiators clearly use the terms as interchangeable synonyms rather than inherently different concepts in their textual discussion.[31]

Perhaps most persuasive is that, even if it is presumed that these terms have different scopes, it is almost impossible to construe any meaningful distinction between them in practice. Looking at the text of GATT 1994 as a whole, it is apparent that 'products' can refer to both input materials in the production of goods,[32] as well as themselves be end-use items of commercial consumption, which can be traded across borders.[33] Goods can also be end-use articles of consumption capable of international trade,[34] in addition to being 'products as understood in commercial practice' which can, in turn, be input materials.[35] They therefore appear to have the same practical application. This, coupled with the fact that their equivalents are mixed and matched in the other language versions version, suggests that they should be considered interchangeable terms.

As such, this chapter undertakes an interpretation of the terms 'products' and 'goods' on the basis that they are generally synonymous under GATT 1994 and should not be read against each other.[36]

2 Dictionary definitions

As discussed in Chapter 2, dictionaries have been recognized as a useful starting point in shedding light on the ordinary meaning of a term.[37] Indeed, in construing the scope of the term 'goods' in Article 1.1(a)(1)(iii) of the Agreement on Subsidies

[30] See eg Proposed Redraft of the Final Text of Chapter IV—Section E (28 February 1948) E/CONF.2/C.8/4/Rev.1 (Central Drafting Committee of GATT 1947), 5 http://www.wto.org/gatt_docs/1946_50.htm (last accessed 10 January 2018); *Report of the Technical Sub-Committee* (11 February 1947) E/PC/T/C.6/55/Rev.1 (Drafting Committee of the Preparatory Committee of the United Nations Conference on Trade and Employment) 47: the phrase 'the *products* of prison labour' was substituted for the phrase 'prison-made *goods*' (emphasis added) http://www.wto.org/gatt_docs/1946_50.htm (last accessed 10 January 2018); *Report of the Legal Drafting Committee of the Tariff Agreement Committee on the Annexes and Schedules Attached to the General Agreement* (23 September 1947) E/PC/T/215 (Second Session of the Preparatory Committee of the United Nations Conference on Trade and Employment) 28: apparent attempt to harmonize the terminology across different language versions <http://www.wto.org/gatt_docs/1946_50.htm (last accessed 10 January 2018).

[31] *Verbatim Report: Twenty-Eighth Meeting of Commission A*, E/PC/T/A/PV/28 (8 July 1947) (Second Session of the Preparatory Committee of the United Nations Conference on Trade and Employment) 6, 15, 19, 24 http://www.wto.org/gatt_docs/1946_50.htm>.

[32] See eg GATT 1994 (n 1) art III.8(a). [33] See eg ibid art VI.1(a).

[34] See eg ibid art III.8(a). [35] See eg ibid ad art XVII.2.

[36] This approach accords with Appellate Body Report, *US—Tax Incentives* [5.9]. Of course, it is recognized that in specific instances in particular provisions they may yield different scopes. For example, GATT 1994 art II limits the term 'products' to only those items listed in Members' binding tariff schedules.

[37] Appellate Body Report, *EC—Chicken Cuts* [175]–[176].

and Countervailing Measures (hereafter SCM Agreement),[38] the Appellate Body in *US—Softwood Lumber IV* began with *Black's Law Dictionary* and the *Shorter Oxford English Dictionary*.[39] As such, it is appropriate to commence an interpretation of the scope of 'products' and 'goods' by consulting their relevant dictionary definitions.

The *Shorter Oxford English Dictionary* defines 'goods' as '[p]roperty or possessions; now in more restricted sense, movable property ... [t]he plural form occurs as a sing.: [p]roperty, an amount of property'.[40] *Black's Law Dictionary* defines 'goods' as '[t]angible or movable personal property other than money; esp., articles of trade or items of merchandise <goods and services>' or as '[t]hings that have value, whether tangible or not (the importance of social goods varies from society to society)'.[41]

While not identical, these definitions do share certain elements—the subsistence of property rights in the item, or the ability to own and possess it, appear in both. Whether an item is tangible and movable also seems to be a relevant, but not necessarily determinative, consideration.

Turning to the term 'products', the *Shorter Oxford English Dictionary* defines it as:[42]

> (a.) An object produced by a particular action or process; the result of mental or physical work or effort. (c.) spec. An article or substance that is manufactured or refined for sale (more recently also applied to services). Now usually denoting goods that are mass produced and commercially marketed.

This can be juxtaposed with the relevant definition in *Black's Law Dictionary*:[43]

> Something that is distributed commercially for use or consumption that is usu. (1) tangible personal property, (2) the result of fabrication or processing, and (3) an item that has passed through a chain of commercial distribution before ultimate use or consumption.

Common features of these definitions are the requirement for some form of human effort to have been expended in the creation of the item, and that the item will have usually entered into channels of commerce. While *Black's Law Dictionary* suggests that the term usually refers to tangible items, the *Shorter Oxford English Dictionary* suggests that the term can extend to the production of services, which tend to be intangible. Although the *Shorter Oxford English Dictionary* does not directly mention 'property', it does state that the term 'products' usually denotes 'goods', which it in turn defines as 'property', as outlined above.

Clearly, the dictionary definitions of 'goods' and 'products' are not definitive in delimiting the scope of these terms the purposes of GATT 1994. They do, however, suggest a spectrum of characteristics that could inform the content of these terms. Whether an item is personal property that can be possessed and traded, whether it

[38] Marrakesh Agreement Establishing the World Trade Organization (n 1) annex IA (Agreement on Subsidies and Countervailing Measures) (SCM Agreement) art 1.1(a)(1)(iii).

[39] Appellate Body Report, *US—Softwood Lumber IV* [59].

[40] *Oxford English Dictionary Online* (OUP 2012) 'good, adj., adv., and n' http://www.oed.com/view/Entry/79925?rskey=79OtP7&result=1&isAdvanced=false (last accessed 28 October 2012).

[41] *Black's Law Dictionary* (9th edn, West 2009) 'goods'.

[42] *OED Online* (n 40) 'product, n.1'.

[43] *Blvack's Law Dictionary* (n 41) 'product'.

can be physically touched and moved, whether some degree of human effort has been exerted in its production, whether it holds economic value, and whether it is intended for commercial distribution and consumption, all seem to be relevant elements.

While not all of these elements appear across the different definitions of 'goods' and 'products', they do illustrate the band of wide and narrow meanings that could be attributed to those terms. For example, on one broad reading, these terms could refer to anything of value that is capable of being possessed and traded. On a more narrow reading, they might refer only to mass-produced, physically tangible objects intended for commercial consumption that have been manufactured or processed in some way and in which property rights subsist. Whether these terms should attract a broad or narrow reading will therefore depend in large part on the context in which they appear, which leads to the next stage of the analysis addressed in section B.

The plausible range of broad and narrow meanings is important in respect of carbon units. On a broad reading, carbon units would likely qualify as 'goods'/ 'products', since they are items with value that are capable of being owned, possessed and traded. On a narrower reading, they would likely not qualify, since they are not tangible, they are not recognized as 'property' under the municipal law of some jurisdictions, and whether they can truly be said to have been 'produced' is doubtful in respect of allowance units.

As discussed in Chapter 2, other international instruments can conceivably shed light on the scope of the ordinary meaning of terms in the WTO Agreement. In this regard, it is noteworthy that, under decisions taken pursuant to the Kyoto Protocol,[44] parties to that treaty agreed that its carbon units do not 'create or bestow any right, title or entitlement to emissions of any kind'.[45] On its face, this text suggests that the carbon units of the Kyoto Protocol should not be construed as proprietary in nature. However, the negotiating history of this provision suggests that it was instead directed at clarifying the nature of countries' mitigation commitments under the Kyoto Protocol, and in particular, issues relating to the grandfathering of historical emissions.[46] It was not intended to shed light on the proprietary status (or otherwise) of carbon units.

Despite having a significantly smaller membership than the WTO Agreement—and thus unlikely to qualify as context under Article 31.3(c) of the Vienna Convention—the United Nations Convention on Contracts for the International Sale of Goods could nonetheless shed light on the ordinary meaning of 'goods' in international commerce and the relevance of tangibility.[47] In particular, its definition of 'goods' explicitly lists certain items that are *not* to be considered 'goods' for

[44] Kyoto Protocol to the United Nations Framework Convention on Climate Change (opened for signature 11 December 1997, entered into force 16 February 2005) 2303 UNTS 148.

[45] Principles, nature and scope of the mechanisms pursuant to Articles 6, 12 and 17 of the Kyoto Protocol, Decision 2/CMP.1, 1st sess (30 March 2006) FCCC/KP/CMP/2005/8/Add.1, 4.

[46] Farhana Yamin and Joanna Depledge, *The International Climate Change Regime: A Guide to Rules, Institutions and Procedures* (CUP 2004) 121.

[47] United Nations Convention on Contracts for the International Sale of Goods (adopted 11 April 1980, entered into force 1 January 1988) 1489 UNTS 3.

its purposes, including inter alia stocks, shares, investment securities, negotiable instruments, money, and electricity. The implication flowing from the structure and nature of this definition is that the term 'goods' would—or at least could—otherwise cover those intangible items.

B Context

Beginning with the immediate context of 'goods' and 'products' in GATT 1994, a number of attributes and characteristics become apparent. Article I.1 refers to 'any product originating in or destined for any other country'.[48] This suggests that 'products' are capable of movement and transportation between different countries. The use of the word 'any' before 'products', which is repeated on numerous occasions in GATT 1994,[49] suggests the broadest possible scope. This accords with WTO jurisprudence on other uses of the term 'any', such as in *Canada—Autos*, where the Appellate Body said that '[t]he words of Article I.1 refer … not to *some* products, but to "*any product*" '.[50]

Article III.1 refers to the 'internal sale, offering for sale, purchase, transportation, distribution or use of products', which suggests that products may be bought and sold, transported and distributed, and capable of use.

References in Article XI to the 'importation of any product' and the 'exportation or sale for export of any product' suggests that they are articles of international trade which can cross borders and be possessed by one actor and re-assigned to another.[51] As articles of international trade, 'products' would also need to have some economic value and be capable of entering channels of commerce. Article XVII.2 refers to the 'consumption' of products, again suggesting that they may be consumed in a commercial sense.

Turning to relevant preambular recitals, it can be observed that GATT 1994 refers to the 'production and exchange of goods' and the WTO Agreement similarly refers to the 'production of and trade in goods'. This suggests that 'goods' are produced, which one panel described as referring to ' "[b]ring[ing] (a thing) into existence" and "bring[ing] into existence by mental or physical labour (a material object)" '.[52]

Furthermore, the absence of any express qualification to the effect that 'goods' and 'products' must be tangible may also be relevant. It could be inferred from this omission that it would be erroneous to try to de facto incorporate that kind of limitation.

Of course, it could be countered that the existence of a dedicated agreement on services under the umbrella of the WTO Agreement suggests that GATT 1994 is

[48] GATT 1994 (n 1) art I.1.
[49] See eg ibid, arts I.1, I.4, II.2, II.4, III.5, VI.3, VI.6, XI.1, XIII.1, XIII.2, XVI.1.
[50] Appellate Body Report, *Canada—Autos* [79] (original emphasis).
[51] GATT 1994 (n 1) art XI.1.
[52] Panel Report, *EC—Salmon (Norway)* [7.114]. See also Voigt, 'WTO Law and International Emissions Trading' (n 11) 55–56.

not intended to deal with intangible articles of commerce. However, the Appellate Body has held that GATT 1994 and GATS should not be read against one another, and specifically that GATS 'does not diminish the scope of application of GATT 1994'.[53] Indeed, both GATT and GATS can regulate the same product[54] and the same measure.[55] Therefore, the fact that GATS covers the intangible services trade should not be taken to mean that GATT 1994 is incapable of extending to intangible items. Further, this kind of argument rests on a flawed assumption that tangibility is the defining marker distinguishing 'goods' from 'services'. Instead, it has been persuasively argued by a number of authors that the ability to own and possess a 'good' vis-a-vis the inability to own and possess a 'service' is the key conceptual distinction.[56] Indeed, as will be discussed further below, WTO jurisprudence has recently recognized that there may be a category of 'intangible products' or 'intangible goods' that are distinct from 'services'.[57]

As discussed in Chapter 2, Article 31.3(c) of the Vienna Convention provides a further matter to be taken into account together with the context of GATT 1994, namely, whether any other relevant rules of international law applicable in the relations between WTO Members may shed light on the scope of 'goods' and 'products'. According to the view set out in Chapter 2, it is unlikely that Article 31.3(c) would provide an avenue for consideration of the norms of the international climate regime in interpreting terms in the WTO Agreement.[58] However, to the extent those norms are relevant, the strong inference can be drawn that measures pertaining to climate change—including measures affecting trade and investment in carbon units—are not intended to be exempted from the international economic regime. Rather, the United Nations Framework Convention on Climate Change (UNFCCC)[59] expressly incorporates the principle from the international economic regime that '[m]easures taken to combat climate change, including unilateral ones, should not constitute a means of arbitrary or unjustifiable discrimination or a disguised restriction on international trade',[60] and the Kyoto Protocol calls on parties to implement their obligations 'in such a way as to minimize adverse effects ... on international trade'.[61] If anything, these provisions emphasize that the international climate regime should be understood to be mutually compatible with the international economic regime to the extent they may overlap. It thus suggests that the international

[53] Appellate Body Report, *Canada—Periodicals* 17–20. [54] ibid.

[55] Appellate Body Report, *EC—Bananas III* [217]–[222].

[56] See Peter Hill, 'Tangibles, intangibles and services: a new taxonomy for the classification of output' in Rohan Kariyawasam (ed), *The WTO, Intellectual Property, E-Commerce and the Internet* (Edward Elgar Publishing 2009) 355–56; Fiona Smith and Lorna Woods, 'A Distinction Without a Difference: Exploring the Boundary Between Goods and Services in the World Trade Organization and the European Union' (2005) 12 *Columbia Journal of European Law* 1, 6, 54–55.

[57] Appellate Body Report, *China—Publications and Audiovisual Products* [364]; Panel Reports, *Canada—Renewable Energy/Canada—Feed-in Tariff Program* [7.229]. But see also Panel Report, *US—Large Civil Aircraft (2nd Complaint) Article 21.5* [8.382].

[58] See above ch 2B and 2D.

[59] United Nations Framework Convention on Climate Change (opened for signature 9 May 1992, entered into force 21 March 1994) 1771 UNTS 107 (UNFCCC).

[60] ibid art 3.5. [61] Kyoto Protocol (n 44) art 2.3.

climate regime should not be readily construed as conflicting with the international economic regime.

In summary, taken as a whole, the context surveyed in this section suggests that the scope of the terms 'products' and 'goods' in GATT 1994 lies somewhere in the midway between the narrowest and broadest possibilities. On the one hand, they appear to be narrower than simply anything of value, because they should be capable of being exported and imported and therefore transported across borders, and should be capable of possession and reassignment to third parties through commercial transactions, in addition to having been produced through some form of human effort. As such, things like public goods or real estate would likely be excluded, despite having economic value. On the other hand, 'goods' and 'products' appear to be broader than tangible objects with a tariff classification in which property rights subsist, since there is no express requirement for tangibility, and since these terms are tied to tariff schedules in only a limited number of provisions in GATT 1994. Therefore, somewhere between these narrow and broad outer limits there is likely to be a range of features and characteristics which could, if present in a given case, result in an item being considered a 'good' or 'product'.

C Object and Purpose

The object and purpose of GATT 1994 and the WTO Agreement may also shed light on the scope of the terms 'goods' and 'products'.

A number of potentially relevant aspects can be drawn out of the preambles of GATT 1994 and the WTO Agreement (see further Chapter 2E). The notion of 'expanding' the production and exchange of goods in both preambles suggests that new and unorthodox classes of goods should not necessarily be excluded from the scope of GATT 1994, even if they were not in existence at the time of its conclusion. The resolve to develop an 'integrated' trading system militates against any interpretation that would leave arbitrary gaps or holes in GATT 1994, and the concept of a 'more *viable* and *durable*' system suggests that GATT 1994 should be capable of adapting to new and changing circumstances over time. Indeed, the Appellate Body in *China—Publications and Audiovisual Products* found that terms used in China's GATS Schedule are 'sufficiently generic that what they apply to may change over time'.[62] In this way, even if the terms 'goods' and 'products' were imagined only to refer to tangible items when they were originally agreed upon, they could nonetheless be capable of broadening to cover intangibles as technology developed and products changed over time.[63]

62 Appellate Body Report, *China—Publications and Audiovisual Products* [396]–[397] n 705.

63 ibid [369]. It is noteworthy that the Appellate Body appeared to endorse a finding in 2009 by the International Court of Justice that the term 'commerce' contained in a 1858 treaty referred to both goods and services, even if it only referred to goods at the time the treaty was concluded (see ibid n 705). See also Appellate Body Report, *US—Shrimp* [129]–[130], finding that the term 'natural resources' was 'evolutionary' in its content and capable of expanding in scope over time.

Additionally, as discussed in Chapter 2, the preamble to the WTO Agreement clearly posits environmental protection, including 'enhancing the means for doing so', as within the scope of the trade and economic relations of WTO Members that fall within its purview. This could be read to suggest that market-based approaches to environmental protection that commodify pollution for international trading could be potentially covered by the WTO Agreement. At a minimum, it suggests that market-based environmental protection mechanisms like emissions trading schemes are not in any way intended to be exempt per se from the purview of the WTO Agreement. In that regard, it is noteworthy that GATT 1994 covers explicitly a number of other toxic or waste products that only have value due to governmental regulations and associated artificially-created markets.[64]

While these elements do not *directly* touch on the scope of 'products' and 'goods' in GATT 1994, they do suggest that its terms are adaptable and capable of expanding to cover new kinds of content as conditions change, and that approaches which would fragment the international trading system should be avoided, and further that environmental protection mechanisms may be subject to the disciplines of GATT 1994. To the extent that there are competing broad and narrow interpretations of 'products' and 'goods', these elements of object and purpose could favour a broader approach that covers carbon units.

D Relevant WTO Jurisprudence

No Appellate Body or panel report has sought formally and methodically to interpret the terms 'products' or 'goods' under GATT 1994.[65] Relevantly, however, the scope and content of these terms have been discussed in the context of *other* covered agreements under the WTO Agreement. While the Appellate Body has cautioned against presuming that the same words in different covered agreements have an identical meaning,[66] it has also noted that they constitute context relevant to each other's interpretation.[67]

Broadly speaking, these cases deal with two questions. First, are the terms 'products' and 'goods' capable of extending to rights and entitlements? Secondly, and relatedly, are these terms capable of extending to intangible items?

The first relevant case is *US—Softwood Lumber IV*, where the Appellate Body was called upon to construe the term 'goods' as it appears in Article 1.1(a)(1)(iii)

[64] Data sourced from the WTO Tariff Download Facility <http://tariffdata.wto.org/TariffList.aspx> (last accessed 20 January 2015). This reveals 4,068 MFN applied tariffs, 5,271 non-MFN, and 1,251 bound tariffs listed in WTO Members' tariff schedules for HS Code 3825, which covers: 'Residual products of the chemical or allied industries, not elsewhere specified or included; municipal waste; sewage sludge; other wastes specified in Note 6 to this Chapter'.

[65] Although the panels in *Canada—Renewable Energy/Canada—Feed-in Tariff Program* were faced with whether electricity qualified as a 'good' or 'product' under GATT 1994, the issue was uncontested by the disputing parties, which meant that there was no systematic interpretation of those terms.

[66] Appellate Body Reports, *Australia—Apples* n 285; *EC—Asbestos* [89].

[67] Appellate Body Report, *Australia—Apples* n 285.

of the SCM Agreement.[68] At issue was whether a right to harvest standing timber fell within the scope of the term 'goods'.[69] Canada had argued that the term 'goods' must be read as limited to tradable and tangible items capable of bearing a tariff classification—and, since 'rights' are intangible and 'standing timber' is fixed to the ground and not in a tradable form, rights to harvest standing timber cannot constitute a 'good'.[70] Canada had also argued that, even if such intangible rights could be considered a 'good', the term 'goods' refers to property rights, and the impugned 'rights' were not considered proprietary under Canadian law.[71]

The Appellate Body rejected these arguments comprehensively. After considering the dictionary definitions of 'goods' extracted above in section A(2), the Appellate Body found that the term was susceptible to a broad scope that did not necessarily exclude immovable property but instead included 'property or possessions' generally.[72] Furthermore, the fact that Canadian law did not recognize rights to standing timber as 'property' was dismissed with the comment that 'the manner in which the municipal law of a WTO Member classifies an item cannot, in itself be determinative of the interpretation of provisions of WTO covered agreements'.[73]

As such, the Appellate Body found that the term 'goods' in Article 1.1(a)(1)(iii) of the SCM Agreement extended to a right to harvest standing timber.[74] In doing so, it dismissed the notion that the term 'goods' inherently refers to movable items or objects capable of bearing a tariff classification. Furthermore, it was willing effectively to 'pierce the veil' of an intangible right to an immovable object, recognizing that the end-result of that intangible right was a tangible article of commerce (timber).

The panels in *Canada—Renewable Energy/Canada—Feed-in Tariff Program* adopted a similar approach with respect to electricity under Article 1.1(a)(1)(iii) of the SCM Agreement and Article III.8 of GATT 1994.[75] Although electricity is intangible and transient—and therefore cannot itself be 'possessed' or 'owned' in any meaningful way in most circumstances—the panel was willing to accept that it could constitute an 'intangible good',[76] and that trade in *entitlements* to electricity were sufficient to qualify as trade in 'goods' or 'products' for the purposes of those provisions.[77] In making these findings, the panel rejected the argument that there must be 'physical possession' of a product for it to be purchased or traded.[78] On appeal, the Appellate Body accepted that electricity could constitute a 'product' under Article III.8 of GATT 1994,[79] finding that a '"product" in the sense of this provision is something that is capable of being traded'.[80] It also upheld the panel's finding that purchases of entitlements to electricity (as an intangible good) fell within the meaning of 'purchases [of] goods' under Article 1.1(a)(1)(iii) of the SCM

[68] Appellate Body Report, *US—Softwood Lumber IV* [59]–[65]. [69] ibid [61].
[70] ibid. [71] ibid [65]. [72] ibid [59]. [73] ibid [65]. [74] ibid [75].
[75] Panel Reports, *Canada—Renewable Energy/Canada—Feed-in Tariff Program* [7.11], [7.136], [7.229], [7.243].
[76] ibid [7.11], [7.229]. [77] ibid [7.136], [7.229], [7.243].
[78] ibid [7.11], [7.228]–[7.229].
[79] Appellate Body Reports, *Canada—Renewable Energy/Canada—Feed-in Tariff Program* [5.60]–[5.63], [5.75]–[5.79].
[80] ibid [5.62].

Agreement, implicitly endorsing the notion that there need not necessarily be any physical possession of the goods or products traded.[81]

In a similar vein, the Appellate Body in *China—Publications and Audiovisual Products* found that the term 'products' in China's GATS schedule could encompass 'both tangible and intangible goods, as well as services'.[82] This is important because, although GATT 1994 is plainly not intended to cover services,[83] the Appellate Body seemed to recognize that the term 'product' can potentially extend to 'intangible' goods or products in certain contexts.

Paradoxically, however, the Appellate Body seemed to reach the opposite conclusion in the same case with respect to the term 'goods' in Article 5.1 of the Protocol on the Accession of the People's Republic of China. Article 5.1 provides that '[a]ll enterprises in China shall have the right to trade in all *goods* throughout the customs territory of China'.[84] Having noted China's argument that intangible content cannot be considered 'goods', and without contradicting it, the Appellate Body stated that '[c]ontent can be embodied in a physical carrier, and the content and carrier *together* can form a good'.[85] The *physical* nature of the combined product was therefore the decisive factor in their reasoning that the impugned measures did indeed affect 'goods'.[86] The corollary of this reasoning is that intangible content would not qualify as a 'good' if not embodied in some tangible or physical medium.

A further case that considered the scope of the term 'goods' is *US—Large Civil Aircraft (2nd complaint)*.[87] As in *US—Softwood Lumber IV*, the panel and Appellate Body in *US—Large Civil Aircraft (2nd complaint)* were called upon to assess the scope and content of 'goods' in Article 1.1(a)(1)(iii) of the SCM Agreement. In particular, the question arose as to whether the term 'goods' in Article 1.1(a)(1)(iii) was capable of extending to certain legal rights to use and improve infrastructure, including roads and rail.[88]

At first instance, the panel rejected the notion that *any* intangible right can be considered a 'good', stating that '[i]t was the *object* of the right that explained why the panel and Appellate Body concluded that the conferral of the right effectively meant the provision of a good' in *US—Softwood Lumber IV*.[89] In other words, the fact that the rights in *US—Softwood Lumber IV* related to a tradable commodity (ie timber) was crucial to the finding that a right to harvest could constitute a 'good' in that case. To avoid any doubt, the panel further stated that '*US—Softwood Lumber IV* cannot be invoked as support for a more general proposition that by granting any kind of rights to a firm, a government is providing goods and services in the sense of

[81] ibid [5.111], [5.128]–[5.129].

[82] Appellate Body Report, *China—Publications and Audiovisual Products* [364].

[83] See eg GATT Secretariat, 'Trade in Services and the GATT: Background Paper by the Secretariat' (6 March 1981) CG.18/49.

[84] Protocol on the Accession of the People's Republic of China (23 November 2001) WT/L/432, art 5.1 (emphasis added).

[85] Appellate Body Report, *China—Publications and Audiovisual Products* [195] (emphasis added).

[86] See also ibid [188].

[87] Appellate Body Report, *US—Large Civil Aircraft (2nd complaint)*.

[88] Panel Report, *US—Large Civil Aircraft (2nd complaint)* [7.387], [7.394].

[89] ibid [7.460] (emphasis added).

Article 1.1(a)(1)(iii) of the SCM Agreement'.[90] This suggests that intangible rights cannot be considered 'goods' in and of themselves, at least for the purposes of Article 1.1(a)(1)(iii). Instead, there must be some nexus to a commercial object.

While this finding was not revisited by the Appellate Body on appeal, it did make a passing comment on the general nature of 'goods':[91]

> 'Goods' are tangible items. They are often contrasted against 'services', which are intangible. There are a number of distinctions usually drawn between services and goods. As opposed to goods, typical features of services include their immaterial, invisible, intangible, non-storable, and transitory nature.

While this comment does not purport to contribute to the interpretation of any particular term or provision, it does seem to reveal the Appellate Body's instinctive view on the ordinary meaning of 'goods'. Tangibility seems to be a core feature of 'goods', in addition to their being material, storable, visible, and permanent. The compliance panel in *US—Large Civil Aircraft (2nd complaint) (Article 21.5—EU)* relied on this observation of the Appellate Body as a basis for rejecting the argument that intellectual property could qualify as a 'good', reasoning that '[w]hile there is wide and uncertain use of the term "goods" in general parlance, the term is typically applied to tangible products, as distinguished from intangible services'.[92] Thus, it was insufficient that intellectual property can be tradable, transferable personal property. Rather, for that panel, physical tangibility was a threshold requirement. The panel's emphasis on tangibility in this regard does not seem consonant with the acceptance of intangible goods (eg electricity) and intangible rights by other panels and the Appellate Body in the cases surveyed above. However, it should be noted that the panel placed strong reliance on a particular element of context in Article 1.1(a)(1)(iii) of the SCM Agreement that is not generally present in GATT 1994. In particular, the panel emphasized the juxtaposition in Article 1.1(a)(1)(iii) between 'goods' on one hand and 'services' on the other hand, in which context they arguably appeared to be mutually exclusive. Thus, even if that particular iteration of 'goods' in Article 1.1(a)(1)(iii) should be construed more narrowly due to the contrasting presence of the term 'services' in that particular provision, the Appellate Body has reached the opposite conclusion in respect of GATT and GATS more generally.[93]

It goes without saying that this body of WTO jurisprudence on the terms 'goods' and 'products' across a range of covered agreements does not provide a definitive answer to the scope of 'products' and 'goods' under GATT 1994. On the contrary, it

[90] ibid [7.460].

[91] Appellate Body Report, *US—Large Civil Aircraft (2nd complaint)* n 1295.

[92] Panel Report, *US—Large Civil Aircraft (2nd Complaint) Article 21.5* [8.382].

[93] See Appellate Body Reports, *Canada—Periodicals* 17–20; *EC—Bananas III* [217]–[222]. Further, the Appellate Body has stated elsewhere that '[t]he terms "goods" and "products" appear in various provisions throughout the SCM Agreement and other covered agreements, and do not appear to be restricted in themselves to specific types of goods, *unless* qualified' (see Appellate Body Report, *US—Tax Incentives* n 38 (emphasis added)).

reveals divergent strands of logic on whether 'goods' and 'products' denote tangible items or additionally extend to 'intangible goods', and the extent to which those terms cover rights and entitlements to other objects.

Nevertheless, perhaps the key lesson to take from this jurisprudence is that 'goods' and 'products' are, in certain contexts, capable of assuming a very broad scope, and are by no means *inherently* or *necessarily* limited to tangible or movable goods contained in WTO Members' tariff schedules. Indeed, in most of the cases discussed above, the specific context in which these terms appeared was crucial to determining their scope.[94] This, in turn, takes us back to the analysis the section above on the context of the terms 'products' and 'goods' under GATT 1994.

E Summary: Delimiting 'Products' and 'Goods' under GATT 1994

The foregoing effort to interpret 'products' and 'goods' demonstrates a number of key elements and criteria in assessing whether an item can fall within their scope under GATT 1994. First, the item should be capable of being exported and imported and therefore transported across national borders. Relatedly, it should be capable of being owned and possessed, with that ownership capable of reassignment to third parties through a commercial transaction. The item should also hold economic value, and should have been subject to some form of processing or other human effort in order to create either the item itself or the economic value subsisting in the item.

While the presence of tangible qualities in an item will make it more likely to qualify as a 'good' or 'product', the jurisprudence from *China—Publications and Audiovisual Products, Canada—Renewable Energy/Canada—Feed-in Tariff Program* and *US—Softwood Lumber IV* suggests that it is not an essential prerequisite. However, if the item is a 'right', 'entitlement', or 'licence', the findings of *US—Large Civil Aircraft (2nd complaint)* and *Canada—Renewable Energy/Canada—Feed-in Tariff Program* suggest that it should correspond to a physical commercial object in order to be considered a 'good', such as electricity or timber. Finally, it is not determinative that the item was never originally envisaged as falling within the purview of GATT 1994. This is because its terms are capable of evolving over time. Further, narrow interpretations that would result in a less-integrated and less-durable trading system should be avoided.

Equipped with these interpretive tools, the next section proceeds to evaluate whether carbon units can be properly considered to fall within the scope of GATT 1994.

[94] See eg Appellate Body Reports, *China—Publications and Audiovisual Products* [365]; *US—Softwood Lumber IV* [59].

F Application to Carbon Units

It is immediately clear that carbon units appear to have many of the hallmarks of 'goods' and 'products' under GATT 1994. They may be imported and exported across borders, particularly where emissions trading schemes are linked, such as through the Kyoto Protocol or through bilateral linking arrangements like those between the EU and Switzerland, and California and Quebec. They have economic value, derived both from their ability to be used to avoid a penalty under an emissions trading scheme, as well as from their other uses (eg as investment goods, as a form of security, and as environmental products on the voluntary market).[95] They are capable of being owned and sold to third parties, and they can be stored in accounts and used in different ways.

However, carbon units have three qualities that cast doubt over their characterization as 'products' or 'goods' under GATT 1994.

First, they represent an intangible right. They cannot be touched or thrown, and exist only as an electronic piece of information that authorizes a certain activity (ie the emission of one tonne of greenhouse gas). While an intangible right was held to fall within the scope of 'goods' in *US—Softwood Lumber IV* for the purposes of Article 1.1(a)(1)(iii) of the SCM Agreement, the right in that case represented a tangible end-product: timber. Greenhouse gas is different to timber because it cannot, in and of itself, be an article of commerce.[96] For example, it cannot be placed in a shipping container and exported overseas. As such, it would not appear to meet the threshold of the test set by the panel in *US—Large Civil Aircraft (2nd complaint)*, namely, that a given right must relate to a tradable commodity.

On the other hand, carbon units represent the only means of effectively commodifying and trading greenhouse gas, owing to its amorphous quality. In a context where governments have imposed scarcity on greenhouse gas and there is an active international market in its trade, it would seem arbitrary to exclude carbon units from the scope of 'goods' and 'products' simply because of the amorphous nature of the substance they represent. It is also noteworthy that most greenhouse gases have an HS Code and would therefore be ordinarily considered to be subject to GATT 1994 when traded in a more orthodox fashion (for example, as a liquid or solid substance, or if piped across borders).[97]

It could be argued that carbon units do not represent a right to greenhouse gas *itself*, but rather to a more limited right to *emit* greenhouse gas. On that basis, it could be argued that carbon units pertain to an activity, as opposed to exhibiting the

[95] See generally ch 3C.

[96] Voigt, 'WTO Law and International Emissions Trading' (n 11) 56.

[97] World Customs Organization, *HS Nomenclature 2012 Edition* (WCO 2012) http://www.wcoomd.org/home_hsnomenclaturetable2012.htm (last accessed 15 January 2016): for carbon dioxide, see 2811.21; for methane (and petroleum gases and other gaseous hydrocarbons generally), see 27.11; for coal gas, water gas, producer gas and similar gases, other than petroleum gases and other gaseous hydrocarbons, see 27.05; for perfluorocarbons and hydrofluorocarbons, see 38.24. For WTO Members' tariff bindings on these products under GATT 1994, see http://tariffdata.wto.org/ReportersAndProducts.aspx.

requisite nexus to a tradable commercial object (such as timber or electricity). This view has merit and is supported by the manner in which emissions trading schemes themselves tend to define carbon units (see further Chapter 3). However, such a view belies the basic structure and functioning of transferable permit schemes. Their very purpose is to convert a public good—namely, the atmosphere in the case of emissions trading schemes—into divisible, privately-owned items with economic value. Despite being a regulatory construct, carbon units are conceptually individual pieces of the aggregate amount of greenhouse gas that a jurisdiction permits to be released into the atmosphere. In other words, within the context of artificially-imposed scarcity, each unit represents a piece of the aggregate quantum of greenhouse gas permitted under an emissions trading scheme.

In any case, even if carbon units were taken to represent a more limited right to emit greenhouse gas, this does not exclude their characterization as 'goods'/'products'. This is because they are personal property in their own right both in economic terms and, in a number of jurisdictions, under municipal law. The ability to trade, store, and possess carbon units—and for them to hold economic value—is conceptually embedded in their existence as units of trade in a transferable permit scheme (see further Chapter 3). Such characteristics alone should suffice for the purposes of 'goods'/'products'.

The second quality of carbon units that complicates their characterization as 'goods' or 'products' is that it is not entirely clear that all carbon units are 'produced'. While carbon units created by private actors through emissions reduction projects—ie offset units—are clearly the output of human and physical effort, units that have been generated by governments or regulators—ie allowance units—are not so obviously 'produced'. They are simply serial numbers that are generated and distributed to private actors, rather than being the result of any meaningful effort on the part of their creators. Of course, on a macro level, they could be viewed as representing a country's collective effort to limit and reduce its emissions of greenhouse gas. However, that would require a somewhat creative understanding of what it means to 'produce' an item.

Thirdly, carbon units can be conceived as a form of *regulatory* property.[98] They are part of a wider family of transferable permit schemes that seek to create fictional property rights out of abstract public goods, such as relating to water use, fisheries, and waste management.[99] This quality has led some authors to suggest that they cannot be considered subject to GATT 1994,[100] and are more akin to a form of 'legal

[98] Karoliina Anttonen, Michael Mehling, and Karl Upston-Hooper, 'Breathing Life into the Carbon Market' (2007) 16 *European Environmental Law Review* 96, 97; Matthieu Wemaere, Charlotte Streck, and Thiago Chagas, 'Legal Ownership and Nature of Kyoto Units and EU Allowances' in David Freestone and Charlotte Streck (eds), *Legal Aspects of Carbon Trading: Kyoto, Copenhagen, and beyond* (OUP 2009) 39.

[99] Ted Gayer and John K Horowitz, 'Market-based Approaches to Environmental Regulation' (2006) 1(4) *Foundations and Trends in Microeconomics* 201, 204–206; Olivier Godard, *Domestic Transferable Permits for Environmental Management: Design and Implementation* (OECD 2001) 11; Olivier Godard, 'Domestic Transferable Permits: Summary of Lessons Learned' in *Implementing Domestic Tradeable Permits: Recent Developments and Future Challenges* (OECD 2002) 11–23.

[100] See eg Wiser (n 5) 558; Charnovitz (n 6) 152.

tender'.[101] The fact that these units subsist in an artificial and potentially volatile market to serve a broader environmental objective that is itself uncertain, unpredictable, and hence prone to governmental intervention, could suggest that carbon units do not have the degree of permanence and stability required for an item to qualify as a 'good' or 'product'. This view is strengthened by the feature of some emissions trading schemes discussed in Chapter 3 in which governments reserve the right to revoke or cancel carbon units unilaterally, and whereby carbon units are expressly denied proprietary status in some jurisdictions.

However, there is nothing in GATT 1994 that expressly excludes regulatory property, and carbon units have a use as a valuable investment item beyond their role in discharging liabilities under an emissions trading scheme.[102] Although greenhouse gases are essentially waste products that only have economic value due to the imposition of emissions trading schemes, many other waste products qualify as 'products' under GATT 1994 despite only having economic value due to government regulation.[103] Further, the increasing linkage of various domestic emissions trading schemes has meant that carbon units have uses beyond the specific regulatory scheme where, and for which, they were first created.[104] As objects, therefore, they are in most instances not inherently tied to or dependent on a specific regulatory framework, but may instead be understood as autonomous items that can be transported across borders. Indeed, the fact that a particular jurisdiction denies proprietary status to a particular item has been found by the Appellate Body to be not dispositive of whether that item constitutes a 'good' or 'product'.[105] The marked inconsistency between jurisdictions on how they classify carbon units—for instance, as property, services, securities, financial products, or commodities—probably renders consideration of municipal law even less relevant or reliable in this context.[106] Rather, the economic reality of that item being susceptible to exclusive possession and use, as well as being capable of being traded across borders, may be more persuasive. This economic reality was the basis for a Californian court finding that Californian carbon units comprise property, despite the statute in question explicitly denuding those units of proprietary status under Californian law.[107]

Indeed, emissions trading schemes can only succeed in achieving their purpose if they stimulate an economy to transition structurally to a low-carbon economy through long-term investments in low-carbon technologies, and such investments will only be made if there is a perception of permanence and stability in the units of trade in emissions trading schemes, namely, carbon units. Even where governments deny carbon units proprietary status, or reserve the right to intervene in the markets created by emissions trading schemes, the underlying economic premise of

[101] See eg Voigt, 'WTO Law and International Emissions Trading' (n 11) 56; Petsonk (n 6) 199–201.

[102] See further ch 3C.

[103] Mirina Grosz, *Sustainable Waste Trade under WTO Law* (Brill 2011) 254–56.

[104] See further ch 3C.

[105] Appellate Body Reports, *India—Patents (US)* [65]–[68]; *US—Section 211 Appropriations Act* [106]; *US—Carbon Steel* [156]–[157]; *US—Softwood Lumber IV* [56].

[106] See further ch 3C.

[107] ibid.

the function of such markets is that carbon units be susceptible to being possessed, stored, and traded.[108]

On balance, the better view is that 'carbon units' qualify as 'products' and 'goods' under GATT 1994. They can be possessed, stored, traded across borders, and hold economic value. The most challenging aspect is the lack of obvious 'production' involved in some classes of units. However, since some units are clearly 'produced', and since all units are fungible and are, to some degree,[109] in a competitive market relationship with one another regardless of how they are created, it would be anomalous if only some classes of carbon units were covered.

G Position under Free Trade Agreements

Over 270 free trade agreements covering trade in goods have been notified to the WTO.[110] While the meaning of the terms 'goods' and 'products' must be construed in light of the particular context, object, and purpose of each of those agreements, the foregoing analysis of those terms can be said with some confidence to apply to many of those agreements. This is because the precedents of many of the world's major trading countries suggest a direct alignment between the meaning of 'goods' and 'products' under GATT 1994, and the meaning of those terms under their free trade agreements. For example, the free trade agreements between Australia and the United States,[111] Korea and the European Union,[112] Mexico and Japan,[113] China and Chile,[114] and Canada and

[108] See eg J H Dales 'Land, Water, and Ownership' (1968) 1 *Canadian Journal of Economics* 791, 792. See also Brian R. Copeland and M Scott Taylor, 'Trade, Tragedy, and the Commons' (2009) 99 *American Economic Review* 725; Tome Tietenberg, 'Tradeable Permits in Principle and Practice', in Jody Freedman and Charles D Kolstad (eds), *Moving to Markets in Environmental Regulation* (2007) 63, 78; Ross Garnaut, *The Garnaut Climate Change Review* (2008) 322–23; Daniel Cole, 'Clearing the Air: Four Propositions about Property Rights and Environmental Protection' (1999) 10(13) *Duke Environmental Law & Policy Forum* 103, 114; Kathy Baylis and Travis Allan, 'Who Owns Carbon? Property Rights Issues in a Market for Green House Gasses' (2005) 7 *Current Agriculture, Food and Resource Issues* 104, 105; Godard, *Domestic Transferable Permits for Environmental Management* (n 99) 67.

[109] See further below ch 8A(3). This book argues that allowance units and offset units are not 'like' under the various standards of likeness in WTO law owing to their different risk profiles, and hence different consumer perceptions, prices, and market frameworks. That notwithstanding, both classes of units are essentially fungible and have the same (or similar) end-uses, and although not rising to the legal standard of 'likeness' in WTO law, they are nonetheless in a competitive market relationship in a broader sense.

[110] See World Trade Organization, *RTA Database* http://rtais.wto.org/ui/PublicMaintainRTAHome.aspx (last accessed 2 June 2015).

[111] *Australia–United States Free Trade Agreement* (Australia–United States) (signed 18 May 2004, entered into force 1 January 2005) [2005] ATS 1, art 1.2.12.

[112] Free Trade Agreement between the European Union and its Member States, of the one part, and the Republic of Korea, of the other part (EU–Korea) (signed 6 October 2010, entered into force June 2010) art 2.2.

[113] Agreement between Japan and the United Mexican States for the Strengthening of the Economic Partnership (Mexico–Japan) (signed 17 September 2004, not yet in force) art 1(h).

[114] Free Trade Agreement between the Government of the People's Republic of China and the Government of the Republic of Chile (China–Chile) (signed 18 November 2005, entered into force 1 October 2006) art 5.

Peru[115] all employ the definition that the '*goods* of a Party means domestic *products* as these are understood in GATT 1994'. Some others do not make an express link between the meaning under GATT 1994 and the meaning under the relevant free trade agreement. For example, the agreements between ASEAN and India,[116] and ASEAN and Australia–New Zealand[117] use definitions such as 'goods means products and/or materials', and 'good means any merchandise, product, article or material'. Nothing in these definitions, however, suggests that they might carry a definition of 'goods' and 'products' *narrower* than that of GATT 1994. Indeed, such an approach would likely be inconsistent with the provision of GATT 1994 that authorizes subsets of WTO Members to enter into free trade agreements in goods. In particular, Article XIV.8(b) of GATT 1994 states that a free trade area must involve the elimination of the duties and other restrictive regulations of commerce on 'substantially all the trade between the constituent territories in products originating in such territories'.[118] A free trade agreement that applies only to a limited subset of the 'goods' and 'products' that fall within the purview of GATT 1994 would be unlikely to meet this threshold, since the duties and other restrictive regulations of commerce applying to trade in goods and products exempted from the free trade agreement would not be 'eliminat[ed]'.

Finally, pursuant to Article 31.3(c) of the Vienna Convention, the interpretation of the terms 'products' or 'goods' under free trade agreements would need to take into account any 'relevant rules of international law applicable in the relations between the parties'. Assuming that all the parties to a free trade agreement are WTO Members, the WTO Agreement would likely be considered to contain 'relevant rules of international law' that could shed light on the meaning of these terms under a free trade agreement, since it too employs identical terms. As discussed above, it appears that a strong argument can be made that 'carbon units' do qualify as 'products' and 'goods' under GATT 1994. This, in turn, informs the meaning of these terms under free trade agreements between WTO Members by virtue of Article 31.3(c) of the Vienna Convention.

H Conclusion: Carbon Units as 'Goods' or 'Products' under GATT 1994 and Free Trade Agreements

In the absence of an express definition, this chapter sought first to delimit the scope of the terms 'products' and 'goods', and then to determine whether carbon units fall

[115] Free Trade Agreement between Canada and the Republic of Peru (Canada–Peru) (signed 29 May 2008, entered into force 1 August 2009) art 105.

[116] Agreement on Trade in Goods under the Framework Agreement on Comprehensive Economic Cooperation between the Association of Southeast Asian Nations and the Republic of India (ASEAN–India) (signed 13 August 2009, entered into force 1 January 2010) art 1(f).

[117] Agreement Establishing the ASEAN–Australia–New Zealand Free Trade Area (ASEAN–Australia–New Zealand) (signed 27 February 2009, entered into force 1 January 2010) [2010] ATS 1, ch 3 art 1(f).

[118] GATT 1994 (n 1) art XXIV(8)(b).

within that scope. It found that, for an item to qualify as a 'good' or 'product', it should be capable of being exported and imported and therefore transported across national borders, as well as being susceptible to ownership and possession, with that ownership capable of reassignment to third parties through a commercial transaction. The item should also hold economic value, and should have been subject to some form of processing or other human effort in order to create either the item itself or the economic value subsisting in the item.

While carbon units exhibit a number of these characteristics, three features in particular inject complexity into their characterization as 'products' or 'goods'. These include their intangibility, the lack of obvious 'production' or human effort in the generation of certain kinds of carbon units, and their status as a form of regulatory property. The most challenging element is the second of these—namely, the lack of obvious 'production' in respect of allowance units, which are simply automatically generated by governments or regulators. However, since offset units are clearly 'produced', and since all units are fungible and are, to some degree, in a competitive market relationship with one another regardless of how they are created, it would be anomalous if only some classes of carbon units were regulated under GATT 1994 and free trade agreements.

It is, of course, possible that a degree of human effort or labour could be found to be a threshold requirement in order for an item for it to qualify as 'goods'/'products'. If so, offset units would qualify but allowance units would not. If, however, the Appellate Body were additionally to determine that tangibility is a threshold requirement of 'goods'/'products', it is clear that no carbon units would qualify. Such an interpretation would, however, have far-reaching consequences, leading to the wholesale exemption of major market segments, such as trade in digital products.[119] Further, it would directly contradict the existing WTO jurisprudence (albeit limited) on the coverage of intangible items such as electricity. Thus, on balance, this chapter concludes that there is a strong argument that carbon units do qualify as 'goods' and 'products' under GATT 1994 and free trade agreements, while recognizing that reasonable arguments could be made to the contrary.

[119] See James Munro, 'Pushing the boundaries of "products" and "goods" under GATT 1994: An analysis of the coverage of new and unorthodox articles of commerce' (2013) 47 *Journal of World Trade* 1323.

5

International Trade in Carbon Units under GATS and Free Trade Agreements

This chapter assesses the extent to which carbon units are covered by services-related obligations under international economic law. It primarily considers this question with respect to the General Agreement on Trade in Services (GATS),[1] which is the premier multilateral instrument governing trade in services. The final section also considers this question with respect to services chapters in free trade agreements, which are largely modelled on GATS.

Unlike the General Agreement on Tariffs and Trade 1994 (GATT 1994),[2] GATS contains a provision delimiting its scope. It provides that GATS 'applies to measures by Members affecting trade in services'.[3] Therefore, the question as to whether GATS applies to carbon units is subtly different to whether GATT 1994 applies, as assessed in Chapter 4. Rather than simply looking at whether carbon units constitute a 'service', the GATS scoping provision calls for a three-pronged approach: (i) the identification of a 'measure', which (ii) can be said to 'affect' (iii) 'trade in services'.[4]

[1] Marrakesh Agreement Establishing the World Trade Organization (opened for signature 15 April 1994, entered into force 1 January 1995) 1867 UNTS 3 annex IB (General Agreement on Trade in Services) (GATS).

[2] Marrakesh Agreement Establishing the World Trade Organization (n 1) annex IA (General Agreement on Tariffs and Trade) (GATT 1994).

[3] GATS (n 1) art I.1.

[4] See Appellate Body Report, *Canada—Autos* [155]; Rudiger Wolfrum, Peter-Tobias Stoll, and Clemens Feinaugle, *WTO—Trade in Services* (Brill 2008) 37.

This chapter evaluates each of these elements. In doing so, the structure of its analysis diverges somewhat from the traditional approach in WTO jurisprudence on services-related disputes. In most cases, it is uncontested whether a certain activity constitutes a service per se—rather, it is contested how that service is characterized, and whether it has been inscribed in a WTO Members schedule of commitments.[5] This chapter, however, addresses the threshold question of whether carbon units themselves can be said to embody a service, which requires a more comprehensive order of analysis. It finds that the laws and regulations on how and when offset units (one of the two major categories of carbon units) may be used in emissions trading schemes are likely to constitute 'measures affecting trade in services', thereby falling under the purview of GATS. However, allowance units—the other major category of carbon units—are unlikely to be covered by GATS.

The analysis in this chapter challenges the view that carbon units cannot be covered as a 'service' due to their nature as a permit or licence.[6] Rather, as will be shown, it is well established in both WTO jurisprudence and in economic literature that a special category of services can be embodied in other objects.[7] The key question, therefore, is whether carbon units embody—or provide a means of trading—a service that has been performed. Although this analysis concurs with those that consider offset units could reflect a form of 'decarobonization service',[8] the analysis in this chapter goes further by interrogating the term and concept of 'service', and thereby determining with greater certainty whether the actual activity underlying offset units falls within this term.

[5] See eg Appellate Body Reports, *China—Publications and Audiovisual Products* [338]–[342]; *US—Gambling* [158]–[161]; *EC—Bananas III* [220] [223]–[233].

[6] See Jacob Werksman, 'Greenhouse Gas Emissions Trading and the WTO' (1999) 8 *Review of European Community & International Environmental Law* 251, 256; Steve Charnovitz, 'Trade and Climate: Potential Conflicts and Synergies' in Pew Center on Global Climate Change, *Beyond Kyoto: Advancing the International Effort Against Climate Change* (Pew Center 2003) 141, 144.

[7] See eg Werner Zdouc, 'Legal Problems Arising under the General Agreement on Trade in Services: Comparative Analysis of GATS and GATT' (PhD Thesis, Universitstät St Gallen 2002) 21–23; Michael Trebilcock, Robert Howse, and Antonia Eliason, *The Regulation of International Trade* (4th edn, Routledge 2012) 474–75; Nicolas Diebold, *Non-Discrimination in International Trade in Services* (CUP 2010) 25; Wolfrum, Stoll, and Feinaugle (n 4) 40; Deepali Fernandes, 'Twins, Siblings or Friends: The Conceptual Case of Goods and Services, Where Do We Stand and Where Could We Be Headed To?' in Kern Alexander and Mads Andenas (eds), *The World Trade Organization and Trade in Services* (Brill 2008) 116; Richard H Snape, 'Principles in Trade in Services' in Patrick A Messerlin and Karl P Sauvant (eds), *The Uruguay Round: Services in the World Economy* (World Bank 1990) 5; Brian Hindley, 'Principles in Factor-related Trade in Services' in Patrick A Messerlin and Karl P Sauvant (eds), *The Uruguay Round: Services in the World Economy* (World Bank 1990) 12.

[8] Felicity Deane, *Emissions Trading and WTO Law* (Edward Elgar Publishing 2015) 102–103; Robert Howse and Antonia Eliason, 'Carbon Trading and the CDM in WTO Law' in Richard Stewart, Benedict Kingsbury, and Bryce Rudyk (eds), *Climate Finance: Regulatory and Funding Strategies for Climate Change and Global Development* (NYU Press 2009) 254, 256–57; Glenn Wiser, 'The Clean Development Mechanism versus the World Trade Organization: Can Free-Market Greenhouse Gas Emissions Abatement Survive Free Trade?' (1999) 11 *Georgetown International Environmental Law Review* 531, 559.

A 'Measures'

Article 31.4 of the Vienna Convention on the Law of Treaties (Vienna Convention)[9] provides that a 'special meaning shall be given to a term if it is established that the parties so intended'. Pursuant to this rule of interpretation, the term 'measure' carries a 'special meaning' under GATS, namely 'any measure by a Member, whether in the form of a law, regulation, rule, procedure, decision, administrative action, or any other form'.[10]

Chapter 8 below elaborates in detail upon the specific measures of different countries that affect carbon units in a way likely to be impugned under international economic law, including GATS. However, since the scoping provision of GATS requires the identification of certain 'measures', it is useful at this stage to give a preliminary overview of the impugned rules and requirements pertaining to emissions trading schemes. They fall into two principal categories.

First, the emissions trading schemes of most jurisdictions contain rules on which types or classes of carbon units are valid for compliance with their schemes.[11] Only by holding and surrendering a *valid* carbon unit may an entity covered by an emissions trading scheme avoid a penalty or fine. These rules often discriminate between carbon units on the basis of their country or jurisdiction of origin, either de jure or de facto. For example, the Californian emissions trading scheme will only accept offset units sourced from greenhouse gas reduction projects in Mexico, Canada, or the United States, thereby excluding offset units sourced from projects in any other country.[12] As another example, Australia's now-repealed emissions trading scheme would only accept allowance units from the EU emissions trading scheme, excluding the allowance units of any other jurisdictions.[13] Since these kinds of rules are contained in legislation and regulations, they would fall within the scope of a 'measure' under Article XXVIII(a) GATS.

The second category relates to rules contained in the emissions trading schemes of many jurisdictions imposing quantitative restrictions on the kinds of carbon units that may be used for compliance. For example, the now-repealed Australian emissions trading scheme required companies covered by its emissions trading scheme

[9] Vienna Convention on the Law of Treaties (opened for signature 23 May 1969, entered into force 27 January 1980) 1155 UNTS 331 art 31.1.

[10] GATS (n 1) art XXVIII(a).

[11] See eg Directive 2003/87/EC of the European Parliament and of the Council of 13 October 2003 establishing a scheme for greenhouse gas emission allowance trading within the Community and amending Council Directive 96/61/EC [2003] OJ L275/32, arts 11(a), 25; California Cap on Greenhouse Gas Emissions and Market-based Compliance Mechanisms 17 Cal Public Health Code § 95820, 95821 (California Market-based Mechanism); Clean Energy Act 2011 (Cth) ss 5, 123; Climate Change Response Act 2002 (NZ) s 4 (definitions of 'unit' and 'approved overseas unit') s 63.

[12] California Market-based Mechanism (n 11) § 95972(c). The law establishing the Californian emissions trading scheme also includes a capacity for offset units from sectoral crediting mechanisms in developing countries to be approved and accepted; however, this has not yet occurred: § 95991.

[13] European Commission, the Hon Greg Combet AM MP, 'Australia and European Commission Agree on Pathway Towards Fully Linking Emissions Trading Schemes' (Media Release, 28 August 2012).

to use a minimum of 50 per cent of Australian-sourced carbon units for compliance with their emissions liabilities.[14] As another example, both the Californian and EU emissions trading schemes place maximum caps on the use of offset units.[15] Again, these kinds of requirements are contained in legislation and regulations, and would also fall within the scope of a 'measure' under Article XXVIII(a) GATS.

Therefore, the rules relating to the different classes and quantities of carbon units that may be used for compliance under an emissions trading scheme will fall within the scope of the term 'measure' under GATS.

B 'Trade in Services'

The expression 'trade in services' is defined in Article I.2 GATS in relevant part as 'the supply of a service from the territory of one Member into the territory of any other Member'.[16] Certainly, the rules on carbon units described above determine whether, and the extent to which, the carbon units generated in the territory of one party may be supplied in the territory of the other party for use in its emissions trading scheme. However, this definition leaves the core concept of a 'service' undefined.[17] This is crucial, because measures affecting carbon units will only be covered if they affect the supply of a *service*.

The 'supply of a service' is, in turn, defined in GATS as including the 'production, distribution, marketing, sale and delivery of a service'.[18] Again, the measures described above certainly affect the distribution, marketing and sale of carbon units. Only valid classes of carbon units will have any value in a given emissions trading scheme, which in turn affects the sale, marketing, and distribution of non-valid carbon units in that scheme. However, this definition also leaves the core concept of a 'service' undefined.

Even the tacit definition of the term 'service' sheds little light on the core concept. Despite clarifying that 'service includes any service in any sector except services supplied in the exercise of governmental authority',[19] it leaves the core concept of a 'service' undefined.[20]

Therefore, in accordance with Article 31 of the Vienna Convention, the term 'service' must be interpreted in good faith in accordance with its ordinary meaning

[14] Department of Climate Change and Energy Efficiency, 'Fact Sheet: Linking and Australian Liable Entities' http://www.cleanenergyfuture.gov.au/linking-and-australian-liable-entities/ (last accessed 15 April 2013).

[15] California Market-based Mechanism (n 11) § 95854; Directive 2003/87/EC (n 11) art 11(a)(8).

[16] Since the impugned measures relate to the cross-border trade in carbon units, the other modes of supply, such as commercial presence and consumption abroad, are unlikely to be relevant.

[17] See Panel Report, *China—Electronic Payment Services* [7.95]. See also Fiona Smith and Lorna Woods, 'A Distinction Without a Difference: Exploring the Boundary Between Goods and Services in The World Trade Organization and The European Union' (2005) 12 *Columbia Journal of European Law* 1, 17–19.

[18] GATS (n 1) art XXVIII(b).

[19] GATS (n 1) art I.3(b).

[20] See Panel Report, *China—Electronic Payment Services* [7.95]. See further Smith and Woods (n 17) 17–19.

in its context and in the light of the object and purpose of GATS and the Agreement Establishing the World Trade Organization[21] (WTO Agreement).[22]

1 Ordinary meaning

As a starting point, and as canvassed in Chapter 1, dictionary definitions can inform the 'ordinary meaning' of a term.[23] Relevant definitions of 'service' in *Black's Law Dictionary* and the *Oxford English Dictionary* include 'an intangible commodity in the form of human effort, such as labour, skill, or advice',[24] and 'the action of serving, helping or benefiting; conduct tending to the welfare or advantage of another … chiefly in to do, render a service'.[25] These definitions suggest that a 'service' involves one person expending effort in order to advantage or benefit another person.

Other definitions of 'service' appear in international guidelines on how to measure and report on trade in services.[26] One particularly noteworthy definition is that contained in the *Manual on Statistics of International Trade in Services 2010*; a document co-produced by the WTO and intended to facilitate, inter alia, the collection of GATS-related statistics.[27] Its definition of 'service' is based on that developed by another group of international organizations in the *System of National Accounts 2008*,[28] a statistical framework for macroeconomic accounts, and is essentially the same as the definition in the International Monetary Fund's *Balance of Payments Manual*.[29] It states that the 'production of services must be confined to activities that are capable of being carried out by one unit for the benefit of another',[30] and that '[s]ervices are the result of a production activity that changes the conditions of the consuming units, or facilitates the exchange of products or financial assets'.[31] It clarifies that the notion of 'changing the condition of the consuming units' refers to a service provider changing the condition of the consumer's goods (eg through cleaning, transporting, or repairing the goods), the physical condition of persons (eg through accommodation, or medical treatment), or the mental condition of

[21] Marrakesh Agreement Establishing the World Trade Organization (n 1) (Agreement establishing the World Trade Organization) (WTO Agreement).

[22] See further ch 2E.

[23] Appellate Body Report, *EC—Chicken Cuts* [175]–[176].

[24] *Black's Law Dictionary* (9th edn, West 2009).

[25] *Oxford English Dictionary Online* (OUP 2015) http://www.oed.com.ezp.lib.unimelb.edu.au/view/Entry/176678?rskey=OpZZsl&result=1&isAdvanced=false (last accessed 23 December 2015) 'service'.

[26] For examples of where panels and the Appellate Body have looked to other international instruments in discerning the 'ordinary meaning' of a term under Article 31.1 of the Vienna Convention, see Panel Report, *EC—Approval and Marketing of Biotech Products* [7.92]; Appellate Body Report, *US—Shrimp* [130].

[27] UN, IMF, OECD, WTO, UNCTAD, EuroStat, UNWTO, *Manual on Statistics of International Trade in Services 2010* ST/ESA/M.86/Rev.1 (United Nations 2011) 1, 109–12.

[28] EC, IMF, OECD, UN and World Bank, *System of National Accounts 2008* (United Nations 2008) [6.17]; UN et al, *Manual on Services Statistics* (n 27) 8–9.

[29] IMF, *Balance of Payments and International Investment Position Manual* (6th edn, IMF 2009) [10.60]; UN et al, *Manual on Services Statistics* (n 27) 8–9.

[30] IMF et al, *System of National Accounts* (n 28) [6.16].

[31] ibid [6.17].

persons (eg through education, or entertainment).[32] This largely accords with Peter Hill's oft-cited definition of a service as a 'change in the condition of a person or of a good belonging to some economic unit, which is brought about as the result of the activity of some other economic unit, with the prior agreement of the former person or economic unit'.[33]

At its core, therefore, the ordinary meaning of service seems to denote 'effort', 'action', and 'conduct' to assist or help another. This assistance can either be rendered by bringing about change to an object or person, or by facilitating the change of ownership of goods, knowledge-capturing products, or financial assets between two or more actors.

Since actions, effort, and conduct cannot be owned, possessed, or touched but are instead things that 'happen', services have been described as an intangible commodity.[34] In this vein, the Appellate Body has stated that 'typical features of services include their immaterial, invisible, intangible, non-storable, and transitory nature … [s]ervices are usually produced and consumed simultaneously'.[35] The WTO Secretariat has also stated that '[s]ervices are, for instance, not normally transferable or storable which means that there is usually a direct relationship between the receiver and the user of a service'.[36] These attributes have also been routinely ascribed to services in the academic literature.[37]

This ordinary meaning presents immediate conceptual difficulties in terms of carbon units. As discussed in Chapter 3, carbon units have a degree of permanence, and are capable of being owned, possessed, and stored over time in accounts. In a number of jurisdictions, they signify property rights under municipal law.[38] As such, carbon units themselves do not constitute 'effort', 'action', or 'conduct'. Instead, they exist with a degree of permanence as a serial number.

However, it should be recalled that whether GATS applies depends not on whether a carbon unit itself constitutes a 'service'. Instead, it depends on whether the rules and requirements applicable to carbon units can be said to *affect* trade in services. As the Appellate Body has indicated, it is immaterial that the principal object of a measure is not itself a service; the fact that a measure is directed towards a

[32] ibid [6.18]–[6.21].

[33] Peter Hill, 'On Goods and Services' (1977) 23(4) *Review of Income and Wealth* 315, 318. See also Fernandes (n 7) 110; Hindley (n 7) 12; Rohan Kariyawasam, 'The classification of electronic intangibles in the WTO' in Rohan Kariyawasam (ed), *The WTO, Intellectual Property, E-Commerce and the Internet* (2009) 362, 384.

[34] See eg Fernandes (n 7) 113; Wolfrum, Stoll, and Feinaugle (n 4) 40.

[35] Appellate Body Report, *US—Large Civil Aircraft (2nd complaint)* n 1295.

[36] GATT Secretariat, 'Trade in Services and the GATT: Background Paper by the Secretariat' (6 March 1981) CG.18/49, 1–2.

[37] See eg Fernandes (n 7) 113; Wolfrum, Stoll, and Feinaugle (n 4) 40; Rolf H Weber and Mira Burri, *Classification of Services in the Digital Economy* (Springer 2012) 3; Diebold (n 7) 24–25; Hindley (n 7) 12; Aly K Abu-Akeel, 'Definition of trade in services under GATS: Legal implications' (1999) 32 *George Washington Journal of International Law and Economics* 189, 191; Rudolf Adlung and Aaditya Mattoo, 'GATS' in Aaditya Mattoo, Robert M Stern, and Gianni Zanini (eds), *A Handbook of International Trade in Services* (OUP 2008) 49; Trebilcock, Howse, and Eliason (n 7) 474.

[38] See above ch 3D. Nevertheless, under Australian domestic law, buying and selling carbon units on behalf of another person is a 'designated service' for the purposes of the Anti-Money Laundering and Counter-Terrorism Financing Act 2006 (Cth) (see item 33 of the table in s 6(2)).

non-service object such as a carbon unit does not a priori exempt it from GATS.[39] Rather, the key issue with such measures is whether they can be understood as having an effect, in broad terms, on another service or service suppliers.[40] As an example, certain measures in respect of bananas (a 'good') were found to 'affect trade in services' in *EC—Bananas* because of the indirect effect they had on the services associated with the distribution of those bananas.[41]

The key question, therefore, is whether carbon units are necessarily or inherently linked to certain services or service suppliers, such that rules on carbon units will inevitably constitute measures affecting trade in a service. For instance, if it can be shown that if the activity and effort involved in generating carbon units falls with the scope of the term 'service', then a measure affecting the distribution, sale, supply, or use of carbon units will necessarily affect the distribution, sale, supply, or use of the service provided in their generation. At this point in the analysis it is useful to separate out allowance units and offset units. This is because of the very different manner in which these categories of units are created.

(a) *Offset units*

As explained in Chapter 3, offset units are generated by private actors and represent the reduction of greenhouse gas emissions outside of an emissions trading scheme as a result of a project which either *removes* greenhouse gas from the atmosphere, for example through planting trees, or which *avoids* emissions of greenhouse gas that would otherwise occur in the absence of the project, for example by installing cleaner technology in a factory leading to lower emissions. On one view, offset units 'embody' a service that has been performed. A number of authors have recognized the existence of a special category of services that can be embodied in other objects.[42] These objects represent the outcome of a service that has been performed or manifest evidence of its performance. Frequently cited examples include architectural drawings, written legal opinions, bank statements, and computer software. Indeed, the European Court of Justice found in one case that, while tangible lottery tickets themselves may not constitute a 'service', they nevertheless *represent* the embodiment of an underlying entertainment or gambling service.[43] This meant that a ban on lottery tickets was tantamount to a ban on the underlying service that they represent.

The activity and effort involved in the generation of offset units seems to correspond directly to the notion of a 'service'. The very purpose of offset projects is the reduction or avoidance of greenhouse gas by one person so that another person may emit greenhouse gas at another time and place, particularly those with liabilities

[39] Appellate Body Report, *EC—Bananas III* [220].

[40] ibid. See also Wolfrum, Stoll, and Feinaugle (n 4) 45.

[41] Appellate Body Report, *EC—Bananas III* [220]–[221].

[42] See eg Zdouc (n 7) 21–23; Trebilcock, Howse, and Eliason (n 7) 474–75; Diebold (n 7) 25; Wolfrum, Stoll, and Feinaugle (n 4) 40; Fernandes (n 7) 116; Snape (n 7) 5; Hindley (n 7) 12.

[43] Case 275/92 *Her Majesty's Customs and Excise Commissioners v Schindler* [1994] ECR I-1039, I-1088 [22]–[25].

under emissions trading schemes. It is an 'action', 'conduct', or 'effort' by one person in order to benefit or advantage another, with the relevant 'action' being the reduction or avoidance of greenhouse gas emissions through a dedicated project.

On the other hand, it could also be argued that this 'action' does not constitute a service activity but simply represents a step in the production of a good, namely, an offset unit. A number of authors have argued that activities which are 'directly incorporated into goods' should not be considered 'services'.[44] According to this perspective, those undertaking offset projects are not supplying a service to others, but are instead undertaking an internal activity for their own benefit in the course of producing a different commercial object (offset units) which they can then sell. Indeed, under the rules pursuant to which such projects are authorized, the sole purpose of greenhouse gas reduction activities should be the generation of offset units.[45] The activity and the end-product are inherently linked. The end-product supplied to the customer is not an activity, but is instead a permanent, storable object that can be possessed.

This perspective perhaps fits better with the description of 'services' in the *System of National Accounts 2008*, which states that services 'cannot be traded separately from their production ... By the time their production is completed, they must have been provided to the consumers'.[46] The production of offset units is the antithesis of this description, insofar as the activity leads to the production of offset units, which in turn may be owned and stored by their producer and traded to customers at a later date. In contrast to this description of services, there is no requirement that production and consumption occur simultaneously with respect to the activity involved in creating offset units.

Relatedly, this perspective also appears to fit better with the emphasis in many descriptions of services on the relationship between the service supplier and its customer.[47] The presence of a direct relationship between these two actors has been described as a 'very important dimension of service activities'.[48] Indeed, since the basic definition of a 'service' requires that the activity be directed at benefiting another person, the presence of a relationship between producer and customer is fundamental; if there is no customer, then there is no person to receive a benefit from the 'action', 'effort', or 'conduct', and hence no service can be performed. However, the production of offset units requires no such 'direct relationship' between producer and consumer. The units may be generated and then sold by the producer to an anonymous buyer on a floating exchange at a later date. This suggests that the 'thing'

[44] Snape (n 7) 5; Wolfrum, Stoll, and Feinaugle (n 4) 43. See also discussion in Trebilcock, Howse, and Eliason (n 7) 474–75.

[45] Carbon Credits (Carbon Farming Initiative) Act 2011 (Cth) s 41; California Market-based Mechanism (n 11) § 95972(a)(9); Modalities and procedures for a clean development mechanism, Decision 3/CMP.1, 1st sess (30 March 2006) FCCC/KP/CMP/2005/8/Add.1, annex [43] (CMP Decision 3); Executive Board of the Clean Development Mechanism, 'Sixty-Second Meeting Report' (15 July 2011) CDM-EB-62, annex 13 [6].

[46] IMF et al, *System of National Accounts* (n 28) [6.17] [6.21].

[47] Fernandes (n 7) 116, 121; Jean-Claude Delaunay and Jean Gadrey, *Services in Economic Thought: Three Centuries of Debate* (Springer 1992) 126; Hill (n 33) 318.

[48] Delaunay and Gadrey (n 47) 126.

traded is not an activity or service but is instead a good or other object, and hence the producers of offset units are not 'service suppliers' but are more akin to manufacturers of an object.

As such, the activity involved in the creation of offset units could be viewed as a step in the production of another commercial object, rather than the supply of a service in its own right.

Although plausible on its face, such a perspective does not represent an entirely accurate reflection of the relationship between an offset unit and the activity that gives rise to its creation. In particular, an offset unit is issued by a government or regulator on the basis of an activity that has been independently measured, monitored, and verified as having in fact occurred and having met all necessary regulatory standards; these are the preconditions to the issuance of most offset units.[49] The function of offset units, therefore, is to provide independent and credible evidence that an activity has occurred. Furthermore, offset units facilitate the breaking down of an aggregate activity into consumable units that can be used in an emissions trading scheme.

Therefore, rather than the relationship between offset units and the activity giving rise to their creation being characterized as a step in the production of a good, the better characterization would be to view offset units as a 'physical support' for the trade of a service. Indeed, the WTO Secretariat has recognized that '[i]n some special cases, goods may simply be physical supports for services—such as exposed film, books, programmed computer tape ... Such goods may, of course, be traded'.[50] Snape has similarly argued that services may be incorporated into goods like 'paper, film, disks and the like' where these goods are 'used to record and transfer the service'.[51] Since the issuance of offset units is the result of a process of measuring, monitoring, and verifying that an activity has been performed, they can be understood as a vessel that 'records' a service performed, and facilitates the transfer of that service. After all, it is the *activity* of reducing or avoiding greenhouse gas emissions that gives offset units their value; the resulting serial number merely records that this activity has occurred, and authorizes its holder to emit one tonne of greenhouse gas (or, in the voluntary market, to secure the reduction of one tonne of greenhouse gas).

Importantly, WTO jurisprudence has also recognized that services may be embodied in goods that serve as their carrier medium. For example, in *Canada—Periodicals*, the Appellate Body found that: 'a periodical is a good comprised of two components: editorial content and advertising content. Both components can be viewed as having services attributes, but they combine to form a physical product—the periodical itself'.[52] The activities involved in producing the editorial and

[49] See eg Department of Climate Change and Energy Efficiency (DCCEE), *Carbon Farming Initiative Handbook* (Commonwealth of Australia 2012) 35–36; CMP Decision 3 (n 41) annex parts H, I, and J; California Air Resources Board (CARB), 'Chapter 6: What are the requirements for offset credits and how are they issued?' in *Cap-and-Trade Regulation Instructional Guidance* (California Air Resources Board 2012) [6.10.2] http://www.arb.ca.gov/cc/capandtrade/guidance/guidance.htm (last accessed 15 January 2013).

[50] GATT Secretariat (n 36) 1–2.

[51] Snape (n 7) 5.

[52] Appellate Body Report, *Canada–Periodicals* 463.

advertising content were not just steps in the production of a good (the periodical), but instead were services in their own right that were carried through another good.

The Appellate Body made a similar finding in *China—Publications and Audiovisual Products*: 'Neither do we consider that content and goods, and the regulation thereof, are mutually exclusive. Content can be embodied in a physical carrier, and the content and carrier together can form a good'.[53]

As such, the Appellate Body found that 'content' (which it accepted in this case constituted a 'service'[54]) could be embodied in another form. In such cases, it rejected the notion that the service and goods components of the end product are 'mutually exclusive', finding that this would involve an 'artificial dichotomy'.[55]

Therefore, the fact that a good contains, embodies, or provides evidence for an activity that has occurred earlier does not exclude that activity from being characterized as a 'service' under WTO law.

It is also noteworthy that, according to WTO jurisprudence, activities undertaken in the process of producing a good can qualify as a 'service', including, in certain instances, where these activities are undertaken internally by the manufacturers of the good.[56] In particular, the Appellate Body has stated that 'even if a company is *vertically-integrated*, and even if it performs *other functions related to the production ... of a product*', it may still be regarded as a service supplier to the extent it supplies a service in relation to the product, including its production.[57] This casts doubt over the notion that an activity undertaken by a company in the pursuit of producing a good cannot be considered a service.

In any case, under a number of offset schemes it is not inevitable that the person undertaking the greenhouse gas reduction activity takes possession of the resulting offset units.[58] Instead, it is possible to structure an offset project such that the *consumer* of the offset units directly receives those units upon their issuance by a regulator. In these kinds of transactions, the object of the transaction between the person undertaking the activity and the consumer is the activity or conduct itself as opposed to the resulting offset units, since these are never actually owned by the person undertaking the activity. The possibility for these kinds of transactions under some offset schemes strengthens the characterization of offset units as the embodiment of, and evidence for, another service that has been performed.

On balance, it seems likely that the greenhouse gas reduction activity undertaken in the generation of offset units is capable of falling within the ordinary meaning of the term 'service' under GATS. At its core, it is an 'action', 'conduct', or 'effort' in the form of reducing or avoiding greenhouse gas in order to benefit another, namely those with liabilities under an emissions trading scheme seeking to offset

53 Appellate Body Report, *China—Publications and Audiovisual Products* [195].

54 ibid [196]. 55 ibid [195].

56 Appellate Body Report, *EC—Bananas III* [227]. See also Wolfrum, Stoll, and Feinaugle (n 4) 46–47.

57 Appellate Body Report, *EC—Bananas III* [227] (emphasis added).

58 See eg CARB, 'Requirements for offset credits' (n 49) [6.10.3]; CMP Decision 3 (n 41) annex [66(b)] (the customer can be listed as a 'project participant' and forwarded all of the CERs). Cf DCCEE (n 49) 28 (only the service supplier may receive offset units under the CFI).

their emissions. The fact that trade in this activity is mediated through a good (offset units) introduces complexity into the analysis, but does not ultimately negate the characterization of this activity as a 'service', according to WTO jurisprudence.

The consequence of this conclusion is that, to the extent offset units represent evidence of a service performed and the means through which that service is traded, any measure affecting trade in offset units will necessarily affect the underlying service. As the WTO Secretariat has stated: '[t]he exceptional cases in which a good acts simply as a necessary support for a service (eg exposed film, books, programmed computer tape) are straightforward – a measure affecting trade in the good automatically affects trade in the service and vice versa'.[59]

(b) *Allowance units*

Unlike offset units, allowance units are not the end result of a project to reduce or avoid greenhouse gas emissions. As explained in Chapter 3, they are simply 'invented' by the regulator or government administering an emissions trading scheme, and then distributed to the market by auctioning, direct sales, or free allocations.

The creation of allowance units and their distribution to the market *by a government or regulator* immediately raises the question of whether their regulation would be exempt from GATS on the basis that the term 'services' expressly excludes 'services supplied *in the exercise of governmental authority*'.[60] Article I.3(c) of GATS defines a services supplied 'in the exercise of governmental authority' to be 'any service which is supplied neither on a commercial basis, nor in competition with one or more service suppliers'. Thus, if the supply of allowance units by a government or regulator meets the two cumulative requirements of not being (i) on a commercial basis and (ii) in competition with one or more service suppliers, it may well invoke the exemption under Article I.3(c) of GATS. While this provision is yet to be interpreted by a panel or the Appellate Body, the concept of 'commercial' has been evaluated in the context of other covered agreements under the WTO Agreement. The Appellate Body has found it to connote an arm's length transaction between a willing seller and a willing buyer, with factors such as the use of market prices, or a profit-orientation on the part of the seller, as relevant indicators.[61] On that basis, the description of a government or regulator's distribution of allowance units to the market as 'commercial' seems problematic and highly contextual. Where allowance units are distributed to the market through competitive auctioning or direct sales at floating market prices, their supply might be considered 'commercial'. However, where allowance units are distributed to market participants directly to customers for no cost, as is the case for large volumes of carbon units in a number of emissions trading schemes,[62] or where they are sold directly within a price collar at the

[59] GATT Secretariat (n 36) 2. [60] GATS (n 1) art I.3(b) (emphasis added).

[61] See Appellate Body Reports, *Canada—Renewable Energy/Canada—Feed-in Tariff Program* [5.70]–[5.71]; *US—Anti-Dumping and Countervailing Duties (China)* [478]–[479].

[62] See Ingrid Jegou and Luca Rubini, 'The Allocation of Emission Allowances Free of Charge: Legal and Economic Considerations' (ICTSD Issue Paper No 18, August 2011) 6–14.

minimum or maximum established price, their supply would be unlikely to be considered 'commercial'. Rather, in such instances, the supply of carbon units is a result of the pursuit of certain policy objectives, rather than a profit-orientation on the part of the seller.

In any case, it seems highly unlikely that the supply of allowance units could be perceived as being *not* in competition with other service suppliers, and thus exempt from GATS pursuant to Article I.3(c). This is because market participants are able to purchase offset units generated by private actors under most emissions trading schemes as an alternative to allowance units, in addition to allowance units generated under the emissions trading schemes of other jurisdictions. These alternatives thus provide a source of competition to the government or regulator selling or distributing allowance units. Further, allowance units that have *already* been distributed to the market and are offered for resale by other private actors provide another source of competition to allowance units supplied by a government or regulator.

That notwithstanding, it is conceivable that an emissions trading scheme could prohibit or tightly restrict the use of offset units, or the allowance units of other jurisdictions, as a source of competition. Further, it is conceivable that an emissions trading scheme could distribute all allowance units at no cost, and thus not in competition with other actors. These kinds of scenarios might make it more likely that Article I.3(c) could be invoked in respect of allowance units. However, the complexities raised by such scenarios are indicative of the problems highlighted in respect of Article I.3(c) by Markus Krajewski.[63] Having examined the negotiating history of this provision, as well as relevant documents of the WTO Secretariat and the positions of various WTO Members, Krajewski concludes that 'there is currently no agreed understanding of this provision among WTO Members or within the Secretariat'.[64]

Assuming that the distribution of allowance units by a government or regulator is not exempted from GATS through Article I.3)(c), it nonetheless seems unlikely that the process involved in generating allowance units would fall within the ordinary meaning of the term 'service'. First, the only effort expended in the creation of each individual unit is the generation of a unique electronic serial number. This is a largely automated process and involves only piecemeal (if any) human effort or labour.[65]

Of course, on an aggregate level, allowance units could be understood to represent the maximum amount of greenhouse gas that may be emitted by the entities covered under the scheme in a given compliance period. This is because the regulator or government administering an emissions trading scheme will not release an amount of allowance units to the market that exceeds the corresponding cap on emissions during the time-period in question. Therefore, on an aggregate level, allowance units

[63] Markus Krajewski, 'Public Services and the Scope of the General Agreement on Trade in Services (GATS)' (Research Paper, Center for International Environment Law 2001).

[64] ibid 6–17.

[65] Partnership for Market Readiness and Forest Carbon Partnership Facility, *Emissions Trading Registries: Guidance on Regulation, Development, and Administration* (World Bank 2016) 57–61.

could be understood collectively to represent a national or subnational 'effort' to reduce overall greenhouse gas emissions in that jurisdiction. They represent the imposition of scarcity on the emission of greenhouse gas in a given jurisdiction during a given time-period—and, usually, they represent the incremental reduction of aggregate emissions over time. In this vein, some authors have argued that a stable climate and clean air should be perceived as a kind of public service to humans.[66]

Importantly, however, the 'effort' expended is not designed to benefit or advantage a given service consumer. Instead, it is implemented in pursuit of a nation's own environmental goals and in the fulfilment of a statutory scheme. It therefore lacks the second key characteristic of a service—that the effort or activity be undertaken to benefit a given service consumer.

Therefore, unlike offset units, allowance units seem to lack the core elements of a service. There is no real effort or action undertaken in the process of generating each individual unit, and on an aggregate level, the 'effort' of aggregate greenhouse gas reductions represented by the generation of allowance units is in pursuit of a jurisdiction's own objectives, rather than serving others.

This chapter now turns to whether the context of the term 'service' sheds light on its coverage of carbon units under GATS.

2 Context

An important element of context is the definition of the term 'service', which includes '*any* service in *any* sector except services supplied in the exercise of governmental authority'.[67] According to the Appellate Body, it can be inferred from the use of the word 'any' that the WTO Membership intended to define services 'very broadly'.[68] This suggests that, where there may be competing broad and narrow interpretations of the term 'service', a broader interpretation should be adopted.

Another important element of context is that WTO Members inscribe the particular service sectors in which they undertake market access and national treatment commitments in specific schedules.[69] By implication, the fact that a certain activity or effort is inscribed in a schedule reveals the intention of the WTO Membership that it should be considered to be a 'service'.[70] Indeed, panels and the Appellate Body have routinely looked to Members' schedules to determine the service at issue in a given case and delimit its scope.[71] It is therefore useful to consider whether Members' schedules list the kind of activity and effort involved in the generation of carbon units as a relevant sector or subsector of a service.

[66] See eg Graciela Chichilnisky, 'International payments for ecosystem services: Principles and practices' in Thomas Koellner (ed), *Ecosystem Services and Global Trade of Natural Resources* (Routledge 2011) 204, 211; Jordan Levine and Kai M A Chan, 'Global human dependence on ecosystem services' in Thomas Koellner (ed), *Ecosystem Services and Global Trade of Natural Resources* (Routledge 2011) 11.

[67] GATS (n 1) art I.3(b) (emphasis added).

[68] Appellate Body Report, *US—Gambling* [180].

[69] GATS (n 1) art XX. See also ibid.

[70] Appellate Body Report, *US—Gambling* [180]. See also Wolfrum, Stoll, and Feinaugle (n 4) 42.

[71] See eg Appellate Body Reports, *Canada—Autos* [157]; *EC—Bananas III* [222]–[228]; Panel Report, *Mexico—Telecoms* [7.35] [7.32] fn 832.

Many WTO Members have made commitments in respect of '[c]leaning services of exhaust gas', with most inscriptions on this sector referring to United Nations Central Product Classification (hereafter UNCPC) No 9404.[72] While the Appellate Body has stated that the UNCPC does not *itself* form part of the 'context' of GATS,[73] the fact that Members' schedules qualify as 'context', together with the fact that most of those schedules refer to the UNCPC[74] to delimit the scope of their inscriptions, mean that it may, through their schedules, be taken into account as context.[75] As such, the UNCPC description of '[c]leaning services of exhaust gases' constitutes a relevant element of context, and states:[76]

> Emission monitoring and control services of pollutants into the air, whether from mobile or stationary sources, mostly caused by the burning of fossil fuels. Concentration monitoring, control and reduction services of pollutants in ambient air, especially in urban areas.

This description is closely aligned to the activity and effort involved in offset projects, which seek to control and reduce air pollutants mainly caused by the burning of fossil fuels. The schedule of Thailand clarifies that this includes 'industrial emission abatement', and the schedule of Tonga clarifies that it includes 'services to reduce exhaust gases and other emissions and improve air quality'.[77] Since the very purpose of offset projects is to reduce emissions of greenhouse gas or remove those gases from the atmosphere, they would appear to fall within the scope of this service sector—or at least be analogous to it.

Alternatively, many WTO Members have also made commitments in respect of '[o]ther environmental protection services', again with most inscriptions on this sector referring to the corresponding UNCPC code to delimit its content.[78] In particular, UNCPC No 9409 describes this sector as: 'Other environmental protection services not elsewhere classified, e.g. acidifying deposition ("acid rain") monitoring, controlling and damage assessment services'.[79]
This description does not directly reference greenhouse gases. However, the example provided includes 'acid rain controlling services'. This is significant, because acid

[72] This data is accessible online through the *WTO Services Database* at http://tsdb.wto.org/. The WTO Members whose schedules refer to UNCPC 9404 include Albania, Armenia, Austria, Cambodia, Canada, Cape Verde, China, Croatia, Ecuador, El Salvador, European Community, Finland, FYR Macedonia, Georgia, Japan, Jordan, Korea, Latvia, Liechtenstein, Lithuania, Moldova, Norway, Oman, Panama, Poland, Saudi Arabia, Sweden, Switzerland, Chinese Taipei, Thailand, Tonga, Ukraine, and Vietnam (accessed 15 January 2015).

[73] Appellate Body Report, *US—Gambling* [178].

[74] ibid [183].

[75] ibid [183]–[186].

[76] *Provisional Central Product Classification (CPC)*, Statistical Papers, Series M No 77 (United Nations 1991) 87 (code 94040).

[77] This data is accessible online through the WTO Services Database at http://tsdb.wto.org/ (last accessed 15 January 2015).

[78] ibid. The WTO Members whose schedules refer to UNCPC 9409 include Austria, Cambodia, Canada, Cape Verde, China, Croatia, Ecuador, El Salvador, European Community, Finland, Georgia, Japan, Jordan, Korea, Latvia, Liechtenstein, Lithuania, Moldova, Norway, Oman, Panama, Saudi Arabia, Sweden, Switzerland, Chinese Taipei, Thailand, Tonga, Ukraine, and Vietnam.

[79] *Provisional CPC* (n 76) 87 (code 94090).

rain is caused by gaseous emissions of sulphur dioxide,[80] which are analogous to greenhouse gas emissions. Services to 'control' such emissions are, in turn, analogous to services that control greenhouse gas emissions through offset projects that reduce emissions or remove greenhouse gas from the atmosphere. As such, it can be inferred from this example that 'other environmental protection services not elsewhere classified' could extend to greenhouse gas reduction and avoidance projects, from which offset units are generated. More broadly, it suggests that the kind of activity and effort undertaken through offset projects can qualify as a 'service'.

Finally, it is pertinent to note that a more recent version of the UNCPC includes another service that seems to match the activity and effort expended in the creation of offset units. In particular, UNCPC No 83326 relates to 'Engineering Services for Waste Management Projects' and covers services 'related to programmes for the collection, treatment, recycling and disposal of industrial air waste'.[81] Since most offset units are generated through dedicated projects that involve some degree of 'collecting' or 'treating' greenhouse gas emissions, which could be considered to be 'industrial air waste', their generation would appear to be covered under this code. Although the Appellate Body has held that more recent versions of the UNCPC cannot be used to interpret the terms of WTO Members' GATS schedules,[82] the appearance of this inscription as a service is nevertheless an important development to note.

These various UNCPC descriptions, the first two of which are referenced in multiple WTO Members' schedules, strongly suggest that the activity and effort involved in the generation of offset units are capable of falling within the scope of the term 'service' under GATS. As such, the foregoing analysis calls into question the respective assertions of Wiser and Petsonk that '[t]he CPC lists no services directly analogous to the sale of decarbonization services represented by CDM offset credits',[83] and that no WTO Member has 'identified emissions reduction and emissions trading-related services as services to which it wished to apply GATS disciplines'.[84] On the contrary, GATS schedules of WTO Members based on the UNCPC appear to cover services very similar to, if not the same as, those involved in the generation of offset units.

As discussed above, it is unlikely that the process involved in generating allowance units also qualifies as a 'service'. There is very limited (if any) activity or effort involved in the generation of each individual allowance unit, and it seems unlikely that this would be tantamount to the 'action', 'effort' or 'conduct' inherent in the concept of a 'service'.

[80] See United States Environmental Protection Agency, *Acid Rain Program SO_2 Allowances Fact Sheet* http://www.epa.gov/airmarkets/trading/factsheet.html.

[81] *Central Product Classification Version 2.0*, Statistical Papers, Series M No 77 (Version 2.0) (United Nations 2008) (code 83326).

[82] Appellate Body Report, *US—Gambling* [193].

[83] Wiser (n 8) 560

[84] Annie Petsonk, 'The Kyoto Protocol and the WTO: integrating greenhouse gas emissions allowance trading into the global marketplace' (1999) 10 *Duke Environmental Law & Policy Forum* 185, 204.

Further, while the UNCPC lists 'public administrative services related to . . . pollution standards' as a service sector under No 91123,[85] no WTO Member has inscribed a commitment pertaining to this kind of service in its schedule,[86] and the broader category of '[a]dministrative services of government' under No 911 is absent from the original documents prepared by the WTO secretariat providing guidance on how to classify service sectors in GATS schedules based on the UNCPC.[87] This suggests an intention not to cover such activities as 'services' under GATS.

As such, while the activity and effort involved in generating offset units would likely be considered a 'service' based on the context of GATS, the same cannot be concluded in respect of allowance units.

Finally, for the reasons discussed in Chapter 2 in sections B and D, it is unlikely that the instruments of the international climate regime would play a direct role through Article 31.3(c) of the Vienna Convention as context in the interpretation of the term 'service' under GATS. However, to the extent they were considered in that regard, a strong inference can be drawn that measures pertaining to climate change—including measures affecting trade and investment in carbon units—are not intended to be exempted from the international economic regime.[88]

3 Object and purpose

As required by Article 31 of the Vienna Convention, the term 'service' must also be interpreted in light of the object and purpose of GATS and the WTO Agreement. The same considerations apply in this respect to the interpretation of 'services' as with 'products'/'goods' discussed in Chapter 3. In particular, there are no relevant preambular elements that are *directly* on point. However, a number of preambular elements—including developing an '*integrated*' and a 'more *viable* and *durable*' trading system, and 'seeking both to protect and preserve the environment and to enhance the means for doing so'—would, if anything, suggest that market-based approaches to environmental protection that commodify pollution for international trading could be potentially covered by the WTO Agreement. At a minimum, those elements do not suggest that such approaches should necessarily be excluded.

In any event, as discussed in Chapter 2, an interpreter should not attach undue importance to arguments concerning the object and purpose of a treaty where the treaty does not contain any relevant explicit statement elements, which likely mitigates against a significant role for this interpretive element when assessing the meaning of 'service' in GATS.

[85] *Provisional CPC* (n 76) 78 (code 91123).

[86] This data is accessible online through the WTO Services Database at http://tsdb.wto.org/.

[87] See GATT Secretariat, 'Services Sectoral Classification List: Note by the Secretariat' (10 July 1991) MTN.GNS/W/120; GATT Secretariat, 'Scheduling of Initial Commitments in Trade in Services: Explanatory Note' (3 September 1993) MTN.GNS/W/164.

[88] See further ch 4B.

C 'Affecting'

The final element in the scope provision of GATS is whether the impugned measures can be said to 'affect' trade in services. This is unlikely to present any obstacles.

First, GATS includes an illustrative list of 'measures affecting trade in services', such as 'measures in respect of the purchase, payment or use of a service'.[89] Since the measures surveyed above determine whether an offset unit may be 'used' for compliance in an emissions trading scheme, they also consequently determine whether the underlying greenhouse gas reduction service may be 'used' for compliance.

Secondly, the Appellate Body has stated that: 'The term of "affecting" reflects the intent of the drafters to give a broad reach of GATS; it implies a measure that has "an effect on", which indicates a broad scope of application; it is wider in scope than such terms as "regulating" or "governing" ...'.[90] Therefore, the term 'affecting' should be construed broadly according to the Appellate Body. It should not matter that the measure is not specifically directed at a service; it matters only whether the measure can be said to 'have an effect' on a service. As such, the fact that the impugned measures govern offset units, rather than the underlying service, does not remove them from the scope of GATS. Instead, the fact that they 'have an effect' on the underlying service is the determinative aspect.

D Summary: Measures Affecting Trade in Services under GATS

In summary, it is likely that GATS extends to the rules and requirements on whether, and to what extent, offset units can be used in emissions trading schemes. This is because such rules and requirements constitute 'measures' which 'have an effect on' the supply of a greenhouse gas reduction and removal service.

On the other hand, it seems less likely that the rules and requirements on the use of allowance units would fall under the purview of GATS. This is because those units do not appear to relate to any underlying 'service'. Individual allowance units are not created through any particular effort or activity, but are merely generated as an electronic serial number. Even if this can be considered an effort or activity, it is not directed at benefiting or assisting a given service consumer, but is instead undertaken in fulfilment of a statutory scheme.

In conclusion, while measures affecting offset units are most likely to be subject to GATS, measures affecting allowance units are not. The key drawback of this conclusion, however, lies in the fungibility between allowance units and offset units in carbon markets. As discussed in Chapter 3, allowance units and offset units have the same or similar end-uses, such as the discharge of liabilities under emissions trading schemes. Further, all carbon units are ultimately intended to be acquired and traded

[89] GATS (n 1) art XXVIII(c).

[90] Appellate Body Report, *EC—Bananas III* [220].

by private actors in commercial markets. From that viewpoint, their fragmented regulation under GATS would appear to be somewhat incongruous.

E Position under Free Trade Agreements

Approximately 120 free trade agreements containing services-related obligations have been notified to the WTO.[91] While it is not feasible to evaluate all of these, an evaluation of a sample of free trade agreements demonstrates that the foregoing analysis in respect of GATS can be largely transposed and applied in respect of free trade agreements. There are a number of reasons for this.

First, many free trade agreements state an intention to *'[b]uild* on their rights and obligations under the WTO Agreement' and *'further* liberalize and expand bilateral trade'.[92] This suggests that the term 'service' in those agreements should, at a minimum, not be interpreted as having a narrower scope than the corresponding term in the WTO Agreement, since this would undermine the resolve to 'build' on services commitments in the WTO Agreement and engage in 'further' liberalization. Any construction of the term 'service' under these agreements that is narrower than that applicable to the WTO Agreement would result a *smaller* range of activities being subject to the liberalizing disciplines of the treaty, and would therefore be inconsistent with the intention to engage in enhanced liberalization beyond the WTO Agreement. Since the activity and effort expended in the creation of offset units is highly likely to fall within the scope 'services' under the WTO Agreement, it is similarly likely to fall within the scope of 'services' under these free trade agreements.

Secondly, and relatedly, many free trade agreements state an intention that they are consistent with Article V GATS.[93] This is important, because Article V of GATS

[91] See World Trade Organization, *RTA Database* http://rtais.wto.org/ui/PublicMaintainRTAHome.aspx (last accessed 2 June 2015).

[92] See eg Australia–United States Free Trade Agreement [2005] ATS 1 (signed 18 May 2004, entered into force 1 January 2005) preambular recitals 2 and 8; Free Trade Agreement between the Republic of Korea and the Republic of Chile, signed 15 February 2003 (entered into force 1 April 2004) preamble; Free Trade Agreement Between Canada and the Republic of Peru, signed 29 May 2008 (entered into force 1 August 2009) preamble; Free Trade Agreement between the Government of the People's Republic of China and the Government of the Republic of Chile, signed 16 November 2005 (entered into force 1 October 2006) art 1 ('encouraging expansion ... of trade between the Parties ... eliminating the barriers to trade in, and facilitate the cross-border movement of ... services between the Parties'); Costa Rica–China Free Trade Agreement, signed 8 April 2010 (entered into force 1 August 2011) preambular recital 3, art 2.1(a); Agreement Establishing the ASEAN–Australia–New Zealand Free Trade Area, signed 27 February 2009 [2010] ATS 1 (entered into force 1 January 2010) art 1(b).

[93] See eg Australia–United States Free Trade Agreement (Australia–United States) [2005] ATS 1 (signed 18 May 2004, entered into force 1 January 2005) art 1.1; Free Trade Agreement between the European Union and its Member States, of the one part, and the Republic of Korea, of the other part (Korea–European Union) (signed 6 October 2010, entered into force June 2010) art 55(c); Free Trade Agreement Between Canada and the Republic of Peru (Canada–Peru) (signed 29 May 2008, entered into force 1 August 2009) art 101; Free Trade Agreement between the Republic of Korea and the Republic of Chile (Korea–Chile) (signed 15 February 2003, entered into force 1 April 2004) art 1.1; Free Trade Agreement between the Government of the People's Republic of China and the Government of the Republic of Chile (China–Chile) (signed 16 November 2005, entered into force 1 October 2006) art 2; Costa Rica–China Free Trade Agreement (China–Costa Rica) (signed 8 April 2010, entered into force 1 August 2011) art 1; Peru–Singapore Free Trade Agreement (Peru–Singapore) (signed 29

requires that an agreement liberalizing trade in services between subsets of WTO Members must have 'substantial sectoral coverage', measured 'in terms of number of sectors, volume of trade affected and modes of supply ... [i]n order to meet this condition, agreements should not provide for the *a priori* exclusion of any mode of supply'.[94] In turn, this suggests that the parties to such agreements intended the services-related commitments to be broad. Given that context, it would appear inappropriate to adopt an interpretation of the term 'services' under those agreements that excludes a particular sector or activity, such as the removal or avoidance of greenhouse gas emissions through offset projects. Indeed, an interpretation of the term 'service' that would result in a *narrower* coverage than the WTO Agreement would likely be inconsistent with the desire to conform to Article V GATS.

Finally, pursuant to Article 31.3(c) of the Vienna Convention, the interpretation of the term 'service' under free trade agreements would need to take into account any 'relevant rules of international law applicable in the relations between the parties'. Assuming that all the parties to a free trade agreement are WTO Members, the WTO Agreement would likely be considered to contain 'relevant rules of international law' that could shed light on the meaning of the term 'service' under a free trade agreement. As discussed above, it is likely that the term 'services' under the WTO Agreement covers the activity and effort expended in the generation of offset units. This, in turn, would inform the meaning of the term 'service' under free trade agreements between WTO Members by virtue of Article 31.3(c) of the Vienna Convention.

For these reasons, it can be stated with some confidence that the term 'service' under many, if not most, free trade agreements will cover measures affecting trade in offset units.

May 2008, entered into force 1 August 2009) art 1; Agreement Establishing the ASEAN–Australia–New Zealand Free Trade Area (ASEAN–Australia–New Zealand) (signed 27 February 2009, entered into force 1 January 2010) [2010] ATS 1, art 2.

94 GATS (n 1) art V.

6

International Trade in Carbon Units and Financial Services*

This chapter assesses the extent to which carbon units are covered by financial services-related obligations under international economic law. It considers this question primarily with respect to the Annex on Financial Services contained in the General Agreement on Trade in Services (GATS).[1] This is the premier multilateral instrument on trade in financial services. While it forms an integral part of GATS, the Annex on Financial Services supplements, better defines, and at times replaces the general disciplines of GATS on account of the unique position of the financial services sector in national economies and international trade.[2]

The final section of this chapter also considers this question with respect to financial services chapters in free trade agreements, which are largely modelled on the Annex on Financial Services.

Like GATS, the Annex on Financial Services contains a provision delimiting its scope. It applies to 'measures affecting the supply of financial services'.[3] In turn, the

* This chapter is a revised and updated version of James Munro, 'Trade in Carbon Units as a Financial Service under International Trade Law: Recent Developments, Future Challenges' (2014) 8(2) *Carbon and Climate Law Review* 106.

[1] Marrakesh Agreement Establishing the World Trade Organization (opened for signature 15 April 1994, entered into force 1 January 1995) 1867 UNTS 3 Annex IB (General Agreement on Trade in Services, GATS).

[2] Rudiger Wolfrum, Peter-Tobias Stoll, and Clemens Feinaugle, *WTO—Trade in Services* (Brill 2008) 621–22; WTO Secretariat, *Guide to GATS: An Overview of Issues for Further Liberalization of Trade in Services* (Kluwer 2001) 340–44.

[3] Annex on Financial Services art 1(a). In order to avoid repetition, see the analysis of 'measures' and 'affecting' in ch 4 ss A and C.

Emissions Trading Schemes under International Economic Law. James Munro.
Published 2018 by Oxford University Press.

'supply of financial services' includes 'the production, distribution, marketing, sale and delivery of a financial service'.[4]

As discussed in Chapter 3, carbon units do not themselves constitute a 'service', and the same is true in relation to 'financial services'. However, carbon units may nevertheless constitute an object regulated by the Annex on Financial Services.

In particular, the Annex on Financial Services contains a substantive definition for the term 'financial service', which provides in relevant part:[5]

> A financial service is any service of a financial nature offered by a financial service supplier of a Member. Financial services include all insurance and insurance-related services, and all banking and other financial services (excluding insurance). Financial services include the following activities: ...
>
> (x) Trading for own account or for account of customers, whether on an exchange, or in an over-the-counter market or otherwise, the following:
>
> (C) derivative products including, but not limited to, futures and options; ...
>
> (E) transferable securities;
>
> (F) other negotiable instruments and financial assets, including bullion.

Based on this definition, if carbon units can be considered a 'derivative product', 'transferable security', 'negotiable instrument', or 'financial asset', then trading in carbon units will constitute a 'financial service' under the Annex on Financial Services. It is important to emphasize that it is not the carbon unit itself that would constitute a 'financial service', but rather a surrounding activity pertaining to it—for instance, trading or supplying units—which would comprise the 'financial service' in question. Relevantly, the description of such activities in Article 5 of the Annex on Financial Services includes not just brokerage services, but also '[t]rading for own account'—that is, where a broker or dealer undertakes a transaction for his or her *own* benefit, rather than that of a client.[6]

This chapter evaluates whether carbon units can fall within the meaning of any of the above-mentioned terms. This question has been the subject of substantial debate in academic literature, with authors reaching a diversity of conclusions.[7] These analyses, however, predate a number of important developments, such as the first ever WTO jurisprudence concerning the Annex on Financial Services,[8] as well as

[4] ibid art 1(a). [5] ibid art 5.

[6] Jonathan Law (ed), *A Dictionary of Finance and Banking* (5th edn, OUP 2014) 'own account trading'.

[7] See eg Jacob Werksman, 'Greenhouse Gas Emissions Trading and the WTO' (1999) 8 *Review of European Community & International Environmental Law* 251; Sikina Jinnah, 'Emissions Trading under the Kyoto Protocol: NAFTA and WTO Concerns' (2003) 15 *Georgetown International Environmental Law Review* 709; Marisa Martin, 'Trade Law Implications of Restricting Participation in the European Union Emissions Trading Scheme' (2007) 19 *Georgetown International Environmental Law Review* 437;; Erich Vranes, 'Climate Change and the WTO: EU Emission Trading and the WTO Disciplines on Goods, Services and Investment Protection' (2009) 43 *Journal of World Trade* 707; Glenn Wiser, 'Frontiers in Trade: the Clean Development Mechanism and the General Agreement on Trade in Services' (2002) 2 *International Journal of Global Environmental Issues* 288; Felicity Deane, *Emissions Trading and WTO Law* (Edward Elgar Publishing 2015) 127–30.

[8] Panel Report, *China—Electronic Payment Services*; Appellate Body Report, *Argentina—Financial Services*.

the recent designation of carbon units as 'financial services' or 'financial assets' under the municipal law of a number of jurisdictions.[9] This chapter concludes that carbon units are unlikely to qualify as 'derivative products', 'transferable securities', or negotiable instruments. However, they are likely to qualify as 'financial assets', and trade in carbon units would in any case be captured by the residual catch-all category 'any service of a financial nature'.

A Derivative Products

Commentators have diverged on whether carbon units constitute 'derivative products' under the Annex on Financial Services. On the one hand, Martin argues that carbon units are 'futures' or 'options' within the meaning of 'derivative products', since most transactions in carbon units occur in the context of derivative contracts.[10] On the other hand, Vranes considers that carbon units 'should not normally be considered to be "derivative products"', since derivatives are based on private law contracts rather than rights issued by a government.[11]

In reality, both are correct in their assessments. Vranes is correct insofar as carbon units *themselves* are not derivative products, and Martin is correct insofar as most transactions involving carbon units are futures or options. This is because trading in carbon units can occur either through spot transactions,[12] whereby units are purchased at current prices for immediate delivery, or as derivative products,[13] which tend to dominate the carbon market.[14] Derivative products are financial instruments whose value derives from an underlying asset (eg carbon units),[15] and in the carbon market they usually take the form of forwards, futures, and options contracts.[16] In basic terms, a forward contract fixes an agreed price for delivery of carbon units at a future date.[17] Futures contracts are essentially the same, but are traded in standardized forms over organized exchanges.[18] Options contracts provide the right—but impose no obligation—to purchase carbon units at some time in the future for an agreed price.[19] These products also offer different ways of structuring

[9] See eg Corporations Act 2001 (Cth) s 764A(1)(kaa); Personal Property Securities Act 1999 (NZ) s 16; European Commission, 'Review of the Markets in Financial Instruments Directive (MiFID) and Proposals for a Regulation on Market Abuse and for a Directive on Criminal Sanctions for Market Abuse: Frequently Asked Questions on Emission Allowances' (Memo/11/719, 20 October 2011) 1.

[10] Martin (n 7) 451. [11] Vranes (n 7) 719.

[12] Andrew Hedges, 'The Secondary Market for Emissions Trading' in David Freestone and Charlotte Streck (eds), *Legal Aspects of Carbon Trading: Kyoto, Copenhagen, and beyond* (OUP 2009) 324–25; Scott Deatherage, *Carbon Trading Law and Practice* (OUP 2011) 257.

[13] See Karan Capoor and Philippe Ambrosi, *State and Trends of the Carbon Market 2008* (World Bank 2008) 64–65.

[14] Alexandre Kossoy and Pierre Guigon, *State and Trends of the Carbon Market 2012* (World Bank 2012) 10, 30; European Commission (n 9) 1.

[15] Martijn Wilder, 'Nature of an Allowance' in Paul Q Watchman (ed), *Climate Change—A Guide to Carbon Law and Practice* (Globe Law and Business 2008) 93, 106; Neil C Schofield, *Commodity Derivatives* (John Wiley & Sons 2008) 1–4.

[16] Schofield (n 15) 255; European Commission (n 9) 1; Hedges (n 12) 324–25.

[17] Schofield (n 15) 2. [18] ibid. [19] ibid 4.

or determining the payment of carbon units at a future date, such as a fixed price per unit, a price pegged to the prevailing market at the time of maturity of the contract, or the use of a floor or ceiling price.[20] They therefore present a means of managing the risk of spikes or collapses in the price of carbon units.

In *China—Electronic Payment Services*, the panel found the ordinary meaning of the term derivative product to be:[21]

> Derivative product: An arrangement or instrument (such as a future, option, or warrant) whose value derives from and is dependent on the value of an underlying asset; or a financial contract the value of which depends on the value of one or more underlying reference assets, rates or indices. For analytical purposes, all derivatives contracts can be divided into basic building blocks of forward contracts, options or combinations thereof.

As such, a derivative product is an instrument whose value is derived from an underlying asset. In the context of the carbon market, carbon units are the underlying asset on which resulting derivative products are based; the product itself is not the unit, but rather a separate financial instrument whose value derives from the unit.

According to the European Commission and the World Bank, the 'lion's share' of trade in carbon units occurs through the medium of derivative products[22] and, in this way, much of the trade in carbon units will be covered under the Annex on Financial Services. However, technically speaking, carbon units themselves are not 'derivative products', and to the extent that carbon units are traded through spot transactions or on the primary market, they will not be covered as 'derivative products'.

B Transferable Securities

On the one hand, both Martin and Jinnah argue that carbon units qualify as 'transferable securities'. They base this on a dictionary definition of 'security' that includes a 'transferable share', and argue that a carbon unit is a 'transferable share' because '(1) it is transferable from one person or government to another person or government; and (2) it represents the ownership of a portion of total allowable carbon dioxide, or carbon dioxide equivalent, emissions'.[23]

Vranes, on the other hand, asserts that while the term 'securities' may vary across jurisdictions and different legal fields, 'it appears to be a common core of this notion that securities are based on contractual relations'.[24] Since carbon units are not founded in a contractual relationship but are instead a government-issued right, Vranes argues that they do not fall within the scope of 'transferable securities'.[25]

[20] Martijn Wilder and Louisa Fitz-Gerald, 'Carbon Contracting' in David Freestone and Charlotte Streck (eds), *Legal Aspects of Carbon Trading: Kyoto, Copenhagen, and beyond* (OUP 2009) 296, 303.

[21] Panel Report, *China—Electronic Payment Services* [7.152].

[22] See European Commission (n 9); Kossoy and Guigon (n 14) 10, 30.

[23] Jinnah (n 7) 741; Martin (n 7) 452.

[24] Vranes (n 7) 719.

[25] In contrast, see Personal Property Securities Act 1999 (NZ) s 16, which includes emissions units within the scope of 'investment securities' in New Zealand. On the other hand, see Securities Act 1978 (NZ) s 5, which expressly exempts emissions units from securities regulation, and similarly Financial

The panel in *China—Electronic Payment Services* clarified the ordinary meaning of the term 'transferable securities'. It found that 'security' referred to:[26]

> Security: A document held by a credit as guarantee of his or her right to payment; a certificate attesting ownership of stock, shares, etc.; the financial asset represented by such a document. Also (US), such a document issued to investors to finance a business venture; or A pledge of financial or physical property to be surrendered in the event of failure to repay a loan. Any medium of investment in the money market or capital market, e.g. a money-market instrument, a bond, a share. A term used to refer only to bonds, and shares, as distinct from money-market assets.

The panel went on to state that 'securities' are defined as 'a means of investment attesting ownership rights and granting financial returns'.[27]

In one sense, carbon units represent a guarantee of a right to avoid a financial liability in the form of a fine for emitting greenhouse gas. This could be considered analogous to the notion of a 'guarantee of a right to payment' in the panel's definition.

On the other hand, Vranes' observation seems apt. There is nothing in the panel's definition that suggests a government-issued instrument in the form of a right or licence can be considered a 'security'. All of the examples listed are private financial instruments, rather than the products of a statutory scheme.

Furthermore, the panel in *China—Electronic Payment Services* demonstrated a reluctance to stretch the interpretation of these types of terms on the basis of analogies or 'common features', particularly since these are listed as discrete terms rather than open-ended categories, and also due to the presence of residual 'other' categories intended to catch items that do not neatly fall within the listed categories.[28]

As such, it seems unlikely that carbon units would fall within the scope of the term 'transferable security' under Article 5(a)(x)(E) of the Annex on Financial Services.

C Negotiable Instruments

As with transferable securities and derivative products, commentators have differed on whether carbon units are 'negotiable instruments' under the Annex on Financial Services.

While Werksman suggests that carbon units could qualify as 'negotiable instruments',[29] Jinnah rejects this on a number of grounds.[30] First, Jinnah points out that carbon units do not contain an 'unconditional promise to pay a specified sum of money', which she asserts is a key component of a 'negotiable instrument'.[31] Secondly, she asserts that carbon units are not 'negotiable'—as a government-issued right defined by a statutory scheme, the unit itself is a fixed, permanent item whose content cannot be 'renegotiated' by private parties.[32]

Service Providers (Registration and Dispute Resolution) Act 2008 (NZ) s 5(i), which also appears to exempt the offering of emissions units to the public from the scope of the term 'financial service'.

26 Panel Report, *China—Electronic Payment Services* [7.152]. 27 ibid [7.160].
28 ibid [7.156]–[7.159]. 29 Werksman (n 7) 256. 30 Jinnah (n 7) 740.
31 ibid. 32 ibid.

The panel in *China—Electronic Payment Services* has since interpreted the term 'negotiable instrument' as follows:[33]

> We consider now the ordinary meaning of the term 'negotiable instruments'. The word 'negotiable' is defined as follows: '[o]f a bill, draft, cheques, etc.: transferable or assignable in the course of business from one person to another simply by delivery.' A 'negotiable instrument' is 'a document of title that can be freely negotiated . . .' or 'unconditional order or promise to pay an amount of money, easily transferable from one person to another'. The characteristics of 'negotiable instruments', as identified in specialized dictionaries, are that they (i) are easily transferable from one person to another, and (ii) can be freely negotiated.

Based on this interpretation, negotiable instruments should exhibit two core qualities. First, they should be easily transferable. Carbon units clearly possess this quality, since they can be easily traded on exchanges and between private parties. Secondly, they should be able to be freely negotiated. According to Jinnah, in the case of carbon units, the instrument itself—the unit—cannot be 'renegotiated' by private parties. While this is correct, the panel appears to have taken a different approach to the term 'negotiable'. It seems to require that the transaction involving the instrument be negotiable, rather than the instrument itself. Indeed, the test for 'negotiable' employed in *China—Electronic Payment Services* was whether an item 'can . . . be traded on a market'.[34] Clearly, carbon units can be traded on a market, and the terms under which they are traded, such as the price, delivery, or nature of the financial product (eg option, future, spot transaction) may be negotiated. Put together, it could be inferred that carbon units do qualify as a 'negotiable instrument'.

However, another element of the panel's definition is that a negotiable instrument constitutes a 'document of title' or an 'unconditional promise to pay an amount of money'. As Jinnah points out, carbon units do not involve a promise to pay money. Furthermore, they are not a 'document of title', but instead exist as an electronic serial number in a person's registry account.

Therefore, as with 'transferable securities', carbon units do not neatly match the ordinary meaning of the term 'negotiable instruments'. Given the panel's apparent reluctance to stretch the interpretation of terms contained in the definition of finance service on the basis of analogies or 'common features',[35] it seems unlikely that a 'document of title' could be stretched to cover an electronic serial number. As such, it seems unlikely that carbon units would be held to constitute a 'negotiable instrument' under Article 5(a)(x)(F) of the Annex on Financial Services.

D Financial Assets

There has also been debate on whether carbon units qualify as 'financial assets'. Both Jinnah and Vranes argue that they are financial assets, emphasizing their ability to be traded on an open market[36] and their status as incorporeal property.[37] In contrast,

[33] Panel Report, *China—Electronic Payment Services* [7.154]. [34] ibid [7.155].
[35] ibid [7.156]–[7.159]. [36] Jinnah (n 7) 741. [37] Vranes (n 7) 719–20.

Wiser argues that financial assets are usually denominated or redeemable in money, whereas carbon units are redeemable as a right to emit and a corresponding avoidance of a penalty.[38]

The panel in *China—Electronic Payment Services* found that the following definitions informed the ordinary meaning of the term 'financial assets':[39]

> Financial assets: '[m]oney and claims, as distinct from physical assets such as land, buildings, or equipment. Financial assets include money, securities constituting a claim to receive money, such as bills or bonds, and shares giving indirect ownership of the physical assets of companies. The claims held as financial assets include the obligations of individuals, companies, and governments, domestic and foreign. Financial assets include shares in financial institutions, and derivatives such as options.' Other definitions describe a 'financial asset' as '[a]n asset that is either cash, a contractual right to receive cash, or the right to exchange a financial instrument with another entity under potentially favourable terms or an equity instrument of another entity"; or "assets in the form of stocks, bonds, rights, certificates, bank balances, etc., as distinguished from tangible, physical assets' ...
>
> Financial: 'of or pertaining to revenue or money matters'.

On this basis, the panel found that the 'ordinary meaning of the term "financial assets" encompasses virtually all financial instruments'.[40] In the specific context of a different occurrence of this term, the panel found that it was narrowed to a sub-class of 'negotiable instruments'.[41] However, the opposite inference appears to be warranted in the context of the term 'financial assets' as it appears in Article 5(a)(x)(F). In particular, since it functions as the residual catch-all category of '*other* negotiable instruments and *financial assets*, including bullion', and since it appears in *addition* to the term 'negotiable instruments', a broad interpretation that is not limited to 'negotiable instruments' appears appropriate.

In particular, the conclusion of Wiser that 'financial assets' are limited to money-related products appears to ignore the express inclusion of 'money market instruments' in Article 5(a)(x). There would be no need to include the residual category of 'other ... financial assets' if this term were limited to money market instruments. The express inclusion of 'bullion' in the term 'financial assets' casts further doubt on Wiser's conception of 'financial assets', since bullion can extend to *non-monetary* precious metals.[42]

Instead, Vranes' broader conception of financial assets as incorporeal property seems more appropriate in the context of Article 5(a)(x)(F). This matches a number of definitions of 'financial assets' cited above by the panel, which point to assets 'as distinct from physical assets' or 'distinguished from tangible, physical assets'.

On a broader conception, carbon units would appear to fall within the scope of 'financial assets' in two ways. First, their use for compliance in an emissions trading scheme discharges the holder from a financial liability. As an asset that relieves the

[38] Wiser, Frontiers and Trade (n 7) 303.

[39] Panel Report, *China—Electronic Payment Services* [7.145].

[40] ibid [7.146].

[41] ibid [7.159].

[42] See eg IMF, *Balance of Payments and International Investment Position Manual* (6th edn, IMF 2009) [9.18].

holder from financial liability, they could therefore be viewed as a 'financial asset'. Secondly, they are liquid assets that can be readily sold for cash through dedicated exchanges, and in that way could also be considered a 'financial asset'.

The object and purpose of GATS appears to confirm an interpretation that carbon units fall within the scope of the term 'financial assets'. In particular, the panel held in *China—Electronic Payment Services* that the 'security and predictability' of GATS-specific commitments would be served by reflecting 'market and regulatory realities' in the classification of items as 'financial assets'.[43] In turn, carbon units are regulated as 'financial products' or 'financial assets', or are generally subject to financial and prudential regulation, under a number of jurisdictions.[44] In Australia, carbon units constitute 'financial products' under the Corporations Act 2001 (Cth) and the Australian Securities and Investments Commission Act 2001 (Cth), which effectively requires providers of financial services concerning carbon units to hold a financial services licence.[45] Similarly, New Zealand regulates carbon units in the same way as currency and other financial instruments for the purposes of futures contracts under its Securities Markets Act 1988 (NZ).[46] Until recently, EU rules only regulated the derivative products of carbon units (options, futures, and forwards) as financial products, with the units themselves not regulated in that way.[47] However, it has now additionally moved to classify the units themselves as financial products subject to financial market regulation.[48] This will likely bring a degree of certainty and harmonization to the classification of units across different EU Member States in financial markets, which varied from expressly classifying units as financial instruments, such as in Sweden, to expressly exempting them from certain financial regulation, such as in Germany.[49]

The prudential regulation of carbon units in this regard reflects the presence of risks to the integrity of domestic carbon markets. Such risks include: (i) gaming and arbitrage in a fragmented global carbon market; (ii) theft and fraud; and (iii) the potential for excessive speculation by financial institutions without liabilities under emissions trading schemes.[50] These kinds of risks justify the prudential regulation of the market by the government or regulator concerned.[51] These kinds of 'market and regulatory realities'—to use the words of the panel in *China—Electronic Payment Services*—would be likely to strengthen the argument that carbon units are properly

[43] Panel Report, *China—Electronic Payment Services* [7.162].

[44] See eg Corporations Act 2001 (Cth) s 764A(1)(kaa); Personal Property Securities Act 1999 (NZ) s 16; European Commission (n 9).

[45] Corporations Act 2001 s 764A(1)(kaa); Australian Securities and Investments Commission Act 2001 s 12BAA(7)(ka).

[46] Securities Markets Act 1988 (NZ) s 37(1).

[47] European Commission (n 9).

[48] ibid.

[49] See Karoliina Anttonen, Michael Mehling, and Karl Upston-Hooper, 'Breathing Life into the Carbon Market' (2007) 16 European Environmental Law Review 96, 98, 103.

[50] Damien Lockie, 'Closing Pandora's Box: The Case for Carbon Market Integrity after the Global Financial Crisis—Conditioning Ownership of the Right to Emit Greenhouse Gases in an Australian Emissions Trading Scheme' (PhD Thesis, Bond University 2011) 154.

[51] ibid 186–220.

classified as 'financial assets' that may be subject to prudential regulation under the Annex on Financial Services.

Therefore, the ordinary meaning of 'financial assets' in its context in Article 5(a)(x)(F) and in light of the object and purpose of GATS points to its coverage of carbon units.

E Any Service of a Financial Nature

Even if carbon units do not fall within the scope of 'financial assets' or any of the other categories under Article 5(a), they may still be regulated under the Annex on Financial Services. This is because the definition of 'financial service' is not limited to the enumerated list in Article 5. Instead, this list provides illustrative examples of the kinds of activities that qualify as a 'financial service', and to that extent they shed light on what may be covered as a 'financial service'. In accordance with WTO jurisprudence, the use of the word 'includes' in Article 5(a) suggests that other items not explicitly listed may nevertheless fall within the scope of the term.[52]

Indeed, the term 'financial service' is defined broadly to mean 'any service of a financial nature ... includ[ing] all ... other financial services'. In turn, the ordinary meaning of 'financial' is 'of or pertaining to revenue or money matters'.[53] The use of the words 'any' and 'all' before 'service' suggests the broadest possible scope, 'manifest[ing] an intention to cover comprehensively the entire spectrum' of things under that term.[54] As such, 'financial service' should be construed to cover comprehensively the entire spectrum of services that pertain to revenue or money matters. The service of trading and supplying of carbon units pertains to revenue or money matters because units are necessary in order to avoid a *financial* liability that is otherwise due; they are also liquid assets traded for cash on dedicated exchanges.

For the same reasons in relation to 'financial assets', the object and purpose of GATS would support an interpretation that trade in carbon units reflects a 'financial service'. In particular, the regulation of trade in carbon units as a financial service suggests that such an interpretation would 'accord with [market and regulatory] realities'.[55] Of course, it would be difficult for a WTO Member that does *not* subject its carbon market to prudential regulation to argue, in effect, that its measures affecting trade in carbon units should obtain the benefit of prudential exceptions under international economic law. Nevertheless, as discussed above, there are sound reasons for subjecting domestic carbon markets to prudential regulation to ensure their integrity, stability, and environmental function, and, in light of those reasons,

[52] Panel Report, *China—Publications and Audiovisual Products* [7.294]; Panel Report, *China—Electronic Payment Services* [7.109].

[53] Panel Report, *China—Electronic Payment Services* [7.145].

[54] Panel Report, *China—Electronic Payment Services* [7.99]; Appellate Body Reports, *US—Wheat Gluten* [51]; *Canada—Autos* [79]; *EC—Asbestos* [188]; *US—Anti-Dumping and Countervailing Duties (China)* fn 157. See also Panel Reports, *US—Steel Plate* [7.57]; *US—Anti-Dumping Measures on Oil Country Tubular Goods* [7.149].

[55] Panel Report, *China—Electronic Payment Services* [7.162].

it would be anomalous for a panel or the Appellate Body to find that the 'market and regulatory realities' do not tend towards the coverage of trade in carbon units as a financial service.

The foregoing suggests that the ordinary meaning of the term 'financial service', in its context and in light of the object and purpose of GATS, extends to cover the trade in, and supply of, carbon units. This remains the case, even if carbon units cannot be considered 'derivative products', 'transferable securities', 'negotiable instruments', or 'financial assets'. If anything, the similarities that carbon units share with a number of those items, as surveyed above, would likely *confirm* their coverage under the residual category of 'all other financial services'.

F Summary

The *sui generis* properties of carbon units make them difficult to classify under the traditional categories of financial instruments, such as 'negotiable instruments', 'transferable securities', and 'derivative products'. However, as an intangible asset that pertains to financial matters—both through their use to avoid financial liability and through their status as liquid assets traded on exchanges for cash—they would appear to fall within the residual catch-all category of 'other financial assets'. In any case, trade in carbon units would appear to fall within the broader residual category of 'any service of a financial nature'. As such, it is highly likely that carbon units constitute objects regulated by the Annex on Financial Services.

It is important to reiterate, however, that it is not the carbon units themselves that would constitute the financial service in question under the Annex on Financial Services. Rather, it is the activity surrounding the carbon unit—namely, the supply or trading of that unit—which would reflect the financial service in question. It is conceivable that a measure could prohibit or restrict the carbon unit of a certain nationality but nonetheless leave the supply or trade of *permitted* carbon units by suppliers of that nationality unrestricted or unaffected. In such instances, it is conceivable that the prohibition or restriction on that carbon unit may not actually hinder the supply of financial services by suppliers of the same nationality, thus probably not engaging the Annex on Financial Services. For instance, while Korea's emissions trading scheme might bar Californian offset units for compliance purposes, it may nonetheless permit financial service suppliers of the United States to freely trade and supply permissible Korean carbon units within the Korean emissions trading scheme on an equal footing with Korean financial service suppliers.

Although potentially significant in some factual matrices, this distinction should not be overstated. It is relevant only where there is minimal or no commercial nexus between the activity (ie *trading* or *supplying* a financial product) performed by a financial service supplier, and the particular financial products being traded or supplied (ie carbon units). It stands to reason that there will often be such a commercial nexus. This is because a financial service supplier of a given jurisdiction will likely have greater proximity to, and expertise in, the carbon units (and associated financial instruments) of its own jurisdiction. Further, in the case of offset units, the financial service supplier may have been involved in the generation of units that it now seeks to trade and, in that regard, it is noteworthy that Article 5 of the Annex on Financial Services refers to '[t]rading *for own account* or for account of customers'. This could cover, for instance, a financial service supplier trading its *own* carbon units,[56] including offset units in whose generation the supplier has participated as an investor.

Finally, it may seem anomalous that a financial product regulated by the Annex on Financial Services could simultaneously comprise a 'good'/'product' regulated by GATT 1994. However, the very definition of 'financial asset' includes 'bullion',[57] which is also a 'good'/'product' in the form of monetary gold.[58] As the Appellate Body has recognized, there is no reason wherefore measures affecting trade in goods under GATT 1994 cannot simultaneously be measures affecting trade in services.[59]

G Position under Free Trade Agreements

Not all free trade agreements include financial services within their scope, and many only reaffirm their existing WTO commitments.[60] However, those that do include financial services in a substantive sense appear to be modelled on the Annex on Financial Services, while some also incorporate the provisions of the Understanding on Commitments in Financial Services.[61] This has resulted in WTO Members usually transposing the definition of 'financial services' in the Annex on Financial

[56] This concept covers instances where a broker or dealer undertakes a transaction for his or her *own* benefit rather than that of a client: see Law (n 6) 'own account trading'.

[57] Annex on Financial Services art 5(a)(X)(F).

[58] World Customs Organization, *HS Nomenclature 2012 Edition* (WCO 2012); for monetary gold see 710820 http://www.wcoomd.org/home_hsnomenclaturetable2012.htm (last accessed 15 January 2015).

[59] Appellate Body Reports, *EC—Bananas III* [220]–[221]; *Canada—Periodicals* 463; *China—Publications and Audiovisual Products* [193]–[196].

[60] See eg Free Trade Agreement between the Republic of Chile and the Republic of Malaysia (Chile–Malaysia) (signed 13 November 2010, entered into force 18 April 2012) art 14.6; Australia–Thailand Free Trade Agreement (Australia–Thailand) (signed 5 July 2004, entered into force 1 January 2005) [2005] ATS 2 art 807; Agreement between Japan and the United Mexican States for the Strengthening of the Economic Partnership (Mexico–Japan) (signed 17 September 2004, not yet in force) art 108, art 109; Peru–Singapore Free Trade Agreement (Peru–Singapore) (signed 29 May 2008, entered into force 1 August 2009) art 11.2.7.

[61] WTO Website, 'Understanding on Commitments in Financial Services' https://www.wto.org/english/tratop_e/serv_e/21-fin_e.htm (last accessed 26 January 2017). See eg Agreement Establishing the ASEAN–Australia–New Zealand Free Trade Area (ASEAN–Australia-New Zealand) (signed 27 February 2009, entered into force 1 January 2010) [2010] ATS 1, ch 8 Annex on Financial Services; Free Trade Agreement between Canada and the Republic of Peru (Canada–Peru) (signed 29 May 2008, entered into force 1 August 2009) ch 11; Agreement between Japan and Chile for a Strategic Economic Partnership (Japan-Chile) (signed 27 March 2007, entered into force 3 September 2007) ch 10; Colombia—United States Trade Promotion Agreement (Colombia–United States) (signed 22 November 2006, entered into force 15 May 2012) ch 12; Australia–United States Free Trade Agreement (Australia–United States) (signed 18 May 2004, entered into force 1 January 2005) [2005] ATS 1, ch 13; Free Trade Agreement between the European Union and its Member States, of the one part, and the Republic of Korea, of the other part (EU–Korea) (signed 6 October 2010, entered into force June 2010) arts 7.37–7.45.

Services directly into their free trade agreements.[62] It also means that the term 'financial service' in free trade agreements appears in a very similar context to the Annex on Financial Services in GATS, since its substantive provisions are largely mirrored in free trade agreements. The corollary is that the foregoing analysis on whether trade in carbon units constitutes a 'financial service' under the Annex on Financial Services will often be applicable to free trade agreements. This is strengthened by the same factors discussed in Chapters 4 and 5 in relation to free trade agreements, namely the object and purpose of many free trade agreements, as well as the Annex on Financial Services constituting 'relevant rules of international law' for the purpose of interpreting free trade agreements under Article 31(3)(c) of the Vienna Convention.

That said, it should be noted that there are some minor variations between the definition of 'financial services' in the Annex on Financial Services and some free trade agreements. For example, the United States' free trade agreements with Colombia and Australia add 'a service incidental or auxiliary to a service of a financial nature' to the general description of 'financial services'.[63] If anything, this would be likely to have the effect of *broadening* the scope of 'financial services' under those free trade agreements.

As another example, the free trade agreement between Japan and Mexico defines a financial service as 'a service of a financial nature, including insurance, and a service incidental or auxiliary to a service of a financial nature'.[64] Although this definition omits any illustrative list of what constitutes a 'financial services', the core definition is the same as the Annex on Financial Services: a 'service of a financial nature'. It would therefore be unlikely to have a materially different scope

Therefore, it seems reasonable to conclude that carbon units will also often be regulated by financial services-related obligations under free trade agreements. That said, the specific definitions, context, and object and purpose of each agreements would need to be consulted on a case-by-case basis to take into account the eccentricities of particular free trade agreements.

[62] See eg Agreement Establishing the ASEAN–Australia–New Zealand Free Trade Area (ASEAN-Australia-New Zealand) (signed 27 February 2009, entered into force 1 January 2010) [2010] ATS 1, ch 8 Annex on Financial Services art 2(a); Agreement Between Japan and Chile for a Strategic Economic Partnership (Japan-Chile) (signed 27 March 2007, entered into force 3 September 2007) art 128; Colombia–United States Trade Promotion Agreement (Colombia–United States) (signed 22 November 2006, entered into force 15 May 2012) art 12.20; Peru–China Free Trade Agreement (China–Peru) (signed 28 April 2009, entered into force 1 March 2010) art 105.7; Australia–United States Free Trade Agreement (Australia–United States) (signed 18 May 2004, entered into force 1 January 2005) [2005] ATS 1, art 13.19.5; Free Trade Agreement between the European Union and its Member States, of the one part, and the Republic of Korea, of the other part, signed 6 October 2010 (entered into force June 2010) arts 7.37–7.45.

[63] Colombia–United States Trade Promotion Agreement (Colombia–United States) (signed 22 November 2006, entered into force 15 May 2012) art 12.20; Australia–United States Free Trade Agreement (Australia–United States) (signed 18 May 2004, entered into force 1 January 2005) [2005] ATS 1 art 13.19.5.

[64] Agreement between Japan and the United Mexican States for the Strengthening of the Economic Partnership (Mexico–Japan) (signed 17 September 2004, not yet in force) art 112(e).

7

Carbon Units as 'Investments' under International Investment Agreements

This chapter assesses the extent to which carbon units constitute objects that are subject to the disciplines of international investment law. As with the foregoing assessment of whether carbon units qualify as 'goods'/'products', 'services', or 'financial services', this question turns on the extent to which carbon units fall within meaning of the term 'investment'.

This chapter commences the legal enquiry into whether carbon units constitute 'investments' with an overview of the typical structure of the definition of that term and the broader nature of international investment law. It then considers whether carbon units fall within the scope of the terms 'property', 'rights', 'licences', or 'assets', and assesses the extent to which they meet the objective criteria for 'investments' such as a commitment of capital, assumption of risk, and a certain duration.

Contrary to earlier analyses, this chapter casts doubt over the view that carbon units necessarily qualify as investments, either as 'property', 'rights', or 'interests in an enterprise'.[1] Rather, as will be shown, the characterization of carbon units

[1] See Lisa Bennett, 'Are Tradable Carbon Emissions Credits Investments? Characterization and Ramifications under International Investment Law' (2010) 85 *New York University Law Review* 1581.

Emissions Trading Schemes under International Economic Law. James Munro. Published 2018 by Oxford University Press.

as 'investments' is highly contextual, depending on factors such as how they are classified under municipal law, how an arbitral tribunal construes 'property' under international law, and the duration and purpose for which carbon units are held by an investor.

A Overview of the Definition of 'Investment' under International Investment Law

Unlike the case for 'goods', 'services', and 'financial services', there is no premier multilateral instrument governing 'investments'. Instead, international investment law is a highly fragmented collection of over 2,750 treaties comprising bilateral investment treaties, plurilateral investment treaties, and free trade agreements with investment chapters, collectively referred to as international investment agreements (IIAs).[2]

Across these IIAs there is no uniform definition of 'investment'.[3] Instead, the precise boundaries of what qualifies as an 'investment' under each IIA will depend on the particular wording of its definition of 'investment', as well as its context and object and purpose. It may also depend on the arbitration rules authorized by an IIA for settling investment disputes.[4]

On the one hand, this makes it problematic to generalize about whether carbon units are regulated as 'investments' under international investment law. This is compounded by the decentralized nature of investor-state dispute settlement under IIAs, in which there is no formal system of precedent, no standing body of adjudicators, and no substantive or unifying appellate mechanism. These systemic features at times have produced conflicting outcomes on questions of law and fact.[5]

However, despite the fragmented nature of international investment law, most definitions of 'investment' have a similar structure.[6] Most define 'investments' broadly as 'every kind of asset', and include a non-exhaustive illustrative list of the

See also Anatole Boute, 'Combating Climate Change through Investment Arbitration' (2012) 35 *Fordham International Law Journal* 613, 627–30; Jacob Werksman, Kevin A Baumert, and Navroz K Dubash, 'Will International Investment Rules Obstruct Climate Protection Policies?' (2003) 3 *International Environmental Agreements: Politics, Law And Economics* 59, 70.

[2] For a listing of all IIAs see the UNCTAD website http://www.unctadxi.org/templates/DocSearch____779.aspx.

[3] See Katia Yannaca-Small, *International Investment Law: Understanding Concepts and Tracking Innovations* (OECD 2008) 46; UNCTAD, 'Scope and Definition' (UNCTAD Series on Issues in International Investment Agreements II, United Nations 2011) 7–8; *Petrobart Limited v Kyrgyz Republic (Arbitral Award)* (Stockholm Chamber of Commerce, Arbitration No 126/2003, 29 March 2005) 69.

[4] Rudolf Dolzer and Christoph Schreuer, *Principles of International Investment Law* (OUP 2012) 65–66; UNCTAD (n 3) 51–60; Yannaca-Small, *International Investment Law* (n 3) 53–60.

[5] For a comprehensive discussion on this see Susan Franck, 'The Legitimacy Crisis in Investment Treaty Arbitration: Privatizing Public International Law through Inconsistent Decisions' (2005) 73 *Fordham Law Review* 1521; Andrew Newcombe and Lluís Paradell, *Law and Practice of Investment Treaties* (Kluwer 2009) 104–07; Frank Spoorenberg and Jorge Vinuales, 'Conflicting Decisions in International Arbitration' (2009) 8 *The Law and Practice of International Courts and Tribunals* 91, 95–96.

[6] Newcombe and Paradell (n 5) 65; Dolzer and Schreuer (n 4) 63; Christopher F Dugan, Don Wallace Jr, Noah D Rubins, and Borzu Sabahi, *Investor-State Arbitration* (OUP 2008) 250; Katia Yannaca-Small, 'Definition of "Investment": An Open-Ended Search for a Balanced Approach' in Katia

kinds of items covered.[7] The precise terms of the illustrative lists vary, but in principle they cover physical property, intangible rights in or relating to property such as shares or intellectual property, and administrative or public rights related to the conduct of investment activities, such as licences or resource concessions.[8] The recently updated IIA between China and Switzerland provides a typical example:[9]

The term 'investment' shall include every kind of asset, and in particular:

(a) movable and immovable property as well as any other rights in rem, such as servitudes, mortgages, liens, pledges and usufructs;
(b) shares, parts or any other kind of participation in companies;
(c) claims to money or to any performance having an economic value;
(d) copyrights, industrial property rights (such as patents, utility models, industrial designs or models, trade or service marks, trade names, indications of origin) know-how and goodwill;
(e) business concessions under public law, including concessions to search for, extract or exploit natural resources as well as all other rights given by law, by contract or by decision of the authority in accordance with the law.

Terms such as 'asset', 'property', and 'business concession' denote the legal categories of items that constitute an 'investment'. In addition to these legal categories, some definitions incorporate an economic dimension to the definition of 'investment'. For instance, the 2012 United States Model IIA states that: '"investment" means every asset that an investor owns or controls, directly or indirectly, *that has the characteristics of an investment, including such characteristics as the commitment of capital or other resources, the expectation of gain or profit, or the assumption of risk*'.[10] This definition then continues with the standard non-exhaustive illustrative list of legal categories such as property and licences.

Yannaca-Small (ed), *Arbitration under International Investment Agreements: A Guide to the Key Issues* (OUP 2010) 245–46.

[7] This is reflected in a representative sample of recent or model IIAs of major jurisdictions: 2012 United States Model Bilateral Investment Treaty (US Model IIA) art 1 www.state.gov/e/eb/ifd/bit/index.htm (last accessed 15 January 2018); Comprehensive Economic and Trade Agreement (EU–Canada) (entered into force provisionally on 21 September 2017) art 8.1; German Model Treaty (German Model IIA) 2008 art 1.1 http://italaw.com/sites/default/files/archive/ita1025.pdf (last accessed 15 January 2018)); Italy Model Bilateral Investment Treaty (Italy Model IIA) 2003 art 1.1 http://www.italaw.com/sites/default/files/archive/ITALY%202003%20Model%20BIT%20.pdf (last accessed 15 January 2018); 2006 French Model Bilateral Investment Treaty (French Model IIA) art 1.1: http://italaw.com/documents/ModelTreatyFrance2006.pdf (last accessed 15 January 2015); Agreement between the Swiss Federal Council and the Government of the People's Republic of China on the Promotion and Reciprocal Protection of Investments (Switzerland–China) (signed 27 January 2009, entered into force 1 April 2010) art 1.1. But see for a contrasting approach Model Text for the Indian Bilateral Investment Treaty (India Model IIA) 2016 art 1 https://www.mygov.in/sites/default/files/master_image/Model%20Text%20for%20the%20Indian%20Bilateral%20Investment%20Treaty.pdf (last accessed 15 January 2018).

[8] M Sornarajah, *The International Law on Foreign Investment* (3rd edn, CUP 2010) 14–15, 190–92.

[9] Swiss–China IIA (n 7) art 1.1.

[10] US Model IIA (n 7) art 1 (emphasis added). As another example see Agreement between the Belgium–Luxembourg Economic Union on the one hand, and the Republic of Colombia on the other hand, on the Reciprocal Promotion and Protection of Investments (Belgium–Luxembourg–Colombia) (signed 4 February 2009) art I.2.3.

These are a similar set of economic criteria to those used by many tribunals arbitrating IIA disputes under the auspices of Convention on the Settlement of Investment Disputes between States and Nationals of Other States (ICSID).[11] Those tribunals have held that a claimant must not only own or control an 'investment' for the purposes of an IIA, but must also own or control an 'investment' for the purposes of ICSID[12] on the basis that ICSID only administers disputes 'arising directly out of an *investment*'.[13] Since the term 'investment' is not defined in ICSID, tribunals have found that economic characteristics of an investment inform its meaning: 'a certain duration, a regularity of profit and return, an element of risk, a substantial commitment and . . . a significant contribution to the host State's development'.[14]

Some tribunals have also applied these economic criteria even in the absence of any requirement in the text of the definition and when not convened under ICSID.[15] Indeed, Zachary Douglas argues that they are an inescapable and inherent component of the ordinary meaning of 'investment', regardless of any textual or contextual guidance in a given IIA.[16]

In light of this general structure of the definition of 'investment', a convenient interpretive method employed by a number of tribunals uses a two-step approach in order to determine whether an item qualifies as an 'investment'.[17] This involves first ascertaining whether the subject item falls within any of the categories expressly included in an IIA's definition of 'investment', such as 'property', 'licences', or 'assets'. If it does, a second step involves assessing whether the item additionally satisfies the economic criteria of an investment.

This is the approach adopted in this chapter with respect to carbon units. It will first consider whether carbon units are capable of being characterized within the major legal categories covered in definitions of 'investment', namely, private property, public law rights, and the residual 'every kind of asset' category. This assessment takes into account both the obvious and subtle variations in the text, context, and object and purpose of different IIAs, showing how these variations may affect the coverage of carbon units. Secondly, it evaluates the extent to which owning carbon units can be construed as meeting the economic criteria of an 'investment'. As will

[11] 575 UNTS 159, (concluded 18 March 1965, entered into force 14 October 1966) art 25(1).

[12] See eg *Phoenix Action Ltd v Czech Republic (Award)* (ICSID Arbitral Tribunal, Case No ARB/06/5, 15 April 2009) [81]–[82]; *Joy Mining Machinery Ltd v Egypt (Award on Jurisdiction)* (ICSID Arbitral Tribunal, Case No ARB/03/11, 6 August 2004) [48]–[53].

[13] ICSID (n 11) art 25(1) (emphasis added).

[14] See eg *Salini Costruttori SpA v Kingdom of Morocco (Decision on Jurisdiction)* (ICSID Arbitral Tribunal, Case No ARB/00/4, 23 July 2001) [52], [54]; *Joy Mining v Egypt* (n 12) [53]; *Biwater Gauff (Tanzania) v Tanzania (Award)* (ICSID Arbitral Tribunal, Case No ARB/05/22, 24 July 2008) [312]–[317].

[15] See eg *Romak SA v Uzbekistan (Award)* (Permanent Court of Arbitration, Case No AA280, 26 November 2009) [177], [207]; *Mytilineos Holdings SA v Serbia and Montenegro, Serbia (Partial Award on Jurisdiction)* (Ad hoc arbitration, UNCITRAL Rules, 8 September 2006) [115]–[120].

[16] Zachary Douglas, *The International Law of Investment Claims* (CUP 2009) 153–65.

[17] See eg *Malaysian Historical Salvors SDN BHD v Malaysia (Decision on the Application for Annulment)* (ICSID Arbitral Tribunal, Case No ARB/05/10, 16 April 2009) [53]. See also *Salini v Morocco* (n 14) and *Joy Mining v Egypt* (n 12). See further Dugan and others (n 6) 259; Yannaca-Small, 'Definition of "Investment"' (n 6) 243, 259.

be shown, this is a complex question that may depend on the context in which carbon units are owned, as well as the individual economic criteria that a given tribunal may choose to apply or emphasize.

Importantly, however, some tribunals have expressly eschewed economic criteria in favour of an exclusive analysis of the legal categories listed in a given IIA's definition of 'investment',[18] including some tribunals convened under ICSID.[19] These tribunals have seen no reason effectively to 'read-in' additional economic criteria into the definition of 'investment' in the absence of any explicit textual requirement to that effect in a given IIA. In those instances, the second step will be irrelevant; the coverage of an item by one of the legal categories in the first step will suffice to qualify as an 'investment'.

B Carbon Units as 'Property'

1 The ordinary meaning of 'property' under international investment law

Almost all IIAs list 'property' as falling within the scope of the 'investments' that they regulate and protect.[20] The question of whether carbon units constitute 'property' under international investment law encounters an immediate and unsettled controversy: how to determine whether something constitutes 'property' for the purposes of international law.[21] Certain characteristics of carbon units compound the complexity, particularly their intangible nature, their quality as a government-issued instrument under a regulatory scheme, and their varying and inconsistent classifications under different municipal legal systems. As discussed in section D of Chapter 3, some municipal legal systems expressly confer proprietary rights on carbon units, others expressly deny them proprietary status, and yet others are either silent as to their classification or confer separate classifications such as a 'securities', 'goods', or 'financial assets'.

The controversy in international law over the proper legal method for determining whether something is 'property' relates to the role of municipal law.[22] On one view, there is no autonomous concept of 'property' in international law.[23] Therefore, the

[18] *White Industries Australia Ltd v India (Final Award)* (Ad hoc arbitration, UNCITRAL Rules, 30 November 2011) 76.

[19] See eg *Malaysian Historical Salvors v Malaysia* (n 17) [75]–[77].

[20] This is reflected in a representative sample of recent or model IIAs of major jurisdictions. See US Model IIA (n 7) art 1; EU–Canada IIA (n 7) art 8.1; German Model IIA (n 7) art 1.1; Italian Model IIA (n 7) art 1.1; French Model IIA (n 7) art 1.1; Swiss–China IIA (n 7) art 1.1.

[21] Monique Sasson, *Substantive Law in Investment Treaty Arbitration: The Unsettled Relationship between International Law and Municipal Law* (Kluwer 2010) 77–96; Zachary Douglas, 'The Hybrid Foundation of Investment Treaty Arbitration' (2003) 74 *British Yearbook of International Law* 151, 197–211.

[22] Sasson (n 21) 77–96; *Barcelona Traction, Light and Power Co Ltd (Belgium v Spain)* [1970] ICJ Rep 3, 272 (Judge Gros), 233 (Judge Morelli), 33–34, 37 (Judgment).

[23] Sasson (n 21) 66; Douglas, 'The Hybrid Foundation of Investment Treaty Arbitration' (n 21) 197; Rosalyn Higgins, 'The Taking of Property by the State: Recent Developments in International Law' (1982) 176 *Recueil des Cours* 263, 270.

only means of determining whether something constitutes 'property' for the purposes of a treaty is to perform a *renvoi* to the municipal legal system in which it purportedly subsists. If that legal system does not recognize the existence of property rights, they will not be protected as 'property' under the treaty. As Douglas explains:

> Customary international law contains no substantive rules of property law. [It] cannot be a source of rights in property. It is therefore the municipal law of the host state that determines whether a particular right in rem exists, the scope of that right, and in whom it vests. There must be a renvoi to a municipal property law ... Investment treaties do not oblige the contracting states to protect intangible property rights that are not recognised in the legal order of the contracting state.[24]

Christoph Schreuer similarly argues that 'the protection of property through an investment treaty or general international law is contingent upon the existence and extent of property rights as determined by the applicable domestic law',[25] and Monique Sasson suggests that terms such as 'property' in international law are 'empty concepts without a renvoi to a municipal legal system'.[26] Underpinning these views is the conceptual difficulty that, if domestic law does not determine the scope and content of intangible, government-issued rights such as carbon units, then what does? Without a touchstone in the municipal law in which they are created and subsist, there is a risk that intangible property rights could morph into 'floating rights ungoverned by any set of rules'.[27]

On another view, international law should not be deferential to classifications under municipal law.[28] Municipal law may, at best, provide factual evidence for the existence or appropriate classification of an object as 'property'.[29] This is the prevailing approach in the jurisprudence of the World Trade Organization (WTO).[30] Under this approach, factual evidence of the position under municipal law sits alongside other relevant factual evidence, such as whether an object has value and may be owned and possessed to the exclusion of others. On this view, the term 'property' should be interpreted like any other term in a treaty, namely, by looking at its ordinary meaning in its context and in light of the object and purpose of the treaty. Since the ordinary meaning of the term property points to economic features such as ownership, value and a degree of permanence,[31] the subsistence of such features in an object will inform whether it is 'property'.[32]

[24] Douglas, 'The Hybrid Foundation of Investment Treaty Arbitration' (n 21) 197.

[25] Christoph Schreuer, 'The Relevance of Public International Law in International Commercial Arbitration: Investment Disputes' (Unpublished Paper, University of Vienna) 21 www.univie.ac.at/intlaw/pdf/csunpublpaper_1.pdf (last accessed 20 February 2015).

[26] Sasson (n 21) 66. [27] ibid 81. [28] *Barcelona Traction* (n 22) 272 (Judge Gros).

[29] ibid. [30] Appellate Body Report, *US—Softwood Lumber IV* [56].

[31] *Black's Law Dictionary* (9th edn, West 2009); *Oxford English Dictionary Online* (OUP 2012) "property" http://www.oed.com.ezp.lib.unimelb.edu.au/view/Entry/152674?rskey=PpbVpD&result=1&isAdvanced=false (last accessed 23 December 2015).

[32] For an analogous focus on economic realities rather than legal formalities conferred under municipal law see *Barcelona Traction* (n 22) 279 (Judge Gros), 337–38 (Judge Riphagen); Appellate Body Report, *US—Softwood Lumber IV* [56]–[65].

In between these two views lie a spectrum of approaches that give differing degrees of primacy to municipal law. Newcombe and Paradell, for instance, argue that there should generally be a *renvoi* to municipal law to determine the existence of property under an IIA—unless such *renvoi* would be 'wholly unreasonable or leads to a result abhorrent to international law'.[33] Presumably, under this approach, economic or other ordinary indicia of 'property' would be used to ascertain whether a *renvoi* to municipal law produces 'wholly unreasonable' results. Another approach is to perform a *renvoi* to municipal legal systems more broadly rather than to the specific municipal legal system of the host state of the investment.[34] Under this approach, general unifying principles relating to property under municipal legal systems, or their general treatment of an object as proprietary or not, play a determinative role in ascertaining whether something is 'property' under international law. If most municipal legal systems treat or recognize a certain item or right as 'property', it would most likely qualify as 'property' in international law under this approach.

The jurisprudence of international investment tribunals reveals a concomitant diversity of views and approaches. Some tribunals have rejected any role for municipal law.[35] The concern appears to be that, if the term 'property' in a given treaty were interpreted by reference to one party's municipal law, this would create the impossible situation where the scope of the term could vary for different parties to the treaty.[36] It would undermine the presumption in international law that the terms of a treaty, which represents a negotiated outcome entered into voluntarily by all parties, must reflect the *common* intention of its parties. On this view, the same word has the same meaning for all parties unless otherwise stipulated.[37]

Other tribunals have looked to municipal law in a more factual way to determine the existence and scope of intangible rights. These tribunals, while recognizing that '[l]egal terms in an international treaty do not necessarily have the same meaning as similar terms in the domestic laws of the Contracting Parties',[38] have viewed the ability to enforce and protect a right or interest under domestic law as important to

[33] Newcombe and Paradell (n 5) 96. [34] *Barcelona* Traction (n 22) 37.

[35] *Saipem SpA v People's Republic of Bangladesh (Decision on Jurisdiction)* (ICSID Arbitral Tribunal, Case No ARB/05/07, 21 March 2007) [121]; *Pope & Talbot v Canada (Interim Award)* (Ad hoc arbitration, UNCITRAL Rules, 26 June 2000) [87]–[97]; *Eureko v Poland (Dissenting Opinion of Partial Award)* (Ad hoc Arbitral Tribunal, 19 August 2005) [10] (identifying the omission of the majority to consider municipal law). See also the approach adopted in *CME Czech Republic v Czech Republic (Partial Award)* (Ad hoc arbitration, UNCITRAL Rules, 13 September 2001); *Wena Hotels Ltd v Arab Republic of Egypt (Decision on Annulment)* (ICSID Arbitral Tribunal, Case No ARB/98/4, 5 February 2002) [29], [31], [34]–[36], [41], [45]. These tribunals were content with prima facie evidence of an economic interest or financial engagement in the host state, regardless of whether this met the threshold of a legally recognized property right under its municipal law.

[36] *Saipem v Bangladesh* (n 35) [124]. This is analogous reasoning to WTO jurisprudence: Appellate Body Report, *US—Softwood Lumber IV* [56].

[37] See eg *Mavrommatis Palestine Concessions, Greece v United Kingdom, Objection to the jurisdiction of the court,* Judgment No 2, PCIJ Series A No 2, ICGJ 236 (PCIJ 1924), 30 August 1924, 19; Vienna Convention on the Law of Treaties (opened for signature 23 May 1969, entered into force 27 January 1980) 1155 UNTS 331, art 33(4); Appellate Body Report, *EC and certain member States—Large Civil Aircraft* [845].

[38] *William Nagel v Czech Republic (Award)* (Stockholm Chamber of Commerce, No 049/2002, 9 September 2003) [296].

its economic value.[39] In the words of one tribunal, 'value is not a quality deriving from natural causes but the effect of legal rules which create rights and give protection to them'.[40] Factually, therefore, the recognition and enforceability of a right or interest under municipal law may inform whether that right or interest exists and holds any economic value.

A further set of tribunals have deferred more reflexively to municipal law, with their legal conclusion automatically flowing from whether the asset at issue is recognized within the domestic legal framework of the host state of the investment.[41] However, one problematic aspect of this automatic *renvoi* to municipal law relates to Article 27 of the Vienna Convention. It provides that '[a] party may not invoke the provisions of its internal law as justification for its failure to perform a treaty'. The denial by a host state of proprietary status in an instrument or interest that would otherwise possess the economic indicia of property could be viewed as using internal law to avoid or subvert the operation of an IIA. The deferential nature of a *renvoi* to municipal law could thus lead to perverse outcomes. As Sornarajah states, 'the content of the treaty obligations could be manipulated simply through changes to laws and regulations'.[42] However, the converse is equally problematic. Leaving the determination of the existence, scope, and content of property rights to a tribunal without requiring a touchstone in the municipal legal system from which they originate confers an undue degree of discretion on tribunals. According to Sasson:

> In circumstances where international law does not contain a substantive definition of the rights that are the subject matter of investment treaties, international tribunals that ignore any municipal law role accord to themselves virtually limitless discretion in inventing the content of such rights and thereby deciding disputes. That limitless discretion has no defensible foundation in international law.[43]

Some advocates of the *renvoi* approach have suggested legal methods of mitigating against the potential for host state abuses. Douglas suggests that the test for determining the existence, scope, and content of intangible rights under municipal law should be at the time at which the investment is made, and that '[s]ubsequent changes to the law of the host state cannot affect the characterisation of intangible property rights as an investment'.[44] If an interest has no legal or proprietary status

[39] *Marvin Feldman v Mexico (Award)* (ICSID Arbitral Tribunal, Case No ARB(AF)/99/1, 16 December 2002) [115]–[116]; *Nagel v Czech Republic* (n 38) [296]–[304]; *Mihaly v Sri Lanka (Award)* (ICSID Arbitral Tribunal, Case No ARB/00/2, 15 March 2002) [47]–[48] (although the tribunal does not appear to have explicitly applied municipal Sri Lankan law in assessing whether the relevant instruments constituted binding obligations). See also *Apotex Holdings Inc and Apotex Inc v United States of America (Award on Jurisdiction and Admissibility)* (ICSID Arbitral Tribunal, UNCITRAL Rules, Case No ARB(AF)/12/1, 14 June 2013) fn 78 [199], [207], [219], [224].

[40] *Nagel v Czech Republic* (n 38) [300].

[41] *EnCana Corporation v Republic of Ecuador (Award)* (London Court of International Arbitration, Case No UN3481, 3 February 2006) [184]; *Bayview Irrigation District and Others v Mexico (Award)* (ICSID Arbitral Tribunal, Case No ARB(AF)/05/1, 11 June 2007) [118].

[42] Sornarajah (n 8) 223 (although writing in relation to textual *renvois*, but the point remains valid for default *renvois*).

[43] Sasson (n 21) xxxi.

[44] Douglas, *The International Law of Investment Claims* (n 16) 172.

at the time it is acquired by an investor, the investor should be on notice that it is not protected by an IIA. Newcombe and Paradell argue that 'well established international law principles of good faith and estoppel' could be deployed to prevent manipulations by a host state to avoid liability under an IIA through denying or terminating legal interests under municipal law.[45]

Perhaps the most effective approach would be for parties to an IIA to clarify these matters in the text of the IIA itself. For instance, the IIA between Argentina and Spain provides that '[t]he content and scope of the rights corresponding to the various categories of assets shall be determined by the laws and regulations of the Party in whose territory the investment is situated'.[46] It thus specifies an automatic *renvoi* approach. The ASEAN IIA contains a similar provision in relation to determining the protected class of intellectual property rights.[47] However the vast majority of IIAs provide no such guidance,[48] and the foregoing discussion reveals the marked uncertainty with which a tribunal might approach the matter.

2 Carbon units as 'property' under international investment law

These differing approaches to determining whether something constitutes 'property' under an IIA could lead to divergent outcomes with respect to carbon units.

Under an automatic *renvoi* approach, carbon units would only constitute 'property' and therefore be protected investments under an IIA if they are recognized as property under the municipal legal system of the host state. While seemingly straightforward, this approach is not without complexity. For instance, California has expressly deprived carbon units under its emissions trading scheme of proprietary status.[49] This suggests that they are not 'property' for the purposes of the United States' IIAs. However, a Californian court found them to be 'property' as between private parties,[50] and the court of another municipal division of the United States, Louisiana, rejected the argument that carbon units are not property under its legal system, instead deciding that 'this court finds that the right to report, transfer,

[45] Newcombe and Paradell (n 5) 97.

[46] Agreement between the Government of the Argentine Republic and the Kingdom of Spain for the Promotion and Reciprocal Protection of Investments (Spain–Argentina) (signed 3 October 1991, entered into force 28 September 1992) art 1.2. See also Agreement between the Government of the United Kingdom of Great Britain and Northern Ireland and the Government of the Republic of Argentina for the Promotion and Protection of Investments (United Kingdom–Argentina) (signed 11 December 1990, entered into force 19 February 1993) art 1(a); *National Grid v Argentina (Award)* (Ad hoc arbitration, UNCITRAL Rules, 3 November 2008) [83]–[84].

[47] ASEAN Comprehensive Investment Agreement (signed 26 February 2009, entered into force 29 March 2012) art 4(c), which limits an 'investment' to 'intellectual property rights which are conferred pursuant to the laws and regulations of each Member State'.

[48] This is reflected in a representative sample of recent or model IIAs of major jurisdictions. See US Model IIA (n 7) art 1; EU–Canada IIA (n 7) art 8; German Model IIA (n 7) art 1.1; Italian Model IIA (n 7) art 1.1; French Model IIA (n 7) art 1.1; Swiss–China IIA (n 7) art 1.1.

[49] California Cap on Greenhouse Gas Emissions and Market-based Compliance Mechanisms 17 Cal Public Health Code § 95820(c).

[50] *California Chamber of Commerce and Others v State Air Resources Board and Others*, Court of Appeal, Third District, California (6 April 2017).

or sell carbon credits is a part of the bundle of rights associated with property ownership'.[51] It is unclear how a *renvoi* to United States' law would thus function with respect to carbon units.

The case of jurisdictions that expressly confer proprietary status on carbon units is not necessarily less complicated. On the one hand, Australia has conferred proprietary status on carbon units in its jurisdiction, thus an automatic *renvoi* should find that they qualify as 'property' under its IIA. However, Australia also regulates carbon units as a 'service' for certain purposes,[52] and—although 'goods' and 'services' are not necessarily mutually exclusive as a matter of WTO law[53]—services have been posited by some economists as the antithesis of property rights.[54] In a similar vein, whereas the European Union (EU) classifies carbon units as 'financial assets' for the purposes of financial regulation,[55] it also considers the transfer of carbon units as a taxable supply of 'services' for the purposes of value-added taxation.[56] To add to the confusion, the European Court of Justice recently expressly avoided addressing whether carbon units qualify as property under Article 17(1) of the Charter of Fundamental Rights of the European Union,[57] whereas an English court found that they qualify as 'property' under English law,[58] and the European Court of Auditors expressly recommended that carbon units be designated as property in under EU law.[59]

Thus, the automatic *renvoi* approach does not necessarily yield a simple, unproblematic answer to the question of whether carbon units should qualify as 'property' under a given IIA.

On the other hand, under the approach that treats municipal law in a manner akin to factual evidence that sits alongside other evidence such as economic realities, carbon units would appear to qualify as 'property'. This is because the classical attributes of property, including ownership and the exclusive right to possession, use, and disposal of a thing,[60] which have been endorsed by past tribunals,[61] apply to carbon units. They can be held and stored in personal accounts to the exclusion of

[51] *Roseland Plantation v United States Fish and Wildlife Service*, 2006 U.S. Dist. LEXIS 29334, 2.

[52] Anti-Money Laundering and Counter-Terrorism Financing Act 2006 (Cth) item 33 of the table in s 6(2).

[53] See ch 4B.

[54] Peter Hill, 'Tangibles, intangibles and services: a new taxonomy for the classification of output' in Rohan Kariyawasam (ed), *The WTO, Intellectual Property, E-Commerce and the Internet* (Edward Elgar Publishing 2009) 355–56. See also *Central Product Classification Version 2.0*, Statistical Papers, Series M No 77 (Version 2.1) (United Nations 2015) [27]–[39].

[55] European Commission, 'Review of the Markets in Financial Instruments Directive (MiFID) and Proposals for a Regulation on Market Abuse and for a Directive on Criminal Sanctions for Market Abuse: Frequently Asked Questions on Emission Allowances' (Memo/11/719, 20 October 2011).

[56] European Environment Agency, *Application of the Emissions Trading Directive by EU Member States—reporting year 2008* (Office for Official Publications of the European Communities 2008) 74–75.

[57] Case T-317/12 *Holcim (Romania) SA v European Commission* (ECJ, 18 September 2014) [161]–[170].

[58] *Armstrong v Winnington Networks* [2012] EWHC 10 (ch) [48]–[49].

[59] European Court of Auditors, 'The Integrity and Implementation of the EU ETS' (Special Report No 6, 2015) 47.

[60] See *Oxford English Dictionary Online* (n 31).

[61] *Pope & Talbot v Canada* (n 35) [87].

others (ie possession), ownership can be transferred to third parties, and they can be used by the party possessing them to meet an emissions liability or as a tradable asset.

From an economic viewpoint, and as canvassed in Chapter 3, the very purpose of carbon units as a form of currency in an emissions trading scheme is of a proprietary nature.[62] J H Dales, who developed the conceptual framework on which emissions trading schemes are based, wrote that the 'existence of a natural pricing system depends crucially on the institution of ownership', and '[p]ollution rights are fully transferable property rights'.[63]

Therefore, if evidence of the economic realities of carbon units is prioritized by a tribunal, they would appear to be covered by the ordinary meaning of the term 'property'.

3 The context, and object and purpose of 'property' under international investment law

According to the customary rule of treaty interpretation, the ordinary meaning of 'property' discussed in the foregoing sections must be interpreted in its context and in light of the object and purpose of an IIA.

There are some elements of context in some IIAs that could influence the interpretation of 'property'.[64] For instance, the term is often predicated by the qualifier 'immoveable or moveable',[65] or 'tangible or intangible',[66] which suggests a broad and unrestricted construction of the term. A small number of IIAs state that the property must be 'acquired in the expectation or used for the purpose of economic benefit or other business purposes'.[67] Any property that does not satisfy this additional requirement will not be covered.[68]

Some more recent IIAs contain provisions relating to the environment from which it can be inferred that environmental protection measures by a host state are ordinarily susceptible to coverage under an IIA. For instance, the IIA between the United States and Uruguay states that: '2. Nothing in this Agreement shall be construed to prevent a Party from adopting, maintaining or enforcing any measure otherwise consistent with this Agreement that it considers appropriate to ensure that investment activity

[62] Daniel Cole, 'Origins of Emissions Trading in Theory and Early Practice' in Stefan Weishaar (ed), *Research Handbook on Emissions Trading* (Edward Elgar Publishing 2016) 9–26. See also Ross Garnaut, *The Garnaut Climate Change Review* (CUP 2008) 322; Kathy Baylis and Travis Allan, 'Who Owns Carbon? Property Rights Issues in a Market for Green House Gases' (2005) 7 *Current Agriculture, Food and Resource Issues* 104, 105; Nicholas Stern, *Stern Review: The Economics of Climate Change* (CUP 2007) 311.

[63] J H Dales 'Land, Water, and Ownership' (1968) 1 *Canadian Journal of Economics* 791, 792.

[64] For a discussion on the role of 'context' in the interpretation of IIAs see J Romesh Weeramantry, *Treaty Interpretation in Investment Arbitration* (OUP 2012) [3.52]–[3.54].

[65] See eg German Model IIA (n 7) art 1.1; Italian Model IIA (n 7) art 1.1; French Model IIA (n 7) art 1.1; Swiss–China IIA (n 7) art 1.

[66] See eg US Model IIA (n 7) art 1; EU–Canada IIA (n 7) art 8; Australia—Chile Free Trade Agreement (Australia–Chile) (signed 30 July 2008, entered into force 6 March 2009) [2009] ATS 6, ch 10 art 10.1(j)(viii); Energy Charter Treaty (signed 17 December 1994, entered into force 16 April 1998) 2080 UNTS 95, art 1(6)(a).

[67] See eg North American Free Trade Agreement (NAFTA) (signed 17 December 1992, entered into force 1 January 1994) art 1139.

[68] See eg *Apotex v United States* (n 39) [209].

in its territory is undertaken in a manner sensitive to environmental concerns'.[69] The qualifier 'otherwise consistent with this Agreement' demonstrates that environmental measures inconsistent with the IIA are capable of falling in its scope. A number of other IIAs contain provisions clarifying the relationship between investment and the environment and providing substantive rules that bar parties from relaxing environment laws to encourage investment.[70] While not specifically directed at climate mitigation measures, these provisions could provide context from which it can be inferred that environmental measures constitute a subject regulated by the IIA.

In an indirect way, these elements of context could suggest that carbon units are not intended to be excluded from the subject matter protected by those IIAs, including 'property'.

In terms of the object and purpose of IIAs, this may be gleaned from the preamble of an IIA, as well as its general structure and substance.[71] While the specific object and purpose may vary between IIAs, there is a universal and unifying theme across all IIAs which is embedded in their internal logic and historical origins.[72] Their penultimate purpose is to stimulate inward flows of capital.[73] Their means of achieving this purpose is to create a stable regulatory environment and investment framework for investors of the other party to an IIA by agreeing to binding protections and guarantees with effective legal mechanisms for enforcing those protections.[74] These two prongs—binding protections coupled with effective enforcement mechanisms—are designed to give confidence to potential investors and reduce their perception of risk in relation to potential future adverse measures by the host state. This underlying logic and structure of IIAs is often reflected in their preambles:[75]

2012 US Model IIA

[R]ecognizing that agreement on the treatment to be accorded such investment will stimulate the flow of private capital and the economic development of the Parties;

Agreeing that a stable framework for investment will maximize effective utilization of economic resources and improve living standards;

Recognizing the importance of providing effective means of asserting claims and enforcing rights with respect to investment under national law as well as through international arbitration; ...

[69] Treaty between the United States of America and the Oriental Republic of Uruguay concerning the Encouragement and Reciprocal Protection of Investment (United States–Uruguay) (signed 4 November 2005, entered into force 1 November 2006) art 1 (emphasis added).

[70] See eg US Model IIA (n 7) art 12.2; Free Trade Agreement between Canada and the Republic of Panama (Canada–Panama) (signed 14 May 2010, entered into force 1 April 2013) art 9.16; Peru–South Korea Free Trade Agreement (Peru–Korea) (signed 14 November 2010, entered into force 1 August 2011) art 9.9.2; EU–Canada IIA (n 7) ch 24.

[71] See Weeramantry (n 64) [3.79].

[72] See eg Newcombe and Paradell (n 5) 40–48; Dolzer and Schreuer (n 4) 19–24, 27; Dugan and others (n 6) 4–9.

[73] See eg *Malaysian Historical Salvors v Malaysia* (n 17) [57].

[74] Newcombe and Paradell (n 5) 113–16 Weeramantry (n 64) [3.83]; Dolzer and Schreuer (n 4) 29–30.

[75] US Model IIA (n 7) preambular recitals 2, 3, and 4; Swiss–China IIA (n 7) preambular recitals 1 and 2.

China – Switzerland IIA

Intending to create and maintain favourable conditions for investments by investors of one Contracting Party in the territory of the other Contracting Party

Recognising the need to promote and protect foreign investments with the aim to foster economic prosperity of both States

As part of the interpretive exercise, therefore, it is useful to ascertain whether the object and purpose of IIAs influences the ordinary meaning of the term 'property' to the exclusion of carbon units and emissions trading schemes. In other words, does the core object and purpose of protecting investments and maintaining a stable regulatory environment lend itself to protecting investors that own carbon units?

On the one hand, the artificial nature of the markets and instruments created by emissions trading schemes lends itself to a high degree of governmental intervention. Since a government is effectively inventing an entirely new market through legally mandating demand, setting the quantum of supply, and creating the product to be traded (carbon units), it is reasonable that it retain a capacity to intervene to ensure that the market operates as intended, and to prevent or mitigate any unanticipated or uncertain outcomes. Relatedly, emissions trading schemes only exist to serve a broader environmental objective, and governments may feel compelled to intervene in the market to ensure that the objective is being met.[76]

The ability to intervene in the market—and potentially interfere with the value or existence of carbon units—runs counter to the objective of stability and predictability in the market, and is one reason why some governments have intentionally refrained from conferring carbon units or similar instruments with proprietary status under municipal law. For instance, this is the case with respect to greenhouse gas emissions trading in California.[77] A requirement to compensate market participants for interfering in the market in a way that damages or destroys the value of their carbon units could restrict a government's policy space to make adjustments that ensure the environmental integrity of the scheme.[78]

Thus, carbon units could reasonably be understood as creations of an artificial market that lends itself to a high level of regulatory intervention. Against that

[76] See eg Australian Government, *Carbon Pollution Reduction Scheme: Australia's Low Pollution Future* (Commonwealth of Australia, Vol 1, 2008) 8-4, 8-5 (discussion on Option 2). See also Daniel W Bromley, *Environment and Economy: Property Rights and Public Policy* (Blackwell 1991) 95–96; Simon Grant and John Quiggin, 'Climate Change and the Precautionary Principle' in John Quiggin and others (eds), *Carbon Pricing: Early Experiences and Future Prospects* (Edward Elgar Publishing 2014) 167, 170–74; Julia Black, 'The Role of Risk in Regulatory Processes' in Robert Baldwin, Martin Cave, and Martin Lodge (eds), *The Oxford Handbook of Regulation* (OUP 2010) 301, 317–23.

[77] California Market-based Mechanism (n 49) § 95820(c). See also Markus Gehring and Charlotte Streck, 'Emissions Trading: Lessons From SO_x and NO_x Emissions Allowance and Credit Systems Legal Nature, Title, Transfer, and Taxation of Emission Allowances and Credits' (2005) 35 *Environmental Law Reporter* 10219, 10221–22.

[78] Baylis and Allan (n 62) 109; Gehring and Streck (n 77) 10222.

background, protecting carbon units as investments under IIAs could be susceptible to Sornarajah's more general critique in respect of protecting public rights as 'investments', namely that their protection 'defeats the very notion of public law rights which are granted with the public interest in mind and become defeasible when they are no longer in the public interest'.[79]

On the other hand, there is a strong argument to be made that the predictability and stability of the market is essential to the effectiveness and success of emissions trading schemes.[80] The overarching objective of an emissions trading scheme is to reduce emissions over time by imposing a cost on emissions and thereby stimulate investment in less carbon-intensive technology and methods of production. However, the kinds of long-term investment-backed decisions required to transition to a low-carbon economy are contingent on a degree of predictability and stability in the operation of the market. Without a requisite degree of confidence relating to the future price of carbon units and the operation or existence of the carbon market generally, market participants will likely be reluctant to make significant low-carbon investments.

Thus, as discussed in Chapter 3, strong property rights in the objects being traded (ie carbon units) and a perception of permanence and stability in the market (eg the absence of governmental intervention) are important elements in emissions trading schemes. This was the major rationale for Australia conferring proprietary rights on its carbon units,[81] and this aspect of emissions trading schemes is essentially aligned to the core object and purpose of IIAs. The maintenance of a stable and predictable environment for investments is both key to the success of emissions trading and the primary objective of IIAs. From this viewpoint, the application of IIAs would be a natural complement to the operation of emissions trading schemes.

Ultimately, these contradictory aspects of emissions trading schemes do not provide definitive guidance on whether the object and purpose of IIAs influences the interpretation of 'property' to the inclusion or exclusion of carbon units. Arguments can be made both ways. That being the case, only limited weight should be accorded to this interpretive element. Tribunals favouring a *renvoi* to municipal law may find value in the first set of arguments canvassed, insofar as they relate to the nature of carbon units under municipal law and the right of governments to define their content, scope, and proprietary status. On the other hand, tribunals that conceive of 'property' as an autonomous concept under IIAs may find the second set of arguments more persuasive with its focus on the investment-oriented economic goals and realities of emissions trading, and this alignment with the objective and purpose of IIAs.

[79] Sornarajah (n 8) 223.

[80] See above ch 3.

[81] Australian Government, *Carbon Pollution Reduction Scheme: Australia's Low Pollution Future* (Commonwealth of Australia, Vol 1, 2008) 8-4, 8-5.

C Carbon Units as an Administrative Right

As mentioned above, 'property' is one of a number of legal categories that fall within most definitions of 'investment'. Another category relates to administrative rights, or rights issued under public law. In textual terms, these rights are expressed in a varying manner in different IIAs, for instance:[82]

China – Switzerland IIA:

> [b]usiness concessions under public law, including concessions to search for, extract or exploit natural resources, as well as all other rights given by law, by contract or by decision of the authority in accordance with the law ...

2012 United States Model IIA:

> [l]icenses, authorizations, permits, and similar rights conferred pursuant to domestic law ...

Australia–Czech Republic IIA:

> [b]usiness concessions and any other rights required to conduct economic activity and having economic value conferred by law or under a contract, including rights to engage in agriculture, forestry, fisheries and animal husbandry, to search for, extract or exploit natural resources and to manufacture, use and sell products ...

Despite the different formulations, these legal categories are directed at the same underlying class of rights and permissions that are granted to an investor by a host state in order to undertake an economic activity.[83] The analogy to carbon units is obvious. They are government-issued instruments that certain enterprises are required to obtain and surrender in order to emit greenhouse gas, or otherwise be penalized, for instance, through a fine. In practical terms, those enterprises may only engage in economic activities that result in greenhouse gas emissions if they obtain a carbon unit for each tonne of greenhouse gas that is emitted. Carbon units could thus be characterized as a kind of 'licence'. Licences ordinarily refer to a 'permission, usually revocable, to commit some act that would otherwise be unlawful',[84] and carbon units permit the emission of greenhouse gas by certain enterprises that would otherwise be penalized. For similar reasons, carbon units could also be characterized as a 'right required to conduct economic activity and having economic value conferred by law'. They are a 'right' because they entitle an enterprise to emit greenhouse gas, they are required to engage in economic activities that result in greenhouse gas emissions, and they are issued under legislation and thus conferred by law.

Importantly, however, most definitions of 'investment' that cover these administrative rights establish a clear link to the law of the host state. For instance, the

[82] US Model IIA (n 7) art 1; Swiss–China IIA (n 7) art 1.1(e); Agreement between Australia and the Czech Republic on the Reciprocal Promotion and Protection of Investments (Australia–Czech Republic) (signed 30 September 1993, entered into force 29 June 1994) [1994] ATS 18, art 1.1(a)(v).

[83] Sornarajah (n 8) 192–93.

[84] *Black's Law Dictionary* (9th edn, West 2009) 'license': 'A permission, usu. revocable, to commit some act that would otherwise be unlawful'.

extracted examples state that the rights or licences must be 'conferred pursuant to domestic law', 'given by law', or 'conferred by law'. Thus, the existence of such rights and their substantive content, including the ability of the host state to vary or terminate the rights, depends on the law of the host state.[85] On that basis, if a host state embeds in a licence an ability to vary its terms or terminate it altogether, the licence will qualify as an 'investment' under an IIA but any adverse variation or termination in accordance with its terms or the law of the host state will not be protected under an IIA. The 2012 US Model IIA takes this one step further, expressly clarifying that:

> Whether a particular type of license, authorization, permit, or similar instrument (including a concession, to the extent that it has the nature of such an instrument) has the characteristics of an investment depends on such factors as the nature and extent of the rights that the holder has under the law of the Party. Among the licenses, authorizations, permits, and similar instruments that do not have the characteristics of an investment are those that do not create any rights protected under domestic law.[86]

Based on this clarification, licences that may be legally terminated or varied by a host state are unlikely even to qualify as 'investments' in the first place. As one example, despite being legally denoted as an 'authorization to emit up to one tonne . . . of any greenhouse gas', carbon units as defined under Californian law would be unlikely to meet the threshold of an 'investment' under the 2012 US Model IIA:

> Each compliance instrument issued by the Executive Officer represents a limited authorization to emit up to one metric ton in CO_2e of any greenhouse gas specified in section 95810, *subject to all applicable limitations specified in this article. No provision of this article may be construed to limit the authority of the Executive Officer to terminate or limit such authorization to emit. A compliance instrument issued by the Executive Officer does not constitute property or a property right.*[87]

By contrast, under the other examples extracted above, carbon units would technically qualify as 'investments' since they are clearly public law rights, or authorizations, to undertake an economic activity. However, in instances where unfettered governmental interference is embedded within the government-issued authorization to emit that forms the basis of the 'investment', it is difficult to envisage any adverse governmental measures that could form the basis of a claim.

Therefore, the extent to which carbon units are protected under an IIA as a 'licence' or other administrative law right will depend in large part on a renvoi to the municipal legal system in which they subsist. This is necessitated by the ordinary meaning of a 'right' or 'licence' granted 'pursuant to domestic law'. There is unlikely to be anything in the context of the relevant terms, or in the object and purpose of IIAs discussed in section B(3), that materially affects this conclusion.

[85] See eg *Middle East Cement Shipping and Handling Co SA v Egypt (Jurisdiction and Liability)* (ICSID Arbitral Tribunal, Case No ARB/99/6, 12 April 2002) [98]–[107].

[86] US Model IIA (n 7) art 1.

[87] California Market-based Mechanism (n 49) § 95820(c).

D Carbon Units as 'Any Kind of Asset'

Even if a carbon unit cannot easily be characterized as 'property' or a 'licence' or other administrative right under an IIA, it may nevertheless fall within the scope of the residual catch-all category of 'any kind of asset'.

While tribunals rarely need to rely on this catch-all term to characterize something as an investment,[88] the specific categories such as 'property' and 'licence' only function as a non-exhaustive, illustrative list of the overarching catch-all term in most instances.[89]

Ordinary dictionary definitions of 'asset' range from any item of value that is owned to something synonymous with 'property'. Different tribunals have used these differing ordinary meanings of the term. For instance, one tribunal found the term 'asset' to mean 'property of any kind'.[90] Another cited an UNCTAD study which described it as 'everything of economic value, virtually without limitation'.[91] A further tribunal stated that '[a]ccording to common practice, 'asset' means a right or claim having economic value and deriving either from law or from contract, towards a given debtor, for the performance of a given obligation'.[92] The tribunal in *Société Générale v Pakistan* also focused on the value of an item, stating that 'the question of what constitutes an asset (whether tangible or intangible) must be viewed more broadly, in terms of the item's economic value'.[93]

Despite the apparent differences in these understandings of the term 'asset', there is a strong line of authority to suggest that an asset-based definition of 'investment' should be interpreted broadly.[94] This is informed by the context of the term 'asset', which is preceded by 'every kind of'[95] or 'any kind of'.[96] Further, the inclusion of

[88] See eg *Saipem v Bangladesh* (n 35); *Société Générale du Surveillance SA v Pakistan (Decision on Objections to Jurisdiction)* (ICSID Arbitral Tribunal, Case No ARB/01/13, 6 August 2003) [83].

[89] See eg *Romak v Uzbekistan* (n 15) [175]–[182]; *Mytilineos v Serbia* (n 15) [102]–[108]; *RosInvestCo UK Ltd v Russian Federation*, SCC *(Award on Jurisdiction)* (Arbitration Institute of the Stockholm Chamber of Commerce, Case No V079/2005, 1 October 2007) [388]. C.f. NAFTA (n 67) art 1139.

[90] *Romak v Uzbekistan* (n 15) [177].

[91] *Mytilineos v Serbia* (n 15) [106].

[92] *Alps Finance v Slovak Republic (Award)* (Ad hoc arbitration, UNCITRAL Rules, 5 March 2011) [230].

[93] *Société Générale du Surveillance SA v Pakistan (Decision on Objections to Jurisdiction)* (ICSID Arbitral Tribunal, Case No ARB/01/13, 6 August 2003) [83].

[94] *Saipem v Bangladesh* (n 35) [121]; *Eureko v Poland (Partial Award)* (Ad Hoc Arbitral Tribunal, 19 August 2005) [137]; *Mytilineos v Serbia* (n 15) [102]; *Bayindir Insaat Turizm Ticaret Ve Sanayi AS v Pakistan (Decision on Jurisdiction)* (ICSID Arbitral Tribunal, Case No ARB/03/29, 14 November 2005) [113].

[95] See eg US Model IIA (n 7) art 1; EU–Canada IIA (n 7) art 8.1; German Model IIA (n 7) art 1.1; French Model IIA (n 7) art 1.1; Swiss–China IIA (n 7) art 1.1.

[96] See eg Italian Model IIA (n 7) art 1.1; Agreement on the Promotion and Safeguarding of Capital Investment Between the Government of State of Kuwait and The Government of Islamic Republic of Pakistan (Kuwait–Pakistan) (signed 17 March 1983, entered into force 15 March 1986) art 1; Agreement on the Reciprocal Promotion and Protection of Investments between the Kingdom of Spain and the Republic of Honduras (Spain–Honduras) (signed 18 March 1994, entered into force 23 May 1996) art I.2.

'property' as a subset of items that constitute an 'asset' suggests that the term should not be limited to property rights narrowly construed.

That notwithstanding, Douglas contends that property rights *must* subsist in an item under municipal law as a prerequisite for to qualify as an 'asset'.[97] He argues this on the basis of the 'proprietary nature' of the examples in the typical illustrative list of what is included as an 'asset'.[98] However, there is nothing in the text of most definitions of 'investment' to sustain this as an inflexible rule,[99] and the context of including 'property' as a subset of the broader term 'asset' gives rise to the reverse inference. If the definition of 'investment' were expressly limited to 'property', as is the case in a handful of older Italian IIAs, this position might be sustainable.[100] However, carbon units provide an example whereby an item lacking proprietary status under municipal law may nevertheless be analogous to one of the other listed categories comprising 'assets'. In particular, IIAs typically include financial instruments in the illustrative list of what constitutes an 'asset',[101] and as discussed in Chapters 3 and 6, carbon units could be credibly characterized in those terms due to their regulation under municipal law as 'financial assets', 'financial securities', and 'transferable securities'.[102] Therefore, regardless of whether they are considered property, carbon units would be analogous to the kinds of financial instruments typically listed as examples of 'assets', suggesting that they are capable of falling within the scope of that term.

Even in the absence of a directly analogous legal category in the illustrative list of items qualifying as 'assets', carbon units are identifiable items that possess economic value, that are capable of possession and trade, and that can be used to generate profits or discharge financial liabilities. As such, it is difficult to envisage any argument that they would not fall within the ordinary meaning of the term 'asset'.

Similar to the analysis of the term 'property', the object and purpose of IIAs would not appear to provide definitive guidance as to the coverage of carbon units in the protected class of 'assets' under IIAs.

[97] Douglas, *The International Law of Investment Claims* (n 16) 163–64. [98] ibid 163.

[99] See eg US Model IIA (n 7) art 1; EU–Canada IIA (n 7) art 8.1; German Model IIA (n 7) art 1.1; Italian Model IIA (n 7) art 1.1; French Model IIA (n 7) art 1.1; Swiss–China IIA (n 7) art 1.1.

[100] See eg Agreement between the Government of the Italian Republic and the Government of the People's Republic of Bangladesh on the Promotion and Protection of Investments (Italy–Bangladesh) (signed 20 March 1990, entered into force 20 September 1994) art 1.1; Agreement between the Government of Jamaica and the Government of the Italian Republic on the Promotion and Protection of Investments (Jamaica–Italy) (signed 29 September 1993, entered into force 9 November 1995) art 1.1.

[101] See eg US Model IIA (n 7) art 1; Agreement between the Belgo-Luxembourg Economic Union and the Government of the Republic of Yemen on the Reciprocal Promotion and Protection of Investments (Belgium–Luxembourg–Yemen) (signed 20 November 2000, entered into force 12 January 2004) art 1.1(b); Swiss–China IIA (n 7) art 1.1(c); Agreement between Canada and the Hashemite Kingdom of Jordan for the Promotion and Protection of Investments (Canada–Jordan) (signed 28 June 2009, entered into force 14 December 2009) art 1(r)(iii), (v).

[102] See above ch 4A, B, C, D, and E.

E Carbon Units as Investments: Economic Criteria

If carbon units fall within the bounds of one of the legal categories that comprise 'investments' under IIAs, they may further be scrutinized against the economic criteria of 'investments'. These economic criteria may either be contained in the definition of 'investment' in an applicable IIA,[103] or mandated by a tribunal's conception of its arbitral rules,[104] or further still, may simply be applied by a tribunal in the absence of any express textual requirement.[105] Equally, some tribunals have eschewed these criteria in the absence of any express textual requirement.[106] For those tribunals, this second step for determining whether carbon units qualify as 'investments' would be an error of law.

Amongst the tribunals that apply these criteria, there is convergence at a high level of abstraction over the kinds of matters to consider, namely the assumption of risk, the commitment of capital, the expectation of gain or profit, and some degree of contribution to the development of the host state.[107] However there has been no such unanimity in relation to the practical application of these criteria, such as whether they are to be analysed as discrete components or in an holistic fashion, or whether the absence of certain criteria in a given case is fatal to its characterization as an 'investment'.[108] Indeed, the actual meaning of certain criteria remains unsettled.[109] Nevertheless, a comprehensive analysis of the intricacies of these divergences is not necessary for the purposes of this chapter. It will instead focus on those elements pertinent to the case study of carbon units.

A prima facie assessment suggests that carbon units are capable of satisfying these criteria. Their purchase through spot trades or through financial instruments will ordinarily involve the commitment of capital, and their use to discharge a financial liability or to on-sell for a higher price at a later date implies an expectation of gain or profit. Further, their ability to be owned and stored suggests a certain degree or permanence and duration, and their purchase could be said to contribute to the development of the host state, since it contributes to that state's sustainable development.

The main difficulty in applying the economic criteria to carbon units relates to their key function as a form of currency to be traded in an open market in an emissions trading scheme. Tribunals have tended to be careful to distinguish between ordinary commercial sales contracts for goods and services on the one hand, and

[103] See eg US Model IIA (n 7) art 1; Belgium–Luxembourg–Colombia IIA (n 10) art I.2.3.

[104] See eg *Phoenix Action Ltd v Czech Republic* (n 12) [81]–[82]; *Joy Mining v Egypt* (n 12) [48]–[53].

[105] See eg *Romak v Uzbekistan* (n 15) [177], [207]; *Mytilineos v Serbia* (n 15) [115]–[120].

[106] *White Industries v India* (n 18) 76; *Malaysian Historical Salvors v Malaysia* (n 17) [75]–[77].

[107] See eg *Salini v Morocco* (n 14) [52], [54]; *Joy Mining v Egypt* (n 12) [53]; *Biwater Gauff v Tanzania* (n 14) [312]–[317].

[108] Dugan and others (n 6) 265–70.

[109] See eg Marek Jeżewski, 'Development Considerations in Defining Investment' in Marie-Claire Cordonnier Segger, Markus W Gehring, and Andrew Newcombe (eds), *Sustainable Development in World Investment Law* (Kluwer 2011) 215.

genuine investments involving some degree of durable economic activity in the host state on the other.[110] As such, carbon units could be perceived as an object of trade handled by speculative traders rather than a legitimate form of investment.

The absence of any tangible economic activity underlying a putative investment is not per se fatal to it meeting the economic criteria.[111] For instance, in its discussion of whether financial investments like securities or shares could meet the criteria, the tribunal in *Société Générale v Dominican Republic* noted that 'this kind might not be as easy to identify as if a factory was built, but this of course does not disqualify financial investments from protection under the Treaty'.[112] However, it seems that there needs to be at least a tacit connection between the purchase of the intangible instrument by the investor, and an activity that has some public or economic utility.[113] In *Société Générale v Dominican Republic,* a nexus between the financial investment and the generation of electricity was important to the tribunal's finding that the investment met the economic criteria.[114] Similarly, in *Fedax v Venezuela*, a promissory note met the economic criteria because it was issued under a Venezuelan law to raise capital 'to undertake productive works, attend to the needs of national interest and cover transitory needs of the treasure'.[115] On that basis, the tribunal found it 'apparent that the transactions involved in this case are not ordinary commercial transactions and indeed involve a fundamental public interest'.[116] Indeed, tribunals have been willing to protect trade in goods and services as investments where this is connected to a more permanent economic activity such as a manufacturing operation.[117]

In contrast, the tribunal in *Joy Mining v Egypt* found that certain bank guarantees were merely incidental to an ordinary commercial sales contract, and that any economic activities associated with discharging that contract were simply a 'special

[110] See eg *Alps Finance v Slovakia* (n 92) [231]–[232], [242]; *Canadian Cattlemen for Free Trade v United States of America (Award on Jurisdiction)* (Ad hoc arbitration, UNCITRAL Rules, 28 January 2008) [144]; *Apotex v United States* (n 39) [233]; *Romak v Uzbekistan* (n 15) [188]; *Global Trading v Ukraine (Award)* (ICSID Arbitral Tribunal, Case No ARB/09/11, 1 December 2010) [51]–[57].

[111] See eg *Abaclat v Argentina (Jurisdiction)* (ICSID Arbitral Tribunal, Case No ARB/07/5, 4 August 2011) [370]–[371].

[112] *Société Générale v Dominican Republic (Jurisdiction)* (London Court of International Arbitration, UNCITRAL Rules, Case No UN 7927, 19 September 2008) [35].

[113] Dolzer and Schreuer (n 4) 73–76. See also Damien Lockie, 'Closing Pandora's Box: The Case for Carbon Market Integrity after the Global Financial Crisis—Conditioning Ownership of the Right to Emit Greenhouse Gases in an Australian Emissions Trading Scheme' (PhD Thesis, Bond University 2011) 206–20. Lockie argues that short-term, speculative trading in carbon units by entities without liabilities under an emissions trading scheme may, in practice, undermine the market integrity and stability of the scheme, ultimately impugning its environmental objective. In such circumstances, it may be difficult to conceive that those kinds of holdings of carbon units could contribute to the development of the host State, or could be said to represent involvement in the carbon market in the spirit for which it was designed.

[114] *Société Générale v Dominican Republic* (n 112) [35].

[115] *Fedax v Venezuela (Jurisdiction)* (ICSID Arbitral Tribunal, Case No ARB/96/3, 11 July 1997) [42].

[116] ibid.

[117] See eg *S.D. Myers v Canada (Partial Award)* (Ad hoc arbitration, UNCITRAL Rules, 13 November 2000) [289]–[297]; *Pope & Talbot v Canada (Claimant's Motion for Interim Measures)* (Ad hoc arbitration, UNCITRAL Rules, 7 August 2000) [19]–[26]. See also Dolzer and Schreuer (n 4) 75–76.

feature of contracts relating to the supply of complex equipment'.[118] The bank guarantees were thus not linked to any meaningful, durable economic activity by the claimant in the host state, and did not meet the economic criteria. Along the same lines, the tribunal in *Apotex v United States* held that even if the particular pharmaceutical approval application at issue constituted property under United States law, its function as merely incidental to the cross-border trade in pharmaceutical products rendered it inadmissible as a protected 'investment'.[119] It had no genuine link to any meaningful economic activity within the United States. Relatedly, some tribunals have expressed reservations about whether assets acquired for purely speculative purposes meet the economic criteria.[120]

These cases suggest that the context in which investors acquire and own carbon units could be pivotal to whether they meet the economic criteria and thus qualify as 'investments'. If, on the one hand, their acquisition and ownership is linked to an underlying economic activity, they are more likely to qualify. For instance, they may be acquired and held as part of an offset project that reduces carbon emissions, or they may be acquired and banked by an enterprise as part of a long term reserve to meet liabilities under an emissions trading scheme. They may also be purchased as an asset to generate longer term returns in competition with other potential investment opportunities, as Garnaut explains:

> A credible market will establish a forward price for permits that reflects expectations about the future demand for permits. The price rises at a rate of interest corresponding to the opportunity cost of capital. This is because investors will be choosing between alternative investments, with an emissions permit being one possible investment. Investors will assess whether the long-term value of holding an emissions permit is higher or lower than the return from an alternative investment. This leads to selling or buying of emissions permits until a forward price curve emerges that causes the expected return from holding a permit to be equivalent to that on alternative investments. The price would therefore rise at a rate of interest corresponding to alternative investments available to holders of permits.[121]

In this context, carbon units could be long term investments from which to generate a return, which would be gauged vis-à-vis other alternative investment opportunities. Even if not directly related to an underlying economic activity, the longstanding and stable nature of such an acquisition of carbon units coupled with the intention of generating longer term returns and the connection to a public interest objective (ie pollution reduction) would likely be sufficient.[122]

On the other hand, if carbon units are acquired and owned in the context of short-term speculative trading on financial markets, they would be less likely to qualify. Such a context would be closer to ordinary commercial sales contracts without any

[118] *Joy Mining v Egypt* (n 12) [55].

[119] *Apotex v United States* (n 39) [207]–[208].

[120] *Alps Finance v Slovakia* (n 92) [236]; *Société Générale v Dominican Republic* (n 112) [34]–[35]. But see, in contrast, *Saluka Investments v Czech Republic (Partial Award)* (Permanent Court of Arbitration, 17 March 2006) [209].

[121] Garnaut (n 62) 319.

[122] See eg *Alps Finance v Slovakia* (n 92) [234]; *Abaclat v Argentina* (n 111) [366], [371].

sense of permanence or a tacit connection to a productive economic activity in the host state.

Further, if carbon units are acquired by an enterprise without charge as part of a free allocation by host states (as may often be the case[123]) and are simply held by that enterprise for future use to discharge liabilities that may arise, they could fail the economic criteria. This is because that kind of context of acquisition and ownership is analogous to contingent liabilities; the ultimate value or use of the units depend on the outcome of a future events, namely, whether an enterprise emits greenhouse gas. Some tribunals have been reluctant to conceive of contingent liabilities as 'investments' because of the absence of any inherent or certain value.[124] Further, the provision of a certain quantity of carbon units without charge to an enterprise by a government involves neither a capital contribution by that enterprise, nor an assumption of risk.[125]

Therefore, whether carbon units satisfy the economic criteria for an 'investment' will require a case-by-case analysis that considers how the investor obtains the units, how it intends to use the units, whether there is any nexus to other economic activity in the host state, and relatedly, the durability or permanence of the investor's acquisition of the units.

F Conclusion

Carbon units are certainly *capable* of constituting investments under international investment law. If all parties to an IIA define the units as 'property' under their municipal law, and if an investor acquired and owns the units with a requisite degree of durability and permanence related to some other economic activity in the host state, they would clearly qualify.

More complex, however, is whether they might qualify if one or more parties to an IIA confer no proprietary status on carbon units, or where the units are not acquired in the context of a meaningful economic activity in the host state.

This conclusion is more nuanced than others who appear to have assumed a determinative role for municipal law, or that carbon units will inevitably qualify as 'property'.[126] It calls for a highly contextual analysis of a given case. Even then, much will depend on a specific tribunal's views on the role of municipal law, and the application of economic criteria, which makes it difficult to speculate on the outcome in a given case.

[123] Ingrid Jegou and Luca Rubini, 'The Allocation of Emission Allowances Free of Charge: Legal and Economic Considerations' (ICTSD Issue Paper No 18, August 2011) 6–14.

[124] *Joy Mining v Egypt* (n 12) [44]–[45]; *Apotex v United States* (n 39) [210], [215], [223].

[125] *Société Générale v Dominican Republic* (n 112) [36], [38].

[126] Daniel Firger and Michael Gerrard, 'Harmonizing Climate Change Policy and International Investment Law: Threats, Challenges and Opportunities' in Karl Sauvant (ed) *Yearbook on International Investment Law and Policy 2010–11* (OUP 2011) 36; Freya Bartens, 'The Kyoto Protocol in Investor-State Arbitration: Reconciling Climate Change and Investment Protection Objectives' in Marie-Claire Cordonnier Segger, Markus W Gehring, and Andrew Newcombe (eds), *Sustainable Development in World Investment Law* (Kluwer 2011) 683, 699; Werksman and others (n 1) 70 Bennett (n 1) 1592–98.

PART III

CONSISTENCY OF EMISSIONS TRADING SCHEMES

8

A Taxonomy of Prima Facie Violations of International Economic Law

Part II of this book, comprising Chapters 4–7 assessed the extent to which carbon units constitute objects that fall within the purview of international economic law. Part III, comprising this chapter and Chapter 9, assesses the consistency of emissions trading schemes and their rules affecting carbon units with international economic law. In particular, this chapter identifies and evaluates the rules in emissions trading schemes affecting the trade, use, and value of carbon units that constitute prima facie violations of that body of law. It considers: (i) the differential treatment of carbon units that engages disciplines on non-discrimination; (ii) the quantitative restrictions on external carbon units that engage disciplines on market access; and (iii) the kinds of governmental interference in carbon markets that engage disciplines on investment. This chapter thereby identifies and catalogues numerous prima facie breaches embedded in the rules of most emissions trading schemes.

Chapter 9 then considers the justifications for these prima facie breaches and assesses whether, if at all, such justifications could ground a defence using a policy-based exception in international economic law, such as relating to the environment, prudential regulation, or procurement.

This chapter is divided into three sections. The first assesses the various ways in which emissions trading schemes accord differential treatment to different kinds of carbon units on the basis of their jurisdiction or the manner of their production, and the extent to which this differential treatment translates into violations of non-discrimination disciplines in international economic law. The second section considers the quantitative restrictions embedded in certain emissions trading schemes, and evaluates whether these are inconsistent with market access disciplines in international economic law. The third section focuses specifically on international investment law, and considers the various kinds of policies and measures pertaining to emissions trading schemes that could be impugned under investment norms.

A Non-discrimination

International economic law contains disciplines aimed at preventing discrimination on the basis of nationality. This section focuses on non-discrimination in WTO law rather than investment law. As will be shown, the impugned discriminatory rules in emissions trading schemes relate to transitory transactions rather than more permanent holdings of units, and therefore are unlikely to engage investment norms.[1]

This section begins with a brief overview of the legal standard of non-discrimination in its various manifestations across the covered agreements of the Agreement Establishing the World Trade Organization (WTO Agreement).[2] In light of this overview, this section then catalogues and categorizes various kinds of differential treatment of carbon units by a number of emissions trading schemes that could raise questions of consistency with non-discrimination rules. It then tests these forms of differential treatment against the non-discrimination rules of the WTO Agreement, with a particular focus on whether different classes of carbon units can be considered 'like' one another.

1 Overview of non-discrimination in WTO law

The economic objective of non-discriminatory treatment is to maximize the efficiency of the allocation of resources.[3] Discriminatory measures that arbitrarily privilege certain goods, services, or service suppliers can distort trade flows and insulate those goods and services from international competition, in turn causing inefficient

[1] See above ch 7. Transitory transactions of carbon units are unlikely to qualify as 'investments', whereas more permanent holdings of units by investors are more likely to qualify.

[2] Marrakesh Agreement Establishing the World Trade Organization (opened for signature 15 April 1994, entered into force 1 January 1995) 1867 UNTS 3 (WTO Agreement).

[3] See eg WTO Agreement (n 2) preamble recital 1 ('optimal use of the world's resources'). See also Petros Mavroidis, *Trade in Goods* (OUP 2007) 120–21; M Rafiquil Islam, *International Trade Law of the WTO* (OUP 2006) 6–12; Mitsuo Matsushita, Thomas J Schoenbaum, and Petros Mavroidis, *The World Trade Organization: Law, Practice, and Policy* (OUP 2003) 143–44, 156–57.

economic outcomes and an overall reduction of welfare. Against this economic motivation, the purpose of non-discrimination rules can be understood as ensuring that there are equal conditions of competition between the goods, services, and service suppliers of different nationalities.[4]

Since ensuring equal conditions of competition is the key purpose of non-discrimination provisions, it can be viewed as a relative or contingent standard of treatment.[5] It depends on how goods, services, and service suppliers are treated compared to others, and whether such treatment alters their relative conditions of competition. As such, an assessment of whether rules on non-discrimination have been violated requires the identification of a comparator, or an equivalent good, service, or service supplier, against which another may be judged.

Another consequence of this key purpose of non-discrimination—ie ensuring equal conditions of competition—is that it should not matter whether discrimination is de jure or de facto.[6] It is not the form of the discrimination that matters, but rather, whether it has the impact of undermining otherwise equal conditions of competition between certain goods, services, or service suppliers.

Relatedly, therefore, it should not matter whether a measure is intended to be discriminatory and protectionist, but rather, whether it has the impact of undermining conditions of competition.[7] Thus, even though a WTO Member does not intend a measure to be protectionist, it can still inadvertently upset the conditions of competition, and therefore have a discriminatory effect that prejudices certain goods, services, or service suppliers, and distorts trade and capital flows, leading to inefficient economic outcomes.[8]

These strands of logic flowing from the underlying economic motivation for non-discrimination provisions have informed their interpretation and application across their various iterations in the WTO Agreement.[9] There are, of course, important qualitative differences in the various iterations of these provisions.[10] One major distinction relates to whether the alleged discrimination occurs between domestic goods, services, and service suppliers vis-à-vis those of other WTO Members ('national treatment'), or whether it occurs between the goods, services, and service suppliers of another WTO Member vis-à-vis those of any other country ('most-favoured-nation treatment'). Another important distinction relates to the differing scopes of the provisions in different instruments. Whereas non-discrimination rules

[4] Appellate Body Reports, *Japan—Alcoholic Beverages II* 16–17; *Korea—Various Measures on Beef* [135]–[137]; Panel Report, *EC—Bananas III* [7.300]–[7.302].

[5] Nicolas Diebold, *Non-discrimination in International Trade in Services* (CUP 2014) 64–69.

[6] Appellate Body Reports, *Korea—Various Measures on Beef* [137]; *EC—Bananas III* [78] [232]–[234].

[7] Mavroidis (n 3) 136–37. See also Appellate Body Reports, *EC—Bananas III* [241]; *Japan—Alcoholic Beverages II* 18–19, 27–28.

[8] See, in contrast, Mavroidis (n 3) 247–53.

[9] Appellate Body Report, *Japan—Alcoholic Beverages II* 16–17. See also Panel Reports, *EC—Bananas III* [7.300]–[7.302]; *EC—Approval and Marketing of Biotech Products* [7.2406]; Appellate Body Reports, *US—Section 211 Appropriations Act* [242]; *EC—Bananas III* [231]–[234].

[10] See eg Won-Mog Choi, *Like Products in International Trade Law* (OUP 2003) ch III; Appellate Body Report, *EC—Asbestos* [89].

for trade in goods tend to be plenary,[11] non-discrimination rules in services tend to depend on whether a WTO Member has expressly agreed to subject a service sector to national treatment,[12] and whether a Member has decided to exempt a service sector from most-favoured-nation treatment.[13] There are also relevant textual and contextual differences between the different provisions.[14]

Despite this, the unifying logic of non-discrimination rules dictates two core elements to their legal standard. First, since it is a contingent or relative concept, an appropriate comparator must be determined against which to assess whether an impugned measure is discriminatory. Secondly, it must be determined whether the impugned measure modifies the conditions of competition between the complainant's goods or services, and the appropriate comparator. Each of these elements is discussed in turn.

The process for determining the appropriate comparator against which to assess the discriminatory nature of a measure is centered on the concept of 'likeness' in WTO law. In general terms a WTO Member must not discriminate between '*like* products' or between '*like* services and service suppliers'. The overarching logic of non-discrimination rules informs the test—two goods or services will be 'like' if they are in a competitive relationship in the marketplace.[15] With respect to goods, there is a largely settled body of jurisprudence on the kinds of indicia that inform whether two goods are in a competitive relationship. These include their physical properties and characteristics, their classification for customs purposes, their end-use, and consumer perceptions, tastes, and habits in relation to the goods.[16]

The jurisprudence on identifying whether services and service suppliers are 'like' is less developed, but emerging.[17] Drawing analogies to the context of trade in goods, the Appellate Body has held that services are 'like' when they are in a competitive relationship with each other, with indicia such as classifications under the United Nations Central Product Classification (UNCPC) and consumer preferences informing a case-by-case analysis.[18]

However, goods and services are also different in important respects. The Appellate Body has considered that the reference to 'service suppliers' in addition to 'services' in the non-discrimination obligations of GATS (and unlike GATT 1994) adds an element to the likeness test under GATS.[19] Although this element

[11] Marrakesh Agreement Establishing the World Trade Organization (n 2) annex IA (*General Agreement on Tariffs and Trade*) arts I, III (GATT 1994).

[12] Marrakesh Agreement Establishing the World Trade Organization (n 2) annex IB (General Agreement on Trade in Services) art XVII.1 (GATS).

[13] ibid art II.2.

[14] See eg Choi (n 10) ch III. See also Appellate Body Reports, *Japan—Alcoholic Beverages II* 21; *US—Tuna II (Mexico)* [212]–[217]; *US—Clove Cigarettes* [88]–[96].

[15] Choi (n 10) 21–33; Diebold (n 5) 334–38. See also Appellate Body Report, *EC—Asbestos* [99]; Panel Report, *China—Electronic Payment Services* [7.699]–[7.702]; Appellate Body Report, *Argentina—Financial Services* [6.25].

[16] Appellate Body Report, *Japan—Alcoholic Beverages II* 25.

[17] Appellate Body Report, *Argentina—Financial Services* s 6.1. See also Diebold (n 5) 118–20, 345–48; Panel Report, *China—Electronic Payment Services* [7.696]–[7.702].

[18] Appellate Body Report, *Argentina—Financial Services* [6.23]–[6.26] and [6.32]. See also Peter Van den Bossche, *The Law and Policy of the World Trade Organization* (CUP 2008) 340.

[19] Appellate Body Report, *Argentina—Financial Services* [6.27]–[6.29].

has not been elaborated upon, it likely flows from the fact that the production—and hence, the producer—of a service is often inseparable from the end-product provided to the consumer, since it is the activity and effort involved in production that is the source of value or demand.[20] Thus, the manner of production is important in understanding both the nature and value of the service as well as in informing consumer perceptions of the service. Such matters may therefore distinguish services from the jurisprudence on goods, whereby the processing and production methods involved in their creation play a decidedly limited role in the analysis (namely, to the extent they influence the competitive relationship between the goods, eg through affecting their physical properties or consumer perceptions).[21]

A related question is the extent to which regulatory objectives and technical standards may feature in a 'likeness' assessment for services.[22] On the one hand, a test that recognizes regulatory distinctions could be open to abuse.[23] A WTO Member could potentially discriminate against the services of another Member on the basis that they are not subject to identical regulatory oversight by the same regulatory body, even if they are in substance the same. Further, GATS incorporates exceptions that reserve policy space for Members to take measures in pursuit of legitimate regulatory interests such as public health, public morals, and prudential regulation.[24] It also includes a quasi-exception to non-discrimination rules that permits Members to recognize certain of each other's regulatory regimes that meet the same or equivalent standards, as long as other WTO Members have the opportunity to demonstrate regulatory equivalence and be accorded the same recognition.[25] This suggests that it would be inappropriate to evaluate differentiation stemming from regulatory objectives and technical standards at the 'likeness' stage of the analysis.

On the other hand, regulations are often directed at ensuring the quality and safety of a service that is ultimately consumed. A service that does not meet certain regulatory requirements may be qualitatively different to one that does. This suggests that services that are differentiated on the basis of regulatory requirements may not be in the same class, and thus not in a competitive relationship.[26]

Thus, while the limited existing WTO jurisprudence on likeness in services favours a market-based approach to determining 'likeness' between services, distinctions between services stemming from technical standards, regulatory objectives,

[20] Diebold (n 5) 345.

[21] Appellate Body Report, *EC—Asbestos* [101]–[104], [113]–[125]. See also Appellate Body Report, *US—Clove Cigarettes*. In that case, the Appellate Body rejected the argument that 'likeness' focuses on the legitimate objectives and purposes of the technical regulation, rather than on the competitive relationship between and among the products, though emphasized that regulatory concerns and considerations may play a role in applying certain of the 'likeness' criteria (that is, physical characteristics and consumer preferences) and, thus, in the determination of likeness under GATT 1994 (see [112]–[117]).

[22] Diebold (n 5) 75–80.

[23] Panel Report, *China—Electronic Payment Services* [7.707].

[24] See GATS (n 12) art XIV and Annex on Financial Services art 3. In contrast see Appellate Body Report, *US—Clove Cigarettes* [101]: the Appellate Body held in that case that the absence of express policy-based exceptions in the Agreement on Technical Barriers to Trade (TBT Agreement) warranted an interpretation that incorporated consideration of legitimate regulatory distinctions in the non-discrimination provision itself. See also Appellate Body Report, *Argentina—Financial Services* [6.113].

[25] GATS (n 12) art VII.

[26] Diebold (n 5) 345–48.

and how/by whom they are produced could serve as probative evidence of their nature and quality.[27] Indeed, the Appellate Body stated as much in *Argentina—Financial Services*. Although the Appellate Body considered that a WTO Member cannot intervene through regulation to *protect* domestic industry, it may be permissible to consider the role played by domestic regulation in shaping, for example, the characteristics of services and service suppliers and consumers' preferences, as part of the 'likeness' inquiry.[28]

If certain 'goods'/'products', 'services'/'service suppliers', or 'financial services'/ 'financial service suppliers' are found to be 'like', the next step of the analysis is to determine whether a measure accords less favourable treatment to those of fellow WTO Members. Despite textual differences between different manifestations of non-discrimination provisions in the WTO Agreement, they all address the same underlying question.[29] Does a measure affecting a good or service adversely impact its competitive opportunities vis-à-vis a like good or service? The process for determining whether the conditions of competition have been modified is more straightforward than 'likeness', particularly in respect of the differential treatment accord to carbon units surveyed in the following sections. It requires an assessment of whether the impugned measure has caused a detrimental impact on the competitive opportunities of the relevant goods or services, and whether this can be explained by their origin.[30] According to WTO jurisprudence, it is immaterial to the assessment whether the alleged less favourable treatment is de jure or de facto.[31] Additionally, with one exception that is outside the purview of this book,[32] it is now settled that the assessment of alleged less favourable treatment does not take into account public policy objectives as a stand-alone component of the legal test.[33] Rather, these are

[27] See eg Appellate Body Report, *Argentina—Financial Services* n 194; Panel Report, *China—Electronic Payment Services* [7.162]; and in respect of 'goods', Appellate Body Report, *US—Clove Cigarettes* [117]. However, in respect of 'goods' at least, the Appellate Body expressly excluded the relevance of legitimate regulatory distinctions in a *direct* sense: Appellate Body Reports, *EC—Seal Products* [5.90]–[5.93], [5.105].

[28] Appellate Body Report, *Argentina—Financial Services* [6.25], [6.39], and n 194.

[29] Appellate Body Report, *Argentina—Financial Services* [6.119].

[30] Van den Bossche (n 18) 341, 369, 384–90, 394–95. See also Appellate Body Reports, *EC—Seal Products* [5.104]; *Japan—Alcoholic Beverages II* 16–17; *Korea—Various Measures on Beef* [135]–[137]; *EC—Bananas III* [214], [231]–[233]. Of course, the means of determining whether differential treatment is explained by the origin of the object has presented difficulties in WTO jurisprudence, and is outside the scope of this book. On this see Diebold (n 5) 40–44; Van den Bossche, *Law and Policy of WTO* (n 18) 384–88.

[31] Appellate Body Reports, *Korea—Various Measures on Beef* [135]–[138]; *EC—Bananas III* [232]–[234].

[32] For non-discrimination claims under the TBT Agreement, an additional element would relate to whether the less favourable treatment stems exclusively from a legitimate regulatory distinction. In light of the function and nature of this additional element, and since the Appellate Body has recognized that it is largely aligned with Article XX of GATT 1994, the discussion on available policy-based exceptions in ch 9 largely covers this element. See Appellate Body Report, *EC—Seal Products* [5.310]–[5.313]: although the panel was found to have erred in that case by transposing the analysis under art 2.1 of the TBT Agreement mutatis mutandis to art XX of GATT 1994, the Appellate Body nonetheless accepted that the substance of the two are, in a general sense, aligned.

[33] Appellate Body Reports, *Argentina—Financial Services* [6.106], [6.119]–[6.122]; *EC—Seal Products* [5.90]–[5.93] and [5.105]–[5.116].

to be examined if general exceptions are invoked to excuse a prima facie violation, which are addressed in Chapter 9.

With this overview in mind, the various forms of differential treatment that engage rules on non-discrimination are identified and described.

2 Description of differential treatment across emissions trading schemes

A possible connection between differential treatment of carbon units and non-discrimination rules under WTO law has been made on a number of occasions.[34] However, these assessments have tended to be somewhat limited and addressing hypothetical scenarios, as opposed to practical real-world examples of differential treatment. This section undertakes a comprehensive review of the types of differential treatment accorded to carbon units by a range of existing emissions trading schemes, and proposes a taxonomy for ordering this treatment. In particular, it reveals that emissions trading schemes accord carbon units differential treatment in two broad ways. First, they accord differential treatment to different classes of carbon units depending on their jurisdiction of origin. Secondly, they accord differential treatment to different classes of offset units based on the manner of their production. Each is discussed in turn.

(a) Differential treatment based on jurisdiction of origin

All of the emissions trading schemes surveyed in this chapter accord differential treatment to different kinds of carbon units, depending on their jurisdiction of origin. This relates primarily to their recognition or non-recognition of allowance and offset units for compliance purposes in their schemes. Some schemes also differentiate between units based on their jurisdiction of origin in terms of their quantitative restrictions on different types of units.

(i) Acceptance of certain countries' allowance units

A number of emissions trading schemes accord differential treatment to allowance units on the basis of their jurisdiction of origin.

For instance, prior to its rescission, the original Australian emissions trading scheme was due to recognize the allowance units of the European Union (EU) for

[34] See eg Christina Voigt, *Sustainable Development as a Principle of International Law* (Brill 2009) 212–15, 241–47; Steve Charnovitz, 'Trade and Climate: Potential Conflicts and Synergies' in Pew Centre on Global Climate Change, *Beyond Kyoto: Advancing the International Effort Against Climate Change* (2003) 141; Jacob Werksman, Kevin A Baumert, and Navroz K Dubash 'Will International Investment Rules Obstruct Climate Protection Policies? An Examination of the Clean Development Mechanism' (2003) 3 *International Environmental Agreements: Politics, Law and Economics* 59, 74; Erich Vranes, 'Climate Change and the WTO: EU Emission Trading and the WTO Disciplines on Goods, Services and Investment Protection' (2009) 43 *Journal of World Trade* 707, 721, 727; Tania Voon, 'Sizing Up the WTO: Trade-Environment Conflict and the Kyoto Protocol' (2000) 10(1) *Journal of Transnational Law & Policy* 71, 106.

compliance after 2015,[35] and the EU emissions trading scheme was due to reciprocate after 2018.[36]

The EU emissions trading scheme will also recognize Swiss allowance units in view of the conclusion of its linking arrangement with Switzerland, and the Swiss emissions trading scheme will similarly accept the allowance units of the EU.[37] The EU emissions trading scheme is also designed to interlink with Norway's emissions trading scheme, thereby recognizing each other's allowance units.[38]

California and Quebec have also finalized a linking arrangement, whereby each other's allowance units will be accepted for compliance under their emissions trading schemes.[39]

The New Zealand, Korean, and Kazakh emissions trading schemes do not presently recognize the allowance units of any other jurisdictions for compliance.[40] While the New Zealand emissions trading scheme mandates that reviews of its scheme must consider the potential for linking to the now-repealed Australian emissions trading scheme,[41] discussions at the officials-level failed to progress to an agreement facilitating the acceptance of each other's units.[42] Kazakhstan and Ukraine have also reportedly expressed a desire to export their allowance units into the EU scheme.[43]

Thus, the degree of market access for allowance units is highly circumscribed. Most jurisdictions with an emissions trading scheme do not accept each other's allowance units for compliance purposes; some accept those of one or two other jurisdictions. However, this is not necessarily attributable to a deliberate policy choice or borne of protectionist or discriminatory intent. In some instances, it may simply be a result of lack of interest or demand. Many jurisdictions provide a legislative framework for

[35] Australian National Registry of Emissions Units Act 2011 (Cth) (ANREU Act) s 4 ('prescribed international unit', 'eligible international emission unit'); Clean Energy Act 2011 (Cth) s 5 ('eligible emissions unit') s 122.1.

[36] Department of Climate Change and Energy Efficiency (DCCEE), 'International Linking' http://www.cleanenergyfuture.gov.au/international-linking/ (last accessed 15 April 2013); European Commission, the Hon Greg Combet AM MP, 'Australia and European Commission Agree on Pathway Towards Fully Linking Emissions Trading Schemes' (Media Release, 28 August 2012).

[37] See further ch 3C.

[38] European Commission, 'Emissions trading: Commission announces linkage EU ETS with Norway, Iceland and Liechtenstein' (Media Release, IP/07/1617, 26 October 2007).

[39] California Air Resources Board (CARB), 'Air Resources Board amends cap and trade program, enhances market security' (News Release, 12–27, 28 June 2012); Regulation respecting a cap and trade system for greenhouse gas emission allowances 2014 (Quebec) appendix B.1; California Cap on Greenhouse Gas Emissions and Market-based Compliance Mechanisms (California Market-based Mechanism) 17 Cal Public Health Code § 95943.

[40] Climate Change Response Act 2002 (NZ) ss 4, 63(1); Climate Change (Unit Register) Regulations 2008 (NZ) r 11; Bloomberg New Energy Finance, *South Korea's Emissions Trading Scheme: White Paper* (Report Prepared by Ernst & Young, 10 May 2013) 12–15, 24; International Emissions Trading Association and Environment Defense Fund, *Kazakhstan* (September 2013), 2 http://www.ieta.org/assets/Reports/EmissionsTradingAroundTheWorld/edf_ieta_kazakhstan_case_study_may_2013.pdf (last accessed 15 January 2015).

[41] Climate Change Response Act (n 40) s 160(5)(g).

[42] Department of Environment, 'Australia and New Zealand advance linking of their emissions trading schemes' (Media Release, GC 333/11, 5 December 2011).

[43] IETA and EDF (n 40) 4–5; Thomas Reuters Point Carbon, 'Ukraine and Kazakhstan eye linkage of ETSs with EU scheme' (Press Release, 12 October 2012).

recognizing new classes of allowance units and linking to new schemes. For instance, Australia's now-repealed emissions trading scheme incorporated a mechanism to accept new classes of units on the basis of, inter alia, Australia's international obligations and objectives, the environmental integrity of the scheme, and the extent to which those units are accepted under the New Zealand and European Union emissions trading schemes.[44] The Australian Government stated that it would 'consider future bilateral links with credible international schemes' on a 'case-by-case basis'.[45]

Under the EU emissions trading scheme, agreements '*should* be concluded with third countries listed in Annex B to the Kyoto Protocol which have ratified the Protocol to provide for the mutual recognition of allowances', and such agreements '*may* be made' with non-Kyoto countries that have emissions trading schemes.[46]

The Quebec and Californian emissions trading schemes also provide for the recognition of other jurisdictions' allowance units on the basis of a reciprocal arrangement or agreement.[47] Both are member jurisdictions of the Western Climate Initiative (WCI), under which they have agreed to accept the allowance units of other WCI member jurisdictions[48] and to consider accepting the allowance units of external schemes that implement a binding and annually declining aggregate total greenhouse gas emissions cap, and that meet certain other safeguards and standards.[49]

These in-built mechanisms for accepting the allowance units of other jurisdictions mitigate the inference that the differential treatment of allowance units is necessarily targeted or protectionist. Rather, they may reflect the reality that linking emissions trading schemes requires a minimum level of technical and policy coordination.[50] Given the manner in which emissions trading occurs between different national registries, it would not be possible, or at least difficult and potentially precarious, to recognize the allowance units of another jurisdiction automatically in the absence of a formal link between the two schemes.[51]

That notwithstanding, these in-built mechanisms also suggest a normative preference for accepting the allowance units of particular jurisdictions—Australia for the New Zealand emissions trading scheme, New Zealand and the EU for the

[44] Clean Energy Act (n 35) s 123. [45] DCCEE (n 36).

[46] Directive 2003/87/EC of the European Parliament and of the Council of 13 October 2003 establishing a scheme for greenhouse gas emission allowance trading within the Community and amending Council Directive 96/61/EC [2003] OJ L275/32, art 25 (emphasis added).

[47] California Market-based Mechanism (n 39) § 95940; Environment Quality Act (Quebec) s 46(14).

[48] Western Climate Initiative, *Recommendations for the WCI Regional Cap-and-Trade Program* (23 September 2008) [7.5].

[49] Western Climate Initiative, *Design for the WCI Regional Program: Detailed Design* (2010) 44.

[50] See eg Partnership for Market Readiness and Forest Carbon Partnership Facility, *Emissions Trading Registries: Guidance on Regulation, Development, and Administration* (World Bank 2016) 80–82; Stefan E Weishaar, *Emissions Trading Design* (Edward Elgar Publishing 2014) 192–206; Michael Mehling, 'Linking of Emissions Trading Schemes' in David Freestone and Charlotte Streck (eds), *Legal Aspects of Carbon Trading: Kyoto, Copenhagen, and beyond* (OUP 2009) 109–33; M J Mace and Jason Anderson, 'Legal and Design Issues Arising in Linking the EU ETS with Existing and Emerging Emissions Trading Schemes' (2009) 6 *Journal of European Environment & Planning Law* 197.

[51] See eg Department of Climate Change and Energy Efficiency and Directorate General for Climate Action, *Registry options to facilitate linking of emissions trading systems: Consultation paper* (Joint Publication of the European Commission and Australian Government 2013) 26–32.

now-repealed Australian emissions trading scheme, other WCI members for the Californian emissions trading scheme, and other Kyoto Protocol parties for the EU emissions trading scheme (although this may recede after the Kyoto Protocol becomes redundant from 2020).

(ii) Acceptance of certain countries' offset units

Most emissions trading schemes surveyed in this chapter accept offset units. However, such acceptance often depends on the jurisdiction in which those units are generated.

For instance, the EU and Switzerland restrict permissible offset units issued after 2012 to those generated in least developed countries (LDCs).[52] The EU explained the rationale for privileging offset units generated in LDCs in terms of the particular vulnerabilities faced by LDCs, namely that they are 'especially vulnerable to the effects of climate change, and are responsible only for a very low level of greenhouse gas emissions', and '[t]herefore, particular priority should be given to addressing the needs of LDCs when revenues generated from auctioning are used to facilitate developing countries' adaptation to the impacts of climate change'.[53] Acceptance of offset units from those countries is thus viewed as a tool for stimulating technology transfer, foreign investment, and wealth transfers to those countries.[54]

It should be noted, however, that the EU emissions trading scheme will not accept *any* international offset units for compliance purposes from 2020 under current policy settings.[55] In that regard, the European Commission explained concerns relating to 'excessive rents and perverse incentives', as well as 'unequal geographical distribution of projects and human rights concerns', and 'a lack of an own contribution to mitigation by the seller'.[56] Further, the Commission considered that there is an existing large surplus of allowance units in its scheme, and thus prohibiting international offset units would assist in stabilizing the EU carbon market and promoting investor certainty. However, it has nonetheless left open the possibility of permitting international offset units pending the outcome of negotiations regarding the implementation of Article 6 of the Paris Agreement.[57] Since domestic offset units are similarly not permitted under the EU emissions trading scheme, the

[52] Directive 2003/87/EC (n 46) art 11a(4); Ordinance for the Reduction of CO_2 Emissions (2012) (Switzerland) art 4.2(b), annex 2.

[53] Directive 2009/29/EC of the European Parliament and of the Council of 23 April 2009 amending Directive 2003/87/EC so as to improve and extend the greenhouse gas emission allowance trading scheme of the Community [2009] OJ L140/63 preambular recital 31.

[54] See also Commission of the European Communities, *Building a Global Climate Change Alliance between the European Union and Poor Developing Countries Most Vulnerable to Climate Change* (COM(2007) 540, 18 September 2007) 6–7.

[55] European Commission (EC), 'Use of International Credits' https://ec.europa.eu/clima/policies/ets/credits_en#tab-0-3 (last accessed 18 January 2018).

[56] European Commission, 'Impact Assessment: Accompanying the document Communication from the Commission to the European Parliament, the Council, the European Economic and Social Committee and the Committee of the Regions A policy framework for climate and energy in the period from 2020 up to 2030' (Staff Working Document, SWD/2014/015 final) section 5.4.2.

[57] EC (n 55).

prohibition on international offset units will not result in discrimination as such—but it may engage market access obligations, as discussed later in this chapter.

California currently accepts two categories of offset units. First, it accepts those issued under its own offset scheme, which expressly limits itself to projects in Canada, the United States, and Mexico.[58] Indeed, two classes of offset units relating to forestry offsets, and another relating to livestock projects, are further restricted to projects undertaken in the territory of the United States.[59] In one of those instances, an explanation is provided for limiting eligible projects to the territory of the United States:

> The Forest Offset Protocol contains data tables, equations, and benchmark data applicable to projects located in the United States. The methods required by this protocol for estimating baseline carbon stocks for Forest Projects cannot currently be applied outside the United States, *as they rely on U.S.-specific data sets and models.* Forest Projects in Alaska and Hawaii are not eligible at this time due to lack of region-specific data.[60]

In addition to offset units issued under its own scheme, the Californian emissions trading scheme accepts offset units issued under the offset scheme of Quebec.[61] Quebec's emissions trading scheme has the same coverage of offset units as California's.[62] This accords with the rule under the umbrella WCI that obliges its member jurisdictions to recognize each other's offset units so that 'all WCI offsets are of equivalent use and fungible throughout the WCI region'.[63] The WCI member jurisdictions also decided to permit the acceptance of external non-WCI offset units, including those generated under the Clean Development Mechanism (CDM), in order to 'support emission reductions on a global scale, and because of concerns that such a limitation may not withstand legal challenges', but only where such offset units meet WCI standards.[64] That notwithstanding, the Californian and Quebecois schemes are yet to extend recognition to any non-WCI offset units.

The law establishing the Californian emissions trading scheme also includes a capacity for offset units from sectoral crediting mechanisms in developing countries to be approved and accepted; however, this has not yet occurred.[65]

[58] California Market-based Mechanism (n 39) § 95972(c).

[59] California Air Resources Board, *Compliance Offset Protocol U.S. Forest Projects* (adopted 20 October 2011) [3.6] 17–18; California Air Resources Board, *Compliance Offset Protocol Urban Forest Projects* (adopted 20 October 2011) [3.1] 4; California Air Resources Board, *Compliance Offset Protocol Capturing and Destroying Methane from Manure Management Systems* (adopted 20 October 2011) [3.1] 6.

[60] California Air Resources Board, *Compliance Offset Protocol U.S. Forest Projects* (adopted 20 October 2011) [3.6] 17–18.

[61] CARB, 'Amendment Announcement' (n 39); California Market-based Mechanism (n 39) § 95942(c), 95942(3), 95802(a)(66).

[62] Regulation respecting a cap and trade system for greenhouse gas emission allowances 2014 (n 39) appendix B.1.

[63] WCI (n 48) 11. [64] ibid 11, 39.

[65] California Market-based Mechanism (n 39) § 95991; California Air Resources Board, 'International Sector-Based Offset Credits' https://www.arb.ca.gov/cc/capandtrade/sectorbasedoffsets/sectorbasedoffsets.htm (last accessed 17 January 2018).

Korea is due to restrict its acceptance of offset units to those generated in its own territory through its domestic offset scheme, as well as potentially CDM projects undertaken in Korea.[66] It will not accept any international offset units until 2021.[67] It is envisaged that the Kazakh emissions trading scheme will accept its own domestic offset units, but will not recognize international offset units for compliance purposes.[68]

China's seven sub-national pilot schemes—intended to be precursors to its nationwide emissions trading scheme—each impose restrictions on offset units.[69] All seven limit permissible offset units to those generated in China, and the Beijing, Guangdong, and Hubei schemes additionally prescribe that certain quantities of permissible offset units must be generated in their local jurisdictions.[70] These restrictions could give an indication of the kinds of design features that might imbue China's nationwide scheme.

New Zealand's acceptance of offset units is limited to those generated in its territory under its own domestic offset scheme in order to inoculate its scheme from low and volatile prices in international carbon markets.[71] However, similar to the EU, New Zealand expects to open its emissions trading scheme to international offset units pending the outcome of negotiations regarding Article 6 of the Paris Agreement.[72] Australia's current baseline-and-credit scheme is similarly limited to offset units generated under its own domestic offset scheme within its territory.[73] However, it has also signalled an intention to open its market to international offset units.[74] Previously, New Zealand and Australia's now-repealed emissions trading schemes had accepted international offset units generated in developing countries under the auspices of the CDM (in addition to domestic offset units generated under their own respective offset schemes).[75]

(iii) Differential quantitative treatment of certain countries' units

Another dimension of differential treatment lies in different *quantities* of units sourced from particular countries or jurisdictions. For instance, the Korean emissions trading scheme accords differential treatment in relation to the quantitative

[66] Bloomberg (n 40) 12–15. [67] ibid 12. [68] IETA and EDF (n 40) 4.

[69] Zhong Xiang Zhang, 'Carbon Emissions Trading in China: The Evolution from Pilots to a Nationwide Scheme' (CCEP Working Paper No 1503, Australian National University April 2015) 10, 13.

[70] ibid.

[71] Climate Change Response Act (n 40) s 4, s 64(1), sch 4. See also New Zealand Government, *New Zealand Emissions Trading Scheme Review 2015/16* (Ministry for the Environment, November 2015) 8 and 20.

[72] See New Zealand's Nationally Determined Contribution under the Paris Agreement http://www4.unfccc.int/ndcregistry/Pages/Search.aspx?k=new%20zealand (last accessed 18 January 2018).

[73] National Greenhouse and Energy Reporting (NGERA) Act 2007 (Cth) s 22XM(1) and s 22XN.

[74] Australian Government, *2017 Review of Climate Change Policies* (Department of Energy and Environment, December 2017) 43–44.

[75] Clean Energy Act (n 35) s 5 ('eligible emissions unit'), s 122(1); ANREU Act (n 35) s 4 ('eligible international emissions unit'); Clean Energy Regulations 2011 (Cth) r 6.1; Climate Change Response Act (n 40) s 4, ('unit') s 63(1). See also Mark Ludlow, 'International carbon permits may be fast-tracked' *Australian Financial Review* (Online) (23 September 2015).

restrictions on offsets units applying from 2020. In particular, it is reported that, from 2020, international offsets can be used for up to 5 per cent of a covered entity's compliance obligation under the scheme, whereas domestic offset units can be used for up to 10 per cent of its compliance obligations.[76] Thus, more domestic offset units may be surrendered for compliance than international offset units.

The now-repealed Australian emissions trading scheme also included a quantitative layer of differential treatment on the basis of jurisdiction of origin. It permitted its own domestic units, both offset and allowance units, to be used for up to 100 per cent of compliance under the scheme.[77] However, the use of allowance units from the EU was due to be capped at 37.5 per cent of compliance, and the use of offset units generated in developing countries under the CDM was due to be capped at 12.5 per cent of compliance.[78] This was to ensure that a minimum level of abatement occurred within the territory of Australia, thus stimulating structural change to decarbonize the Australian economy.[79]

By contrast, the Californian emissions trading scheme expressly incorporates non-discriminatory treatment for the allowance and offset units of jurisdictions with which it links.[80] Such non-discriminatory treatment is mandated by the WCI with respect to the carbon units of other WCI member jurisdictions. However, WCI rules also require that the recognition of carbon units of emissions trading schemes that are not part of the WCI be capped at 49 per cent in order to ensure that a majority of abatement occurs within the territory of the WCI member jurisdictions.[81]

(b) Differential treatment based on manner of production

Most emissions trading schemes also differentiate between offset units for reasons related to their production. These kinds of differentiation fall into two broad categories. The first relates to the external consequences and impacts of the activity that results in the avoidance or reduction of emissions. The second relates to the activity itself that results in the avoidance or reduction of emissions.

(i) Consequences/impact of emissions reduction activity

The EU, New Zealand, Norwegian, and the now-repealed Australian emissions trading schemes deny recognition for offset units generated under the CDM from large-scale hydro power projects, unless they comply with international criteria and guidelines such as those contained in the 2000 report of the World Commission on Dams.[82] The Swiss emissions trading scheme goes further by prohibiting offset

[76] Jeff Schwartz and others, 'Republic of Korea: An Emissions Trading Case Study' (IETA, EDF, SFOC, CRIK Joint Publication 2016) 5.

[77] DCCEE (n 36); Clean Energy Act (n 35) s 121.

[78] DCCEE (n 36). See also 'Australia—EU Linking Emissions Trading Schemes' (n 36).

[79] DCCEE (n 36).

[80] California Market-based Mechanism (n 39) § 95942(b), 95942(c).

[81] WCI (n 48) 38–41.

[82] Norwegian Ministry of the Environment, *Norwegian National Allocation Plan for the Emissions Trading System in 2008–2012* (March 2008) [5.2]; Climate Change (Unit Register) Regulations 2008 (NZ) (n 40) r 8B; Directive 2003/87/EC (n 46) art 11(a), art 11(b); Directive 2004/101/EC of

units from large-scale hydro power projects, regardless of compliance with any international criteria.[83]

The targeting of this class of offset unit was initiated by the EU emissions trading scheme out of an expressed concern for the 'negative environmental or social impacts ... identified by the World Commission on Dams' in relation to large-scale hydro.[84] By contrast, the original iteration of Australia's emissions trading scheme initially rejected this restriction.[85] It considered that the broader social and environmental impacts of an offset project do not relate to the emissions reduction benefits arising from that project, and it is not appropriate to address such impacts through an emissions trading scheme.[86] However, it ultimately adopted the same rule, presumably to ensure compatibility with the EU scheme in order to facilitate a link.[87]

The New Zealand emissions trading scheme adopted this restriction out of concerns relating to loss of biodiversity, the displacement of local communities, and adverse impacts on land-use.[88] It was also interested in 'improving prospects for future international links', presumably with the EU and Australian schemes.[89] The Norwegian scheme adopted the restriction as part of its broader harmonization with EU standards.[90]

The New Zealand, Norwegian, EU, and now-repealed Australian emissions trading schemes preclude acceptance of offset units generated from projects involving nuclear energy. While this may be understood in terms of a pre-existing ban on such units under Kyoto Protocol offset rules,[91] the underlying origins of the restriction are probably better understood in terms of broader environmental or foreign policy concerns over nuclear energy and proliferation.[92]

the European Parliament and of the Council of 27 October 2004 amending Directive 2003/87/EC establishing a scheme for greenhouse gas emission allowance trading within the Community, in respect of the Kyoto Protocol's project mechanisms (Linking Directive) [2004] OJ L338 art 11(b)(6); Clean Energy Regulations 2011 (Cth) r 6.1(2)(b)(ii).

[83] Ordinance for CO_2 Reduction (n 52) art 4.2(b), annex 2 s 1(c).

[84] Linking Directive (n 82) preambular recital 14.

[85] Australian Government, *Carbon Pollution Reduction Scheme (CPRS): Australia's Low Pollution Future* (Commonwealth of Australia, Vol 1, 2008) 11–12.

[86] ibid.

[87] The precise motivations of the policy change are unclear; however, it is noteworthy that Australia undertook a range of policy changes to ensure compatibility and harmonize its scheme with the EU. See eg Department of Climate Change and Energy Efficiency, *Implementing links to overseas emissions trading schemes—Draft legislation Explanatory Note* (31 August 2012) 4–5.

[88] New Zealand Government, *Consultation on proposed regulations restricting the use of certain international units in the NZ ETS* (Ministry of Environment, November 2012) 2.

[89] ibid.

[90] Norwegian Ministry of the Environment, *Norwegian National Allocation Plan for the Emissions Trading System in 2008–2012* (n 82) [5.2].

[91] Modalities and procedures for a clean development mechanism as defined in Article 12 of the Kyoto Protocol, Decision 17/CP.7, 7th sess (10 November 2001) FCCC/CP/2001/13/Add.2, preamble; Directive 2003/87/EC (n 46) art 11(a), art 11(b); Linking Directive (n 82) art 11(a)(3)(a).

[92] See eg UNFCCC Secretariat, Ad Hoc Working Group on Long-term Cooperative Action (14th sess), 'Views on the elaboration of market-based mechanisms: Submissions from Parties' (Ad Hoc Working Group on Long-term Cooperative Action, 14th sess) FCCC/AWGLCA/2011/MISC.2, 10, 59; 'Work Programme on Mechanisms (Decisions 7/CP.4 AND 14/CP.5) Note by the President Addendum' (24 November 2000) (UNFCCC Conference of the Parties, 6th sess, FCCC/CP/2000/CRP.2/Add.1, 16; 'Work Programme on Mechanisms (Decisions 7/CP.4 AND 14/CP.5) Report by the

The Swiss emissions trading scheme takes a broader approach, barring any offset units that 'would contravene Swiss foreign and development policy', as well as any 'emission reductions were achieved in violation of human rights' or that were 'achieved under conditions that had significant negative social or ecological effects'.[93]

A unifying characteristic of these forms of differentiation is that they are grounded in policy concerns wholly unrelated to the objective of mitigating climate change. They differentiate between classes of units regardless of whether they have genuinely resulted in the removal or avoidance of one tonne of greenhouse gas.

(ii) Differential treatment based on the manner of emissions reduction

Most emissions trading schemes also accord differential treatment on the basis of the activity itself that results in the avoidance or reduction of greenhouse gas emissions.

The EU, New Zealand, and the now-repealed Australian emissions trading schemes deny recognition for compliance purposes of offset units that are generated from the destruction of hydrofluorocarbon-23 or the destruction of nitrous oxide (N_2O) resulting from the production of adipic acid.[94] The origins of this restriction lie in concerns over the environmental integrity of offset units generated from these activities.[95] In particular, there was a concern that recognition of these offset units created a perverse incentive for *increasing* production of the relevant industrial gases, which gave rise to doubts over whether the units genuinely represented one tonne of avoided greenhouse gas.[96]

The EU emissions trading scheme also bars offset units from 'land use, land use change and forestry activities' out of similar concerns relating to their environmental integrity.[97] In particular, it cites concerns over 'issues of non-permanence, additionality, [and] leakage' in relation to the generation of offset units from forestry activities. In large part, these concerns stem from uncertainties in relation to the measurement and verification of land-based and forestry emissions reduction activities. In contrast to more tangible and measurable activities such as renewable energy production and energy efficiency programmes, the EU appears to consider

Co-Chairmen of the negotiating group' (19 July 2001) (UNFCCC Conference of the Parties, 6th sess) FCCC/CP/2001/CRP.2 1.

[93] Ordinance for CO_2 Reduction (n 52) art 4.2(b), annex 2.

[94] Commission Regulation (EU) No 550/2011 of 7 June 2011 on determining, pursuant to Directive 2003/87/EC of the European Parliament and of the Council, certain restrictions applicable to the use of international credits from projects involving industrial gases [2011] OJ L149/1 art 1; Clean Energy Regulations 2011 (Cth) r 6.1(2)(a); Climate Change (Unit Register) Regulations 2008 (NZ) (n 40) r 8A.

[95] See eg UNFCCC Secretariat, 'Implications of the establishment of new hydrochlorofluorocarbon-22 (HCFC-22) facilities seeking to obtain certified emission reductions for the destruction of hydrofluorocarbon-23 (HFC-23): Submissions from Parties' (23 August 2006) (Subsidiary Body for Scientific and Technological Advice, 25th sess) FCCC/SBSTA/2006/MISC.11; UNFCCC Secretariat, 'Issues arising from the implementation of potential project activities under the clean development mechanism: the case of incineration of HFC-23 waste streams from HCFC-22 production: Technical paper' (26 April 2005) FCCC/TP/2005/1.

[96] New Zealand Government, *Consultation* (n 88) 2; Commission Regulation (EU) No 550/2011 (n 94) preambular recital 8.

[97] Linking Directive (n 82) art 11(a)(3)(b).

that the measurement, reporting, and verification of emission reductions through forestry projects is currently too unreliable to permit such units in their scheme. This is because it is usually measured through statistical modelling and projections rather than actual, precise recordings of emissions reductions,[98] and because it is difficult to measure and verify the future permanence of the removals of greenhouse gas from the atmosphere since trees ultimately die and decompose, or are used as fuel, thus releasing carbon dioxide back into the atmosphere.[99]

In addition, the EU emissions trading scheme seems to be concerned with broader 'impacts on biodiversity and natural ecosystems' arising from forestry and land-based activities.[100] Further, a report commissioned by the European Commission speculated that the 'sheer quantity of potential credits arising in the [forestry and land-based] sector (if introduced as an offset mechanism) could undermine the carbon market' in the EU. This may offer a different explanation for their non-recognition of such credits relating to price and market integrity.[101] Norway has adopted the same restriction in order to harmonize with EU standards.[102]

By contrast, the Californian, New Zealand, and (both former and current) Australian schemes recognize offset units generated from forestry or land-based activities undertaken in their own jurisdictions.[103] They consider that their methodologies and safeguards are sufficient to guarantee the environmental integrity of those offset units.[104] For instance, in order to guarantee that the sequestration of greenhouse gas emissions through forestry and land-based activities is permanent, both California and Australia maintain so-called 'buffers' to reserve a portion of offset units as a contingency for future reversals.[105]

[98] Intergovernmental Panel on Climate Change, *Special Report on Land Use, Land-Use Change, and Forestry* (2000) [2.4.1.1] http://www.ipcc.ch/ipccreports/sres/land_use/index.php?idp=78 (last accessed 15 April 2013).

[99] Commission of the European Communities, *Green Paper on greenhouse gas emissions trading within the European Union* (COM(2000) 87 final, 8 March 2000) n 2. However, this perspective could be changing as multilateral negotiations process on reducing emissions from deforestation and forest degradation see: UNFCCC Secretariat, 'REDD+ Web Platform http://unfccc.int/land_use_and_climate_change/redd_web_platform/items/4531.php (last accessed 26 January 2018).

[100] Linking Directive (n 82) art 11(a)(3)(b).

[101] Peter Kruikman and others, *Policy options for including LULUCF in the EU reduction commitment and policy instruments for increasing GHG mitigation efforts in the LULUCF and agriculture sectors: Synthesis Report* (Report commissioned by European Commission, November 2006).

[102] Norwegian Ministry of the Environment, *Norwegian National Allocation Plan for the Emissions Trading System in 2008–2012* (n 82) [5.2].

[103] California Market-based Mechanism (n 39) § 95973(2)(c)(3), 95973(2)(c)(4); Climate Change Response Act (n 40) pt 5 subpt 1; Clean Energy Act (n 35) s 5 ('eligible emissions unit') s 122.1; Carbon Credits (Carbon Farming Initiative) Act 2011 (Cth) s 53, 53A and 54; NGERA Act (n 73) s 22XM(1)(a).

[104] See eg Carbon Credits (Carbon Farming Initiative) Act (n 103) s 133; California Market-based Mechanism (n 39) § 95970, 95972, § 95973.

[105] California Air Resources Board, 'What Are the Requirements for Offset Credits and How Are They Issued?' in *Cap-and-Trade Regulation Instructional Guidance* (2012) 64 http://www.arb.ca.gov/cc/capandtrade/guidance/chapter6.pdf; Department of Environment, Australian Government, *Permanence* (undated) Australian Government Climate Change Website http://www.climatechange.gov.au/reducing-carbon/carbon-farming-initiative/activities-eligible-and-excluded/permanence.

However, notwithstanding its acceptance of its own domestic forestry and land-based offset units, the New Zealand scheme expressly bars international forestry units generated under the CDM.[106] Like the EU, this is because certain special features and limitations associated with those units give rise to a higher degree of risk and contingent liability for the jurisdiction in which they are held.[107] These special features originate from attempts to mediate concerns about the non-permanence of carbon stored in forest sinks.[108]

The Swiss emissions trading scheme takes a broader approach by barring any offset units that are not generated through the use of renewable energy or improved energy efficiency.[109] By implication, this precludes forestry and land-based offset units, as well as offset units generated from the destruction of the industrial gases mentioned above.

(c) *Summary: differential treatment*

The foregoing has identified various instances of differential treatment of carbon units in the rules of the emissions trading schemes of the EU, Switzerland, New Zealand, Norway, California, Quebec, Korea, and Australia. In broad terms, this treatment arises from differentiations on the basis of jurisdiction of origin or on the basis of the manner of production of the units. The following sections (A(3)–(5)) assess the extent to which this differential treatment violates rules on non-discrimination under the WTO Agreement.

3 Likeness

The first step in assessing whether the measures described above constitute prima facie violations of non-discrimination rules is to determine the 'likeness' of carbon units that are subject to differential treatment.

The few attempts in existing literature to assess the 'likeness' of different kinds of carbon units have been somewhat passing. One analysis concluded that nothing inherent in allowance units and offset units suggests that they are 'unlike', but different kinds of offset units must be 'sufficiently similar' in order to be considered 'like'.[110] Another found that units created by different jurisdictions under different regimes would not be 'like'.[111] This section seeks to address this question in a methodical

[106] Climate Change (Unit Register) Regulations 2008 (NZ) (n 40) r 8, r 9.

[107] New Zealand Government, *The Framework for a New Zealand Emissions Trading Scheme* (2007) 44. Australia's now-repealed scheme had a similar restriction; see Australian Government, *CPRS* (n 85) 11–13; DCCEE (n 36); ANREU Act (n 35) s 4 ('eligible international emission unit'); Clean Energy Act (n 35) s 5 ('eligible emissions unit'), s 123.

[108] See eg Modalities and procedures for afforestation and reforestation project activities under the clean development mechanism in the first commitment period of the Kyoto Protocol, Decision 5/CMP.1, 1st sess (30 March 2006) FCCC/KP/CMP/2005/8/Add.1, annex, part K.

[109] Ordinance for CO_2 Reduction (n 52) art 4.2(b), annex 2 s 1(d).

[110] Felicity Deane, *Emissions Trading and WTO Law* (Edward Elgar Publishing 2015) 78–79, 108–09.

[111] Voigt (n 34) 215–16.

and comprehensive manner by evaluating the key characteristics of different classes of carbon units and determining whether, based on their respective similarities and differences, they can be considered 'like'.

The differential treatment occurs between the two major categories of carbon units—offset units and allowance units—as well as within those categories between subsets of allowance units and offset units. Further, differential treatment occurs between domestic units and units originating from other countries or jurisdictions. This makes it necessary to assess 'likeness' on four levels. First, whether offset units and allowance units may, in general terms, be considered 'like' one another. Secondly, whether different classes of offset units, such as units generated through forestry-based carbon sequestration and units generated renewable energy projects, are 'like' one another. Thirdly, whether different classes of allowance units, namely those generated by different jurisdictions, are 'like' one another. Fourthly, whether there are any inherent qualitative differences between domestic and foreign units that might justify them not being 'like'. This is particularly salient in the context of the principle of 'supplementarity' under the Kyoto Protocol.

This section finds that offset units and allowance units are not 'like' one another, however different classes of offset units will often constitute 'like services' and 'like products' depending on the process leading to their generation, and allowance units stemming from different jurisdictions are also likely to be 'like products'. Similarly, the trading of offset units and the trading of allowance units do not constitute 'like financial services', but the trading of each of these subsets is likely to be a 'like financial service'.

(a) Likeness of offset units and allowance units

Since measures affecting allowance units do not relate to a service,[112] the question of 'likeness' as between offset units and allowance units is limited to whether they constitute 'like products' and whether their trade constitutes a 'like financial service'.

In relation to 'like products', at first glance offset units appear to be in a competitive relationship with allowance units. Both categories of units enable their owner to emit one tonne of greenhouse gas and avoid a penalty for doing so under an emissions trading scheme.[113] In that sense, they are fungible; they have an identical use. Further, both classes of carbon units exist as a unique serial number comprising component numbers that represent information such as their jurisdiction of origin or year of creation and both are stored in accounts in the same national registries.[114] They thus exhibit similar properties and characteristics.

In other respects, however, offset units and allowance units exhibit a number of key qualitative differences. Offset units function as valid evidence or a representation that one tonne of greenhouse has been removed from the atmosphere or whose emission was avoided.[115] Their value and eligibility in emissions trading schemes is, in large part, contingent on the accuracy of that representation. The risk that

[112] See ch 5B(1)(b). [113] See ch 3B. [114] ibid. [115] ibid.

the eligibility of offset units may be revoked in the event that they are found to lack environmental integrity, or that a given project or activity produces less emissions reductions and hence fewer offset units than anticipated, influence their price, and consumer perceptions.[116] Indeed, these risks have given rise to a suite of risk-management financial products in the primary trade of offset units through which they are traded.[117] Allowance units, by contrast, do not represent evidence of any underlying activity. They are created by a government for the specific purpose of use in its own emissions trading scheme, and there is no concomitant risk relating to their environmental integrity and eligibility as for offset units.[118]

The supply of offset units is determined by the private actors that undertake the removal or avoidance of greenhouse gas emissions,[119] and their existence and value is not solely contingent on the operation of an emissions trading scheme. Even in the absence of an emissions trading scheme, they may be traded on voluntary carbon markets by environmentally minded customers seeking to purchase a greenhouse gas emissions reduction service. The supply of allowance units, by contrast, is fixed by a government, which creates the units for the specific purpose of use in its own emissions trading scheme. They cannot exist or have value in the absence of an emissions trading scheme.[120]

Further, as discussed in more detail below, offset units are generated outside of an emissions trading scheme, which has led many schemes to set quantitative restrictions on their use. This is designed to ensure that a minimum amount of abatement is undertaken by major emitters covered by an emissions trading scheme, or undertaken within the geographic bounds of a jurisdiction. Allowance units originate from within an emissions trading scheme, and hence there is no concomitant need to impose any quantitative restrictions on their use to guide where, and by whom, emissions reductions occur. No emissions trading scheme surveyed in this chapter imposes quantitative restrictions on the use of their own allowance units.

These core distinctions have informed consumer perceptions of difference between the classes of units, which has in turn led to their trades occurring at different prices.[121] As a number of economists have recognized, offset units and allowance

[116] Fatemeh Nazifi, 'Modelling the price spread between EUA and CER carbon prices' (2013) 56 *Energy Policy* 434, 441–42; Alexandre Kossoy and Pierre Guigon, *State and Trends of the Carbon Market 2012* (World Bank 2012) 37–38.

[117] See eg Martijn Wilder and Louisa Fitz-Gerald, 'Carbon Contracting' in David Freestone and Charlotte Streck (eds), *Legal Aspects of Carbon Trading: Kyoto, Copenhagen, and beyond* (OUP 2009) 296, 302–06; Neil C Schofield, *Commodity Derivatives* (John Wiley & Sons 2008) 258.

[118] There are, of course, other risks in relation to allowance units, such as measures to remedy over-supply or variations in price collars; however, none are in relation to the verification of emissions reductions.

[119] Nazifi (n 116) 437; Weishaar (n 50) 63–64.

[120] Allowance units may, of course, be purchased and cancelled by actors in the voluntary market, but only if there is a compliance market operating in parallel through an emissions trading scheme. If there is no binding cap on allowance units, they will have no environmental effectiveness and hence no value in the voluntary market.

[121] Nazifi (n 116) 445; Pauline Barrieu and Max Fehr, 'Integrated EUA and CER price modeling and application for spread option pricing' (Working Paper No 50, Centre for Climate Change Economics and Policy, March 2011) 5.

units (namely, offset units under the Kyoto Protocol and allowance units in the EU emissions trading scheme) operate in practice under different market frameworks.[122]

It could be argued that consumer perceptions of difference themselves stem from the impugned discriminatory treatment and regulation, rather than any innate or actual differences. In other words, the subsistence of different prices and different market frameworks for each class of unit could be viewed as a result of governmental discrimination, the absence of which would facilitate a true competitive relationship of 'likeness'.[123] On that basis, it could be argued that these differences between offset units and allowance units should not be used to assess whether they are 'like'.[124]

However, the salience of this line of argument would be limited largely to the quantitative restrictions on the use of offset units, which are themselves derived from the different features and properties of offset units and allowance units. The other key differences informing price and consumer perceptions, such as differential risks relating to eligibility and delivery or the different determinants of supply,[125] stem from the fundamental distinction between offset units as evidence of an activity undertaken by the private sector and allowance units as government-issued instruments that do not represent any underlying activity.

On balance, the evidence relating to consumer perceptions, properties and differential price spreads suggests that the nature and extent of the competitive relationship between offset units and allowance units is somewhat limited. Of course, the precise scope of 'like products' depends on the particular provision in which the term appears.[126] However, even on the broadest reading of the term, it seems unlikely that they would meet the threshold of 'like products'.

The same conclusion appears warranted with respect to 'like financial services'. While both allowance units and offset units are traded for the same ultimate purpose of discharging liabilities under an emissions trading scheme by the same actors on the same platforms, they operate under different market frameworks. Trades in each class of unit, therefore, are not 'like' one another.

(b) *Likeness of classes of offset units*

As surveyed above, different classes of offset units are often treated differently by an emissions trading scheme. One class may be eligible for use in an emissions trading scheme, whereas another may not. Some may be subject to higher quantitative restrictions than others. This makes it necessary to determine whether different classes of offset units are 'like' one another. For instance, is one tonne of greenhouse gas removed from the atmosphere through planting trees and verified

[122] Bruce Mizrach, 'Integration of the Global Emissions Trading Markets' (Working Paper, Rutgers University, December 2009) 26–27, 39.

[123] Barrieu and Fehr (n 121) 5.

[124] See eg Appellate Body Report, *Korea—Various Measures on Beef* [143]–[151].

[125] Nazifi (n 116) 436, 442–43.

[126] Appellate Body Report, *Japan—Alcoholic Beverages II* 16–17.

by Australia's domestic offset regulator 'like' one tonne of greenhouse gas whose emission was avoided through a renewable energy project and verified by the CDM Executive Board?

All things being equal, different classes of offset units are clearly 'like' one another. As a means of allowing emitters covered by an emissions trading scheme to outsource their emissions reductions, they have the same end-use. As a representation of one tonne of greenhouse gas that has been removed or avoided, they have the same nature and properties. Similar risks relating to eligibility and environmental integrity apply to the different classes of offset units, since they must all meet satisfy certain auditing or verification procedures to validate that the claimed emissions reductions have occurred.[127]

However, qualitative differences in the *process* for verifying and auditing whether an activity has resulted in the removal or avoidance of emissions could have material implications for the 'likeness' analysis. In particular, a less stringent or flawed process could produce offset units that do not genuinely represent the removal or avoidance of one tonne of greenhouse gas. This, in turn, changes the nature of the offset unit generated by the activity subject to that process. Rather than constituting evidence of one tonne of greenhouse gas reduction, an offset unit generated through a flawed process might be evidence in real terms of half of one tonne or some other undetermined lesser amount.[128] This is essentially a question of fact. For two classes of offset units to be 'like', they would need to be subject to the same or equivalent degree of stringency in their production, or at least to a standard that is sufficient to assure that it genuinely represents one tonne of greenhouse gas avoided or removed. In cases where two classes of offset units are subject to the same process by the same regulator, for instance the CDM Executive Board, there would be a strong presumption that they are 'like'—the same entity applying the same rules and level of stringency has attested to both classes of units representing one tonne of greenhouse gas removal or avoidance. This is significant because, in a number of instances surveyed above, an emissions trading scheme permits one class of offset units but rejects another authorized by the same regulator, such as units generated from industrial gas destruction under the CDM.

In cases where two classes of offset units are subject to different processes by different regulators, a complainant would need to establish as a matter of fact that its processes produce offset units that represent one tonne of greenhouse gas removal or avoidance, or are issued to the same degree of stringency as the other class of units.

These considerations are equally relevant to the determination of both 'like services' and 'like products'. While the focus on the process for producing offset units as a key point of difference appears to jar with WTO jurisprudence on the role of process and production methods in assessing 'like products',[129] its fundamental role in determining the very properties and nature of the end-product offset units warrants

[127] See ch 3B.

[128] See eg *LMS Energy Pty Ltd v Clean Energy Regulator* [2014] AATA 709 [44]–[46].

[129] Van den Bossche (n 18) 341; Christiane R Conrad, *Processes and Production Methods (PPMs) in WTO Law* (CUP 2011) 178–89; Appellate Body Report, *US—Clove Cigarettes* [115]–[121].

its prominence in this case. A flawed or less stringent process in producing offset units would also impact consumer perceptions of the quality of the offset unit, and affect the risks relating to its eligibility in an emissions trading scheme and hence its price and marketability vis-à-vis other offset units.

Thus, the extent to which different classes of offset units qualify as 'like products' or 'like services' depends largely on factual evidence relating to their production. On the one hand, if it can be demonstrated that one class of offset units was generated by a procedure that assured they represent one tonne of greenhouse gas removed or avoided, or that they were subject to a similarly stringent procedure as the other class of units, they will qualify as 'like'. On the other hand, if it can be demonstrated that one class of offset units were generated by a procedure that was flawed and did not assure that they genuinely represent one tonne of greenhouse gas removed or avoided in contrast to another class, they will unlikely qualify as 'like'. The same considerations apply to the question of whether trades in different classes of offset units constitute 'like financial services'.

(c) Likeness of classes of allowance units

As surveyed above, different classes of allowance units are often treated differently by an emissions trading scheme. The allowance units of one jurisdiction may be eligible for use in an emissions trading scheme, whereas those of another may not. Since measures affecting allowance units do not relate to a service,[130] the question of 'likeness' as between different classes of allowance units is limited to whether they constitute 'like products' and whether their trade constitutes a 'like financial service'.

In relation to 'like products', the allowance units of different jurisdictions would appear to be 'like' one another. All allowance units represent the tradable, correlative right of the owner of the unit to emit one tonne of greenhouse gas under an emissions trading scheme, thus exhibiting the same end-use. They all constitute the quantum of a binding cap on emissions of greenhouse gas, and all exist in the same form as a unique electronic serial number in electronic registries.

Of course, differences in the level of ambition of different jurisdictions' climate mitigation policies will affect the stringency of the caps of their respective emissions trading schemes, which in turn affects both the supply of allowance units as well as demand for allowance and offset units in that scheme, and hence the prevailing price for carbon units in that scheme. A lower level of mitigation ambition will correlate to a larger supply of allowance units and a lower price for allowance and offset units in that scheme. This will result in a lower level of investment in decarbonizing an economy, thus reducing the environmental effectiveness of that scheme. There may also be differences in the sectoral coverage of different schemes.

Consumers in a jurisdiction that does not recognize another jurisdiction's allowance units for compliance in its scheme could perceive the cheaper allowance units of less environmentally effective emissions trading schemes to be qualitatively

[130] See above ch 5B(1)(b).

different to those of jurisdictions that implement a higher level of ambition with more expensive units.[131] To that extent, these kinds of differences in ambition and stringency could affect the competitive relationship between the allowance units of different jurisdictions, and thus influence the assessment of whether they are 'like products'. However, differences in mitigation ambition between different jurisdictions are matters of environmental policy set by a government that do not *directly* flow from the competitive relationship between allowance units and should not, in and of themselves, be taken into account in the 'like products' assessment. They are rather matters relating to the environmental integrity and effectiveness of an emissions trading scheme to be considered in the application of general exceptions.[132] The same considerations apply to the question of whether trades in different classes of allowance units constitute 'like financial services'.

(d) *Likeness of domestic and foreign carbon units*

Differences in levels of mitigation ambition also raise questions of the interaction between international economic law and the international climate regime. That is because, at least to some extent, differences in levels of ambition are a reflection of the norms and commitments in the international climate regime. The principle of 'common but differentiated responsibilities' suggests that developed countries should have a higher level of mitigation ambition, and the principle of 'supplementarity' under the Kyoto Protocol suggests that the primary source of abatement should be *domestic*, which means, in practical terms, that a minimum amount of domestic units be used.[133]

These kinds of principles provide differing indications insofar as whether domestic and foreign carbon units (both allowance and offset) are 'like'. The principle of 'supplementarity' suggests that domestic units are qualitatively different, since abatement occurring domestically vis-à-vis abatement occurring in foreign jurisdictions are—at least in ethical or normative terms—treated as conceptually different pursuant to that principle. The principle of common but differentiated responsibilities, in contrast, suggests that even if the schemes of different jurisdictions have differing levels of ambition and thus divergent prices flowing from different relative quantities of carbon units, their units should not necessarily be considered 'unlike'. Pursuant to this principle, when equity in sharing the burden of mitigating climate change is accounted for, these respective schemes are, in reality, equivalent—notwithstanding their differing levels of ambition and divergent prices.

Such considerations are, however, largely academic. As explained in Chapter 2, the principle of 'supplementarity' under the Kyoto Protocol is largely inutile due to the limited coverage of that treaty and the fact that its present round of commitments have not, and may never, enter into force. Further, the operational meaning

[131] See eg the debate over certain allowance units under the Kyoto Protocol constituting 'hot air': Voigt (n 34) 365–66.

[132] See Appellate Body Report, *Argentina—Financial Services* [6.117]–[6.118], [6.120]–[6.122].

[133] See ch 2B.

of equity and common but differentiated responsibilities is unsettled in the international climate regime, and countries' individual levels of ambition are not, in a technical sense, legally binding under the Paris Agreement. Thus, it is difficult to envisage how such principles might provide a touchstone for interpreting the term 'like' in international economic law insofar as it applies to domestic vis-à-vis foreign carbon units. In view of the settled competition-based focus of 'likeness' in WTO jurisprudence, it is more likely that, if such principles were to play any role assessing the consistency of emissions trading schemes with international economic law, it would be in discerning whether prima facie violations are 'arbitrary' or 'unjustifiable' in the context of applicable exceptions, rather than whether foreign and domestic units are 'like'.

4 Less favourable treatment

In respect of the differential treatment surveyed above, it seems to be relatively straightforward that the conditions of competition are modified as between carbon units to the extent they are 'like' and comprise (or embody) 'goods' or 'services'. By either rendering a certain class of carbon unit as ineligible for use in its emissions trading scheme or imposing a stricter quantitative limit on one class of units vis-à-vis another, the differential treatment places those units at a competitive disadvantage. Their ability to access the market and compete with other like units is either limited or prevented entirely. Importantly, this only applies to *like* classes of units—for instance, offset units that are at a competitive disadvantage vis-à-vis allowance units will not give rise to a violation of non-discrimination provisions because those units are not 'like'.

There may be some scope to argue that the rules on differential treatment of offset units based on their manner of production are origin-neutral, and thus do not discriminate on the basis of national origin. In such cases, a complainant would need to elicit evidence sufficient to demonstrate 'a genuine relationship between the measure at issue and its adverse impact on competitive opportunities for imported versus like domestic products to support a finding that imported products are treated less favourably' (or vis-à-vis a group of imported products of other origin in respect of most-favoured-nation treatment). For instance, the origin of two kinds of offset units that are now routinely barred, namely those created under the CDM by the destruction of industrial gases or through forestry projects, is limited to a narrow, discrete group of WTO Members. This would likely be a sufficient nexus to establish a case for de facto discrimination.[134]

[134] Appellate Body Report, *EC—Seal Products* [5.104]. For instance, for industrial gas destruction from HCFC-22 production, most units are generated in China and India (see methodology AM0001 at 'CDM: Project Activities' http://cdm.unfccc.int/Projects/projsearch.html), and most units from afforestation and reforestation projects are generated in India, Colombia, and Brazil (see methodologies AR-AM0001 to AR-AM0014 at 'CDM: Project Activities' http://cdm.unfccc.int/Projects/projsearch.html).

It is also worthwhile to reiterate at this juncture that, in respect of financial services, it is not the carbon units themselves that would constitute the financial service in question under the Annex on Financial Services. Rather, it is the activity surrounding the carbon unit—namely, the supply or trading of that unit—which would reflect the financial service in question. It is therefore conceivable that measures according differential treatment regarding carbon units will not necessarily result in less favourable treatment regarding the activities surrounding units generally. However, as discussed in Chapter 6, this distinction is relevant only in the limited factual circumstance whereby where there is minimal or no commercial nexus between the activity performed by a financial service supplier, and the particular financial products being traded or supplied.

5 Prima facie violations of non-discrimination provisions

In summary, some but not all of the instances of differential treatment between carbon units described above give rise to prima facie violations of non-discrimination provisions.

The differential treatment between offset units and allowance units is unlikely to be impugned under non-discrimination provisions. This is because they operate under different market frameworks and would not be considered 'like products', 'like services' or 'like financial services'.

The differential treatment amongst offset units is more likely to engage non-discrimination provisions. However, this too turns on the question of 'likeness'. If factual evidence can be elicited to demonstrate that the process for verifying and authorizing a given class of offset units is lacking, those units will likely have sufficiently different properties to distinguish them from others that genuinely do represent one tonne of greenhouse gas that has been removed or whose emissions was avoided. On the other hand, it could be difficult to justify differential treatment between offset units that have been verified by the same or substantially equivalent rules, or by the same regulator.

The differential treatment between allowance units on the basis of their jurisdiction of origin involves a more straightforward case of discrimination. It is, however, noteworthy that most emissions trading schemes have an in-built mechanism to recognize the allowance units of others. This could mitigate the prospect of a challenge.

These findings are, of course, subject to the potential applicability of exceptions, such as those relating to the conservation of natural resources, those necessary to protect human health and plant life, or those relating to LDCs. These are discussed in Chapter 9. Further, the specific services obligations of particular WTO Members will vary depending on their schedules and exemptions. As noted earlier, many have made inscriptions in potentially relevant service sectors; however, the extent to which these apply will depend on a given case.

B Market Access

International economic law contains disciplines aimed at facilitating uninhibited market access for goods, services, and capital flows. As with the foregoing section on non-discrimination, this section focuses on market access in WTO law rather than investment law. This is because the impugned market access rules in emissions trading schemes relate to transitory transactions rather than more permanent holdings of units, and therefore are unlikely to engage investment norms. However, to the extent that quantitative restrictions constitute de facto local content requirements in relation to investments, these are discussed in the next section.

This section begins with a brief overview of market access rules in their various manifestations across the covered agreements of the WTO Agreement. In light of this overview, it describes the various quantitative limitations and absolute prohibitions on carbon units imposed by a number of emissions trading schemes that could raise questions of consistency with market access rules. It then tests these restrictions and prohibitions against those rules. It finds that, to the extent carbon units are characterized as 'goods', the quantitative restrictions will not ordinarily violate Article XI GATT 1994 because they tend not to be measures applied at the border or affecting the physical importation of the units. However, to the extent offset units represent or embody a 'service' for which a WTO Member has made a specific commitment, the quantitative restrictions will likely give rise to a prima facie breach of Article XIV GATS. These findings are, of course, subject to Chapter 9 concerning the potential applicability of exceptions.

1 Overview of the legal standards in WTO law

In general terms, the WTO Agreement proscribes WTO Members from imposing quantitative restrictions on the import of goods and services from other Members.

Article XI GATT 1994 contains the relevant provision in respect of goods, and provides that: 'No prohibitions or restrictions other than duties, taxes or other charges, whether made effective through quotas, import or export licences or other measures, shall be instituted or maintained by any contracting party on the importation of any product of the territory of any other contracting party'. Thus, according to this provision, quantitative restrictions on the import of goods are prohibited. Importantly, however, it is concerned primarily with the physical entry of goods into the market place, rather than measures affecting goods following their importation.[135] This makes it important to discern whether a measure is an import ban or whether it is more appropriately characterized as an internal measure.[136] If it is the latter, the rules on non-discrimination will apply rather than those on market access.[137]

[135] Panel Report, *India—Autos* [7.257]–[7.263].
[136] See Van den Bossche (n 18) 346–47, 447–50.
[137] See, in contrast, GATT (n 11) ad art III.

Article XVI GATS contains the market access rules relating to services. Importantly, and in contrast to the plenary nature of Article XI GATT 1994, it only applies to the service sectors where WTO Members have made specific commitments in their individual schedules.[138] It provides, in relevant part, that WTO Members shall not maintain or adopt:

> limitations on the total value of service transactions or assets in the form of numerical quotas . . .; [or]
>
> limitations on the total number of service operations or on the total quantity of service output expressed in terms of designated numerical units in the form of quotas . . .

In effect, this provision proscribes quantitative restrictions on the total value of service transactions or assets, or the total number of service operations or quantity of service output. Unlike the equivalent for goods, this provision is not expressly limited to the *importation* of services. However, the requirement that the limitation applies to the 'total' value, volume, or number suggests that it must be a market-wide limitation. Although emissions trading schemes do not technically represent the totality of the carbon market, they do represent such an overwhelming source of demand[139] that restrictions on access to emissions trading schemes would likely be de facto 'total'.[140]

2 Description of the market access restrictions

The market access restrictions of emissions trading schemes can be grouped into three broad categories. First, most emissions trading schemes impose limitations on the quantity of offset units that entities with liabilities are permitted to use for complying with their liabilities. Secondly, in some instances where emissions trading schemes have recognized the allowance units of other jurisdictions for compliance purposes, quantitative restrictions have been imposed on their use. Thirdly, most emissions trading schemes prohibit the import or use of certain classes of carbon units, which is effectively a quantitative restriction of zero. Each is discussed in turn.

(a) Limitations on amount of offset units

The EU, Swiss, Californian, Quebecois, Korean, and the now-repealed Australian emissions trading schemes impose quantitative restrictions on the amount of international offset units that may be used for compliance. Australia's now-repealed scheme set a limitation of 12.5 per cent,[141] the EU and Swiss limitations vary for different companies but are generally set at around 11 per cent and 4.5 per cent

[138] GATS (n 12) art XVI.2.

[139] World Bank, Ecofys, and Vivid Economics, *State and Trends of Carbon Pricing 2017* (World Bank 2017) 24 and 40 (the World Bank valued emissions trading schemes and carbon taxes at US$52billion, compared to the voluntary carbon market at US$191 million).

[140] Panel Report, *US—Gambling* [6.344]–[6.347] (finding that de facto prohibitions may constitute 'total' limitations); Appellate Body Report, *US—Gambling* [264].

[141] Clean Energy Act (n 35) s 123A(g).

respectively (although the EU will bar all international offset units from 2020),[142] and California and Quebec both set limitations of 8 per cent generally (although California maintains lower limitations of 2.5 per cent and 5 per cent for international offset units generated through sectoral crediting mechanisms in developing countries—none of which has yet been approved for use in its scheme in any case).[143] Through its prohibition on international offset units until 2020, the Korean emissions trading scheme could also be understood as setting a quantitative restriction of zero.[144] China's seven pilot emissions trading schemes similarly do not permit international offset units.[145]

There are twin rationales for limiting international offset units. The first is to ensure that a minimum amount of emissions reductions are undertaken by the facilities engaged in major polluting activities in the jurisdiction of the emissions trading scheme.[146] This accords with one of the major goals of emissions trading schemes, which is to stimulate long-term investments in clean energy and lower emissions technology.[147] An unlimited usage of offset units could allow the largest emitters of greenhouse gas to meet their liabilities under an emissions trading scheme without making the necessary structural changes or investments to reduce their emissions.[148]

The second rationale is to guarantee that a minimum amount of abatement occurs within the territory of the jurisdiction of an emissions trading scheme.[149] This is to ensure that the domestic economy covered by an emissions trading scheme engages in a meaningful process of restructuring and decarbonization, rather than outsourcing the responsibility for undertaking emissions reductions to other jurisdictions.[150] Further, the structural economic change stimulated by requiring abatement to occur domestically would likely enable a jurisdiction to take on progressively more ambitious and deeper reductions in greenhouse gas emissions over time.[151] It accords with the principle of 'supplementarity' in the Kyoto Protocol, which requires that the principal and primary effort for reducing emissions occurs within a given party.[152] For Quebec and California, this rationale applies with

[142] Directive 2003/87/EC (n 46) art 11a(8); Ordinance for CO_2 Reduction (n 52) art 48.

[143] California Market-based Mechanism (n 39) § 95854, 95942(b), 95942(c); Regulation respecting a cap and trade system for greenhouse gas emission allowances 2014 (n 39) r 20 appendix B.1.

[144] See Appellate Body Report, *US—Gambling* [250]–[251] [264].

[145] Mengya Zhang, Yong Liu, and Yunpeng Su, 'Comparison of Carbon Emission Trading Schemes in the European Union and China' (College of Management and Economics, Tianjin University, Tianjin, September 2017) 7–8.

[146] WCI (n 48) 10.

[147] Weishaar (n 50) 46–47, 63; Commonwealth, *Parliamentary Debates*, House of Representatives, 13 September 2011, 9845 (Prime Minister Julia Gillard) (Second Reading Speech of the Clean Energy Bill 2011); WCI (n 48) 41.

[148] See, in contrast, New Zealand Government, *The Framework for a New Zealand Emissions Trading Scheme* (n 107) 43–44; Australian Government, *CPRS* (n 85) 11–17, 11–18.

[149] Linking Directive (n 82) preambular recital [7]; DCCEE (n 36); WCI (n 48) 41.

[150] DCCEE (n 36); WCI (n 48) 38–41.

[151] Froukje Maria Platjouw, 'Reducing Greenhouse Gas Emissions at Home or Abroad? The Implications of Kyoto's Supplementarity Requirement for the Present and Future Climate Change Regime' (2009) 18 *Review of European Community and International Environmental Law* 244, 254.

[152] See ch 2B. See also Voigt (n 34) 79–80, 363–64.

respect to external emissions trading schemes not covered under the WCI, rather than between different schemes operating under the WCI.[153]

By contrast, the New Zealand emissions trading scheme was at first designed not to introduce any quantitative restrictions on international offset units.[154] The nature of greenhouse gas is such that it does not matter where or when it is emitted, nor where or when such emissions are sequestered or avoided, and thus, on one view, there is no net benefit to the climate mitigation objective by promoting *domestic* reductions or reductions by large emitters. [155] However, since 2015, New Zealand has prohibited all international offset units. This was in response to low and volatile prices for such units, which disrupted the scheme's objective of incentivizing investment in less carbon-intensive means of production.[156]

Similarly, the original iteration of Australia's emissions trading scheme imposed no limits on international offsets.[157] Economic modelling suggested that domestic abatement would occur regardless of any quantitative restrictions.[158] This was then revised to a 50 per cent quantitative restriction in order to ensure that at least half of abatement occurs domestically in Australia, followed by a reduction to 12.5 per cent in order to harmonize with the EU emissions trading scheme. The current Australian baseline-and-credit scheme prohibits international offset units; however, it intends to accept international offset units pending the outcome of negotiations concerning Article 6 of the Paris Agreement.[159]

(b) Limitations on amount of other countries' allowance units

The now-repealed Australian emissions trading scheme imposed a quantitative restriction of 37.5 per cent on the amount of European Union allowance units that could be used for compliance.[160] Similarly, while not imposing quantitative restrictions on each other's allowance units, the emissions trading schemes of the member jurisdictions of the WCI (currently California and Quebec) have determined to impose an external quantitative restriction of 49 per cent on the allowance units of non-WCI emissions trading schemes.[161]

As with quantitative restrictions on offset units, this may be understood in terms of guaranteeing that a minimum amount of abatement occurs within the territory of the jurisdiction of the emissions trading scheme.[162] This is intended to prompt an

[153] WCI (n 48) 38–41.

[154] New Zealand Government, *The Framework for a New Zealand Emissions Trading Scheme* (n 107) 43–44.

[155] See Kumi Kitamori, 'Domestic GHG Emissions Trading Schemes: Recent Developments and Current Status in Selected OECD Countries' in *Implementing Domestic Tradeable Permits: Recent Developments and Future Challenges* (OECD 2002) 73; WCI (n 48) 41.

[156] New Zealand Government, *New Zealand Emissions Trading Scheme Review 2015/16* (n 71) 8–9 and 21.

[157] Australian Government, *CPRS* (n 85) 11–17, 1118.

[158] ibid.

[159] NGERA Act (n 73) s 22XM(1) and s 22XN; Australian Government, *2017 Review of Climate Change Policies* (n 74) 43–44.

[160] DCCEE (n 36).

[161] WCI (n 48) 38–41.

[162] DCCEE (n 36); WCI (n 48) 38–41.

economic transition to a low-carbon economy in the jurisdiction of the emissions trading scheme.[163]

(c) *Prohibition on types of unit*

As surveyed above, a number of jurisdictions impose prohibitions on the types of carbon units that may be used for compliance purposes. These prohibitions may take the form of an import ban, under which such units are barred from entering the registry of a jurisdiction. They may also take the form of a ban on using such units for compliance purposes. Under this approach, a carbon unit may be imported into the registry of a jurisdiction, but may not be used to meet liabilities in its emissions trading scheme. This denudes units of their main underlying value in an emissions trading scheme.

For instance, New Zealand imposed a ban on the importation of offset units generated from nuclear energy.[164] By contrast, its restriction on offsets generated from the destruction of industrial gases relates to their use for compliance with liabilities under its emissions trading scheme rather than their importation; they may still be imported into New Zealand and be traded between and held in New Zealand accounts (eg for use in the voluntary market), but may not be used in its emissions trading scheme.[165]

3 Prima facie violations of market access rules

In respect of market access rules for goods, a threshold question is whether the relevant measure operates in relation to the *importation* of carbon units. Amongst the emissions trading schemes surveyed in this chapter, the quantitative limitations on allowance units and offset units relate to their eligibility for use in the scheme rather than their importation. This means that an entity may import an amount of units *in excess of* the limitations into the territory of the jurisdiction. The limitation is not imposed at the border or the point of importation, and does not relate to their physical entry into the jurisdiction. Rather, it is imposed at the time that an entity covered by the emissions trading scheme seeks to discharge its liabilities under the scheme by using a certain amount of offset units or allowance units subject to the limitation.[166] This would likely remove those measures from the purview of Article XI GATT 1994.

By contrast, the *prohibitions* on certain classes of carbon units are, on occasion, applied at the border and the prohibited units are physically blocked from entering

163 Commonwealth, *Parliamentary Debates*, House of Representatives, 13 September 2011, 9845 (Prime Minister Julia Gillard) (Second Reading Speech of the Clean Energy Bill 2011); WCI (n 48) 38–41.

164 Climate Change (Unit Register) Regulations 2008 (NZ) (n 40) r 10.

165 ibid r 8A.

166 See eg Clean Energy Act (n 35) ss 123, 123A; California Market-based Mechanism (n 39) § 95854; Ordinance for CO_2 Reduction (n 52) art 48; Directive 2003/87/EC (n 46) art 11a(8) (all of these schemes apply the restriction to the surrender, rather than the trade, of units). See also Vranes (n 34) 721.

the jurisdiction. This blockage can arise either through an express rule prohibiting the importation of units or through the absence of a functioning link to an external trading platform where those external units subsist. In such instances, Article XI GATT 1994 will be engaged. It is important to note, however, that in other cases the prohibitions relate to the eligibility of certain classes of units for use in an emissions trading scheme rather than their importation. In those instances, Article XI GATT 1994 would not apply.

There is no analogous threshold question in respect of market access rules for services. Thus, the question in respect of services is relatively straightforward: do the quantitative limitations and prohibitions on the use of different classes of offset units surveyed above limit the total number of service operations, the total quantity of service output, or the total value of service transactions or assets in terms numerical quotas?

As discussed above, the quantitative limitations for the use of offset units in emissions trading schemes are 'total' because those schemes are overwhelmingly the predominant source of demand for greenhouse gas reduction services. Through an overall cap on the amount of offset units that may be used for compliance, the number of greenhouse gas reduction service operations and output is limited. For instance, California caps the use of offset units in its emissions trading at 8 per cent,[167] which in turn translates into a maximum use of greenhouse gas reduction services of slightly over 200 million mega tonnes of greenhouse gas.[168]

Since these limitations take the form of maximum percentage thresholds that translate into a maximum tonnage of greenhouse gas reductions, they can be said to be 'expressed in terms of designated numerical units in the form of quotas'. Even though they are not expressly designated as 'quotas', WTO jurisprudence has clarified that a measure is covered if it is 'quantitative in its thrust and therefore, limits the supply of a service as a quota would do'.[169]

These limitations could also be said to limit the total *value* of service transactions or assets. Of course, the amount that may be spent on offset units (and therefore, greenhouse gas reduction services) is not *directly* capped by these kinds of measures. However, by capping the total use of those services, there will necessarily be a consequential cap on the value of the services that may be used. For example, if there is a cap of 200 million mega tonnes of greenhouse gas, and the reduction services provided of each mega tonne sells on average for one dollar, there will be a de facto cap on the value of service transactions of US$200 million.

This analysis reveals a relatively straightforward case that the quantitative limitations on offset units constitute prima facie violations of Article XVI GATS for Members that have made relevant commitments. According to WTO jurisprudence, this analysis is equally applicable to instances where a limitation operates only

[167] California Market-based Mechanism (n 39) § 95854.

[168] See New Forests, 'The California Carbon Market: Implications for Forest Carbon Offset Investments' (2012) 2; American Carbon Registry, 'Compliance Offset Supply Forecast for California's Cap-and-Trade Program (2012–2013)' (2012) 1.

[169] Panel Report, *Electronic Payment Services* [7.592].

in respect of a particular mode of supply. For instance, restrictions that apply only to international offset units place effective limitations on the cross-border supply of greenhouse gas reduction services.

C Investment

Two features of international investment law make it difficult to undertake a comprehensive assessment of the kinds of measures relating to carbon units that will breach its norms. First, it is a sprawling and diffuse body of law contained in over 2,750 treaties that often comprise similar yet differently worded disciplines. Secondly, most of its core disciplines are, in general terms, directed at protecting specific investors and investments against adverse and usually unanticipated treatment following the making of an investment. The array of potential actions by a host state that could negatively impact holdings of carbon units is vast and not susceptible to the same degree of categorization and interrogation as for the measures engaging non-discrimination and market access rules surveyed above.

Therefore, this section (8C) does not aim to undertake a complete analysis of all measures that might violate all iterations of investment norms. Rather, it will consider, in broad terms, the kinds of measures and actions affecting carbon units that may be impugned under the relevant core disciplines of international investment law. It begins with an overview of the potentially applicable investment disciplines. Drawing on recent examples, it then considers the conceivable kinds of government interference in the carbon market that could infringe international investment law.

1 Overview of the core disciplines in international investment law

Expropriation and fair and equitable treatment are two core disciplines contained in most international investment agreements (IIAs) that may protect investors' interests from harm or damage caused by governmental interference in the carbon market. Rules on performance requirements constitute a third discipline contained in a minority of more recent IIAs that engage the local content requirements of some emissions trading schemes in relation to carbon units. A brief overview is given of each of these disciplines.

IIAs usually prohibit expropriations unless four conditions are met: they must be for a public purpose, be non-discriminatory, be against compensation, and due process must be accorded.[170] While governmental interference in the carbon market

[170] This is reflected in a representative sample of recent or model IIAs of major jurisdictions: 2012 United States Model Bilateral Investment Treaty (US Model IIA) art 6 www.state.gov/e/eb/ifd/bit/index.htm (last accessed 15 January 2018); Comprehensive Economic and Trade Agreement (EU–Canada) (entered into force provisionally on 21 September 2017) art 8.12.1; German Model Treaty 2008 art 4 http://italaw.com/sites/default/files/archive/ita1025.pdf (last accessed 15 January 2018); Italy Model Bilateral Investment Treaty 2003 art 4 http://www.italaw.com/sites/default/files/archive/ITALY%202003%20Model%20BIT%20.pdf (last accessed 15 January 2018); 2006 French Model Bilateral Investment Treaty art 4 http://italaw.com/documents/ModelTreatyFrance2006.pdf (last accessed 15 January 2015); Agreement between the Swiss Federal Council and the Government of the

will not usually involve the formal seizure of title or ownership in carbon units, there is a widespread understanding in international investment law that investors are also protected against *indirect* expropriations.[171] The legal standard for identifying an indirect expropriation is whether an investor suffers a substantial and lasting deprivation of its investment,[172] for instance through the destruction of the value of the investment,[173] the effective loss of control of the investment,[174] or the effective neutralization of the benefit of the investment to its owner.[175] As such, if a given instance of governmental interference in the carbon market has the effect of destroying the value of an investor's investments in carbon units, it could result in a breach of expropriation disciplines in IIAs.

Importantly, however, investment tribunals have recognized that the legitimate exercise of regulatory powers in the public interest, such as to protect public health or the environment, does not constitute an indirect expropriation.[176] While the dividing line between legitimate regulatory measures and indirect expropriations can be at times ambiguous and unpredictable, tribunals will generally take into account whether the measure is non-discriminatory, whether it is proportionate to the purported public policy objective,[177] and the extent to which it is inconsistent with an investor's legitimate expectations.[178] As such, governmental interference in

People's Republic of China on the Promotion and Reciprocal Protection of Investments (Switzerland–China) (signed 27 January 2009, entered into force 1 April 2010) art 1.1; Model Text for the Indian Bilateral Investment Treaty 2016 art 5.1 https://www.mygov.in/sites/default/files/master_image/Model%20Text%20for%20the%20Indian%20Bilateral%20Investment%20Treaty.pdf (last accessed 15 January 2018).

171 See eg Andrew Newcombe and Lluís Paradell, *Law and Practice of Investment Treaties* (Kluwer 2009) 322.

172 See eg *Saluka Investments v Czech Republic (Partial Award)* (Permanent Court of Arbitration, 17 March 2006) [263]–[264]. For an in-depth discussion on indirect expropriation see Newcombe and Paradell (n 171) 321–70.

173 *CME Czech Republic v Czech Republic (Partial Award)* (Ad hoc arbitration, UNCITRAL Rules, 13 September 2001) [599] and [609].

174 *Toto Costruzioni Generali v Republic of Lebanon (Decision on Jurisdiction)* (ICSID Arbitral Tribunal, Case No ARB/07112, 8 September 2009) [185].

175 *CME v Czech Republic* (n 173) [604].

176 *Suez v Argentina (Decision on Liability)* (ICSID Arbitral Tribunal, Case No ARB/03/17, 30 July 2010) [128] [147]–[148]; *Fireman's Fund Insurance Company v Mexico (Award)* (ICSID Arbitral Award, Case No ARB(AF)/02/01, 17 July 2006) [176(j)]; *Saluka v Czech Republic* (n 172) [254]–[255], [257]–[258], [261]–[262], [275]–[276]; *Técnicas Medioambientales Tecmed v Mexico (Award)* (ICSID Arbitral Tribunal, Case No ARB(AF)/00/2, 29 May 2003) [119], cf [121]; Katia Yannaca-Small, 'Indirect Expropriation and the Right to Regulate: How to Draw the Line?' in Katia Yannaca-Small (ed), *Arbitration under International Investment Agreements: A Guide to the Key Issues* (OUP 2010) 445, 470–72; August Reinisch, 'Expropriation' in Peter Muchlinski, Federico Ortino, and Christoph Schreuer (eds), *The Oxford Handbook of International Investment Law* (OUP 2011) 407, 433, cf 437–38. But see, in contrast, *Patrick Mitchell v Democratic Republic of Congo (Decision on Annulment)* (ICSID Ad hoc Committee, Case No ARB//99/7, 1 November 2006) [53]; *Pope & Talbot v Canada (Interim Award)* (Ad hoc arbitration, UNCITRAL Rules, 26 June 2000) [99]; *Compañía del Desarrollo de Santa Elena v Costa Rica (Final Award)* (ICSID Arbitral Tribunal, Case No ARB/96/1, 17 February 2000) [71]–[72].

177 *LG&E Energy Corp v Argentina (Decision on Liability)* (ICSID Arbitral Tribunal, Case No ARB 02/1, 3 October 2006) [195]. See also *Fireman's Fund v Mexico* (n 176) [176(j)]; *Azurix v Argentina (Award)* (ICSID Arbitral Tribunal, Case No ARB/01/12, 23 June 2006) [311]–[312]; *Tecmed v Mexico* (n 176) [122], [132].

178 *Fireman's Fund v Mexico* (n 176) [176(k)].

the carbon market that is designed to achieve a genuine public policy objective, such as ensuring the environmental integrity of the emissions trading scheme, and that is non-discriminatory, is not discordant with the legitimate expectations of investors and the market, and is proportionate to achieving that objective, will be unlikely to give rise to a compensable indirect expropriation.

The 'fair and equitable treatment' standard contained in most IIAs may provide another means of protecting investors' interests in the carbon market from undue government intervention.[179] Not only does the fair and equitable treatment standard protect against government conduct that embodies a manifest denial of natural justice and due process—such as arbitrary, grossly unfair, unjust, discriminatory, or non-transparent treatment[180]—but it is generally recognized as protecting investors' legitimate expectations in relation to a host state's legislative framework.[181] This is particularly so where a government has made a 'specific assurance or commitment to the investor so as to induce its expectations'[182] or has created 'reasonable and justifiable expectations'[183] '*in order to induce* investment'.[184]

Therefore, where market participants make investments in the carbon market on the basis of bona fide, justifiable expectations as to the nature and operation of the market, subsequent government interventions that subvert those expectations could violate the fair and equitable treatment standard. Protected investors under a given IIA could thus seek compensation for any harm or damage suffered to the value or use of their carbon units. Indeed, investors have done so in respect of climate mitigation measures that were originally designed to stimulate investment but were unwound or rescinded.[185]

[179] It is, of course, a contested area as to whether fair and equitable treatment in investment treaties is limited to the customary minimum standard or whether it is its own autonomous, potentially broader standard founded on the text of a given treaty rather than rooted in customary principles. This controversy lies outside the scope of this book. However, it suffices to note that more restrictive understandings of fair and equitable treatment that relate only to due process or natural justice could offer more limited remedies to market participants in the carbon market. See Tania Voon, James Munro, and Andrew Mitchell, 'Importing WTO General Exceptions into International Investment Agreements: Proportionality, Myths and Risks' *Yearbook on International Investment Law and Policy* (forthcoming, OUP 2018).

[180] *Waste Management, Inc v Mexico (Award)* (ICSID Case No ARB(AF)/00/3, 30 April 2004) [98]. See also eg *Loewen v United States (Award)* (ICSID Case No ARB(AF)/98/3, 26 June 2003) [132]; *International Thunderbird Gaming Corporation v Mexico (Award)* (Ad hoc arbitration, UNCITRAL Rules, 26 January 2006) [194]; *Merrill & Ring Forestry LP v Canada (Award)* (ICSID-Administered Tribunal, UNCITRAL Rules, 31 March 2010) [236]; *Mobil Investments Canada Inc v Canada (Decision on Liability)* (ICSID Case No ARB(AF)/07/4, 22 May 2012) [152(2)]; *TECO Guatemala Holdings LLC v Guatemala* (Award) ((ICSID Case No ARB/10/17, 19 December 2013) [492].

[181] Newcombe and Paradell (n 171) 278–89.

[182] *Glamis Gold Ltd v United States (Award)* (Ad hoc arbitration, UNCITRAL Rules, 14 May 2009) [620] (see also [767] [799]–[800] [807]). See also *EDF (Services) Ltd v Romania (Award)* (ICSID Case No ARB/05/13, 8 October 2009) [219].

[183] *Thunderbird v Mexico* (n 180) [147].

[184] *Glamis v United States* (n 182) [621] (original emphasis) (see also [627], [802]).

[185] As recent examples see *Eiser Infrastructure Limited and Energía Solar Luxembourg Sàrl v Kingdom of Spain (Final Award)* (ICSID Arbitral Tribunal, Case No ARB/13/36, 4 May 2017) [363]; *Eskosol SpA in liquidazione v Italian Republic (Decision on Respondent's Application Under Rule 41(5))* (ICSID Arbitral Tribunal, Case No ARB/15/50, 20 March 2017) [25]; *Windstream Energy LLC v Government of Canada (Award)* (Permanent Court of Arbitration, UNCITRAL Rules, 27 September 2016) [363]–[364] and [380].

That said, it is important to note that the fair and equitable treatment standard does not, as one tribunal stated, function an 'insurance polic[y] for bad business judgments'.[186] For instance, if it can be reasonably anticipated from the broader political or economic context that there may be future government interventions or regulatory changes impacting on an investment, it will not ordinarily be protected against such changes by disciplines on fair and equitable treatment. Indeed, one tribunal noted that 'no investor may reasonably expect that the circumstances prevailing at the time the investment is made will remain totally unchanged'.[187] Thus, the fair and equitable treatment standard may protect investors against sudden or unanticipated interventions in the carbon market that cause harm. However, regulatory measures that ought to have been foreseeable, or at least plausible, at the time the investment made will be unlikely to constitute a breach of fair and equitable treatment.[188] This may include, for instance, reasonable and proportionate public welfare measures.[189]

Prohibitions on certain performance requirements, including local content requirements, have tended to be included in more recent IIAs, and are also included in the TRIMS Agreement.[190] A typical example is found in the US Model IIA:

> 1. Neither Party may, in connection with the establishment, acquisition, expansion, management, conduct, operation, or sale or other disposition of an investment of an investor of a Party or of a non-Party in its territory, impose or enforce any requirement, or enforce any commitment or undertaking, to: …
>
> (b) achieve a given level or percentage of domestic content; …[191]

Based on this provision, requirements to achieve a minimum percentage of domestic content in the purchase or disposal of carbon units are proscribed. The TRIMs Agreement similarly prohibits measures requiring: '[t]he purchase or use by an enterprise of products of domestic origin or from any domestic source, whether specified in terms of particular products, in terms of volume or value of products, or in terms of a proportion of volume or value of its local production'.[192] Thus, it is not permissible under the TRIMs Agreement to require enterprises to purchase a specified or minimum amount domestic carbon units.

[186] *Emilio Agustín Maffezini v Kingdom of Spain* (ICSID Arbitral Tribunal, Case No ARB/97/7 13 November 2000) [64].

[187] *Saluka v Czech Republic* (n 172) [305].

[188] According to some tribunals, the high threshold for violation allows policy space to pursue public welfare objectives: *Frontier Petroleum v Czech Republic (Award)* (Ad hoc arbitration, UNCITRAL Rules, 12 November 2010) [527]. According to other tribunals, there exists a 'right to regulate' in respect of fair and equitable treatment that effectively excuses violations vis-à-vis public welfare measures: see *Saluka v Czech Republic* (n 172) [305].

[189] For an analysis of the precise and diverging manner in which public policy space is reflected in the 'fair and equitable treatment' standard see Tania Voon, James Munro, and Andrew Mitchell, 'Importing WTO General Exceptions into International Investment Agreements: Proportionality, Myths and Risks' *Yearbook on International Investment Law and Policy* (forthcoming, OUP 2018).

[190] Marrakesh Agreement Establishing the World Trade Organization (n 2) annex IA (Agreement on Trade-Related Investment Measures) (TRIMs Agreement); 2012 US Model IIA (n 170) art 8.

[191] US Model IIA (n 170) art 8.

[192] TRIMs Agreement, annex clause 1(a).

2 Violations of international investment law

In general terms, governmental interventions in carbon markets that significantly affect the value of carbon units may raise issues of consistency with expropriation and fair and equitable treatment.

Recent experience demonstrates that the potential reasons for governmental interventions are as diverse as the forms they may take. For instance, the Australian Government rescinded the minimum price floor for carbon units in its now-repealed emissions trading scheme in order to facilitate a link with the EU emissions trading scheme, which offered access to significantly cheaper external units.[193] This price floor would have guaranteed a minimum price for carbon units, thus giving investors in the carbon market a degree of certainty and stability in making their investments in carbon units.[194] The Australian Government also reduced its quantitative cap on offset units generated under the Kyoto Protocol from 50 per cent to 12.5 per cent as part of its link to the EU scheme, thus significantly reducing demand for those units in Australia's emissions trading scheme.[195] It is a truism that significant reductions in demand for a product can result in a substantial devaluing of the investments in that product.

As another example, the New Zealand Government withdrew recognition of carbon units generated by industrial gas destruction projects, rendering those units ineligible for use in its emissions trading scheme.[196] This stemmed from concerns over the environmental integrity of those units.[197] The EU has also recently intervened in its emissions trading scheme by withholding the supply of allowance units in order to inflate the price of carbon units in its market artificially.[198] There had been concerns that the market price was too low to stimulate significant low-carbon investments.[199]

Perhaps the most extreme form of governmental interference is the wholesale rescission of a carbon market, as occurred in Australia.[200] For units whose only or major source of demand had been the Australian market, this intervention effectively nullified their value and use.[201] The reason for this interference was to replace

[193] Department of Climate Change and Energy Efficiency, *Fact Sheet: Linking and Australian Liable Entities* http://www.cleanenergyfuture.gov.au/linking-and- australian-liable-entities/ (last accessed 15 January 2012).

[194] Explanatory Memorandum, Clean Energy Bill 2011 (Cth) 32.

[195] Department of Climate Change and Energy Efficiency, *Fact Sheet: Linking and Australian Liable Entities* http://www.cleanenergyfuture.gov.au/linking-and- australian-liable-entities/ (last accessed 15 January 2012).

[196] Climate Change (Unit Register) Regulations 2008 (NZ) (n 40) s 8A.

[197] New Zealand Government, *Consultation* (n 88).

[198] Ewa Krukowska, 'EU Adopts Emergency Carbon Fix Law to Curb Permit Glut' *Bloomberg* (17 December 2013). But see also Directive 2003/87/EC (n 46) art 29a.

[199] European Commission, *Report from the Commission to the European Parliament and the Council: The state of the European carbon market in 2012* (Report COM(2012) 652 final, 2012) 6, 9–11.

[200] Department of the Environment, *Repealing the Carbon Tax*, http://www.environment.gov.au/climate-change/repealing-carbon-tax (last accessed 15 January 2018). However, this has since evolved into a baseline-and-credit emissions trading scheme (see ch 3A).

[201] For instance, this would be the case for offset units issued under the Carbon Farming Initiative, or for allowance units issued by the Australian regulator.

a mandatory market-based approach to climate mitigation with a voluntary market-based approach driven by government procurement of carbon units.[202]

These are examples of governmental interventions in the carbon market with potentially significant impacts on the value of carbon units. Whether these impacts give rise to compensable investment claims depends largely on the context surrounding a given intervention.

For claims founded on indirect expropriation, the reduction of value in the carbon units would need to be particularly severe. The intervention would likely need to result in either a collapse in their market price, or undermine their ability to be used or traded in carbon markets. For instance, a government ban on a particular kind of carbon unit for use in its emissions trading scheme could destroy the value and utility of that unit to an investor. However, if that unit could nonetheless be sold into external carbon markets, and thus retained a degree of value and utility, the ban would be less likely to constitute an indirect expropriation. Further, if the ban were undertaken in a non-discriminatory and proportionate manner to serve a public purpose, for instance if the units were found not to represent real emissions reductions, it would not qualify as an indirect expropriation. Thus far, the introduction by governments of bans on particular kinds of carbon units that were previously eligible for compliance have tended to apply prospectively and with grace periods to minimize impacts on investors.[203] Retrospective invalidations of existing units tend to be limited to instances where they were issued through fraud or where they are found not to represent real emissions reductions.[204] These kinds of safeguards and limitations mitigate the potential for a successful indirect expropriation claim on carbon units devalued through government actions.

Claims relating to fair and equitable treatment will turn on whether investors holding carbon units had a legitimate expectation at the time of their purchase that the actions affecting their units would not be taken. Legitimate expectations can arise through government conduct and guarantees that they will refrain from certain actions, and potentially also through commitments contained in a legislative framework (depending on their degree of specificity).[205] For instance, the Australian Government assured market participants that there would be a price floor of around AUD$15 per unit operating in its emissions trading scheme until 2018. As mentioned above, this was designed to provide stability and certainty to the market, which would in turn assure potential investors in market of a minimum value for their investments.[206] The subsequent rescission of this floor in 2012 occurred in

[202] Department of the Environment, *Clean Air* http://www.environment.gov.au/clean-air (last accessed 15 January 2018).

[203] See eg Clean Energy Act (n 35) s 123; Decision No 406/2009/EC of the European Parliament and the European Council of 23 April 2009 on the effort of Member States to reduce their greenhouse gas emissions to meet the Community's greenhouse gas emission reduction commitments up to 2020 [2009] OJ L140/136, art 5(1).

[204] See eg Carbon Credits (Carbon Farming Initiative) Act (n 103) s 175; Climate Change Response Act (n 40) s 7(2).

[205] Newcombe and Paradell (n 171) 278–89; Rudolph Dolzer and Christoph Schreuer, *Principles of International Investment Law* (OUP 2012) 145–50. See also *Glamis v United States* (n 182) [620].

[206] Explanatory Memorandum, Clean Energy Bill 2011 (Cth) 32.

a context of significantly lower international prices for carbon units, with some trading at that time as low as AUD$3.60.[207] If an investor had made investments in carbon units on the assumption of government assurances of a minimum price of AUD$15 per carbon unit, the rescission of the price floor would have substantially undermined the value of those investments contrary to earlier government assurances. This mixture of circumstances, including a government assurance intended to provide certainty and stimulate investment in the carbon market, coupled with the unanticipated and unforeseen nature of its rescission, would likely give rise to a strong claim based on fair and equitable treatment.

The manipulation of the price of its allowance units by the EU through its 'back-loading' amendments offers a more nuanced example. On the one hand, it occurred after the parameters of the 2013–2020 trading period had already been set.[208] The EU had made representations to the carbon market about the supply of allowance units and the timing with which they would be released to the market.[209] Its regulations did not foresee any tool or capacity for short-term interventions to increase the price of its allowance units artificially.[210] To that extent, investors in its carbon market were entitled to make investments in the market on the basis of the anticipated supply of allowance units, which is a significant determinant of their price and value. On the other hand, the EU had made no express representations that it would not make adjustments to supply under any circumstances.[211] Its intervention was designed to avoid a wholesale collapse in the price of its allowance units flowing from its economic recession, and thus to safeguard the environmental objective of the emissions trading scheme to stimulate investments in low-carbon technology and commerce.[212] The absence of unambiguous and express assurances that the supply and price of units would not be manipulated, coupled with the fact the intervention was neither unreasonable nor arbitrary in light of the underlying purpose of the carbon market, make it less likely that a fair and equitable treatment claim would succeed in this kind of case.

Performance requirements relating to local content originally appeared in both the Australian and Korean emissions trading schemes. Under the now-repealed Australian scheme, covered entities were required to use a minimum 50 per cent of domestically sourced carbon units to cover their liabilities.[213] Under the Korean scheme, it was reported that the number of international offset units submitted for compliance with liabilities would not be able to exceed the number of domestic offset units submitted for each compliance year.[214]

[207] See Alexandre Kossoy and others, *Mapping Carbon Pricing Initiatives: Developments and Prospects* (World Bank 2013) 43–44.

[208] Krukowska (n 198).

[209] Directive 2003/87/EC (n 46) arts 9 and 10.

[210] See eg Directive 2003/87/EC (n 46) art 29a. The EU only included a tool to make adjustments to lower the price in the event of excessively *high* price fluctuations.

[211] See eg *William Nagel v Czech Republic (Award)* (Stockholm Chamber of Commerce, No 049/2002, 9 September 2003) [164]; *International Thunderbird Gaming Corporation v Mexico (Award)* (Ad hoc arbitration, UNCITRAL Rules, 26 January 2006) [30].

[212] European Commission, *Report from the Commission to the European Parliament and the Council: The state of the European carbon market in 2012* (n 199) 6, 9–11.

[213] DCCEE (n 36); Clean Energy Act (n 35) s 121.

[214] Bloomberg (n 40) 7.

Both measures would appear to infringe investment rules on performance requirements. In respect of the TRIMs Agreement, the Australian rule required the use by an enterprise of products of domestic origin to discharge their liabilities under its emissions trading scheme, and the Korean rule required similarly requires the use of domestic products 'in terms of volume' proportionate to international equivalents. These would be relatively straightforward violations of the TRIMs Agreement. In respect of the performance requirements ordinarily contained in more recent IIAs, the Australian rule required covered entities to achieve a given percentage of domestic content in the discharge of its liabilities, and thus the use and disposition of its investments, through surrendering carbon units for compliance. Although it operates differently by relating the volume of domestic offset units that must be used to the volume of international offset units that are used, the Korean rule also reportedly requires a that a given level of domestic content be achieved in relative terms. Thus, despite that they may be designed to adhere to the principle of 'supplementarity' or to ensure that abatement occurs domestically, these rules may nonetheless represent relatively straightforward violations of the performance requirements common to more recent IIAs, including those of a number to which Australia and Korea are party.[215]

The foregoing demonstrates that, to the extent holdings of carbon units constitute investments, governmental measures that significantly affect their value or use, or that impose local content requirements, may engage disciplines under international investment law. The forms of government intervention that may affect the value of carbon units are innumerate, and whether they rise to the level of a breach of expropriation or fair and equitable treatment provisions is largely context dependent. In general terms, bona fide actions that are proportionate to pursue a legitimate public objective will be less likely to give rise to a breach. By contrast, actions that are unanticipated or inconsistent with governmental representations at the time an investment is made, which involve a degree of capriciousness or unreasonableness, and which lack due process, will be more likely to constitute an indirect expropriation or a violation of fair and equitable treatment.

[215] See eg Australia–United States Free Trade Agreement, signed 18 May 2004 [2005] ATS 1 (entered into force 1 January 2005) art 11.9; Free Trade Agreement between the Republic of Korea and the Republic of Peru, signed 14 November 2010 (entered into force 1 August 2011) art 11.9; TRIMs Agreement art 2.

9

Exceptions

This chapter provides an overview of the availability and applicability of exceptions that could potentially save aspects of emissions trading schemes that otherwise violate international economic law. Drawing on the justifications set out in respect of those impugned aspects of emissions trading schemes in Chapter 8, this chapter explains which of those justifications might be permissible under international economic law, and the kind of evidence that would be required to make out a successful defence.

This chapter begins with an overview of the three broad kinds of justifications for violations that were surveyed in Chapter 8. It then assesses the availability and applicability of the primary exceptions contained in Article XX of General Agreement on Tariffs and Trade 1994 (GATT 1994)[1] and Article XIV of the General Agreement on Trade in Services (GATS).[2] Finally, it assesses the availability and applicability of other ad hoc exceptions under international economic law. These ad hoc exceptions might be particularly relevant to justifications based on objectives and considerations unrelated to the reduction of greenhouse gas emissions, such as transferring finance and technology to Least Developed Countries (LDCs), discouraging the

[1] Marrakesh Agreement Establishing the World Trade Organization (opened for signature 15 April 1994, entered into force 1 January 1995) 1867 UNTS 3 annex IA (General Agreement on Tariffs and Trade) (GATT 1994).

[2] Marrakesh Agreement Establishing the World Trade Organization (n 1) annex IB (General Agreement on Trade in Services) (GATS).

development of nuclear energy, prudential regulation of financial markets, or avoiding the negative socio-economic impacts of large-scale hydro.

This chapter finds that justifications that are rationally connected to the goal of mitigating climate change or safeguarding financial markets, and which deploy the least trade-restrictive means possible, could form the basis of a defence in many instances. However, justifications that are grounded in other economic or social policy goals, or for which there is a less trade-restrictive means of achieving that end, will be less likely to save a measure that is otherwise a violation of international economic law.

A Overview of the Justifications for Prima Facie Violations

Before considering which exceptions might apply under international economic law, it is useful to recall and distil the principal justifications provided for the prima facie violations set out in Chapter 8. These purported justifications fall into three groups.

One set of violations is justified, in broad terms, on the grounds of ensuring the environmental integrity of the emissions trading scheme in question. In other words, the particular aspects of the relevant scheme that infringe international economic norms are intended to safeguard or enhance the ability of the scheme to mitigate climate change by reducing greenhouse gas emissions.

For instance, the European Union (EU) and New Zealand emissions trading schemes refuse to recognize offset units generated from the destruction of hydrofluorocarbon-23 or the destruction of nitrous oxide (N2O) resulting from the production of adipic acid out of doubts over whether the units genuinely represent one tonne of avoided greenhouse gas.[3] As another example, the EU emissions trading scheme bars offset units from 'land use, land use change and forestry activities' out of concerns over the measurement and verification of those activities and whether they represent actual, precise recordings of emissions reductions.[4]

Another set of violations are justified on the grounds of ensuring that emissions reductions occur within the jurisdiction of the emissions trading scheme concerned, or within particular sectors in that jurisdiction. This is in order to ensure that a minimum degree of investment promoting less carbon-intensive economic activity is made *within* that jurisdiction, thereby prompting the necessary structural changes to enable a transition to a low-carbon economy. This justification flows from the perspective that achieving a low-carbon economy is a long-term process of structural change, and that it is difficult to commit to progressively ambitious and deep emissions reductions over time without such structural change.[5] For some, this justification could also conceivably flow from the principle of 'supplementarity',[6] which posits the outsourcing of actual emissions reductions to other jurisdictions

[3] See ch 8A(2)(b)(ii). [4] ibid. [5] See ch 8A(2)(a).
[6] See ch 2A and ch 82(a).

as unethical, requiring emissions reductions to occur principally within one's own jurisdiction.

For instance, the EU, Swiss, Korean, and the now-repealed Australian emissions trading schemes impose quantitative restrictions on the amount of international offset units that may be used for compliance.[7]

A further set of violations are justified on grounds unconnected to the reduction of greenhouse gas emissions by an emissions trading scheme, but based on other public policy concerns. These include concerns over the ecological, social, and human rights impacts of emissions reduction activities, as well as concerns to avoid promoting nuclear energy or to stimulate technological and financial transfers to LDCs. While these kinds of concerns are not connected to emissions reductions per se, they could potentially be framed as part of addressing climate change more generally. This is because the international climate regime acknowledges that:[8]

> [Since] climate change is a common concern of humankind, Parties should, when taking action to address climate change, respect, promote and consider their respective obligations on human rights, the right to health, the rights of indigenous peoples, local communities, migrants, children, persons with disabilities and people in vulnerable situations and the right to development, as well as gender equality, empowerment of women and intergenerational equity ...

The international climate regime also notes the 'importance of ensuring the integrity of all ecosystems, including oceans, and the protection of biodiversity ... and noting the importance for some of the concept of "climate justice", when taking action to address climate change', and recognizes 'the intrinsic relationship between climate change, poverty eradication and equitable access to sustainable development'.[9] Thus, at a high level of abstraction, violations that are justified on the basis of matters such as human rights, indigenous rights, poverty eradication, or sustainable development could be linked to addressing climate change in a general sense.

B Exceptions under Article XX of GATT 1994 and Article XIV of GATS

The exceptions that might save the prima facie violations surveyed in Chapter 8 are primarily contained in Article XX of GATT 1994 to the extent that carbon units are 'goods'/'products', and in Article XIV of GATS to the extent that the activity underlying offset units constitutes a 'service'.[10] These provisions have the same structure and use similar terminology, and are therefore discussed in tandem in this section.

[7] See above ch 7B.2(a).

[8] Paris Agreement (opened for signature 22 April 2016, entered into force 4 November 2016) preambular recital 11.

[9] ibid preambular recitals 8 and 13.

[10] These same provisions are replicated in free trade agreements covering goods and services. See eg Australia–United States Free Trade Agreement (Australia–United States) (signed 18 May 2004, entered into force 1 January 2005) [2005] ATS 1, art 22; Free Trade Agreement between the European Union and its Member States, of the one part, and the Republic of Korea, of the other part (EU–Korea) (signed

Other ad hoc exceptions for 'goods'/'products', as well as exceptions for 'investments' and 'financial services', are discussed below in section C.

Article XX of GATT 1994 and Article XIV of GATS introduce the matters that may justify prima facie violations with the following chapeau:

> Subject to the requirement that such *measures* are not applied in a manner which would constitute a means of arbitrary or unjustifiable discrimination between countries where the same conditions prevail, or a disguised restriction on international trade, *nothing in this Agreement shall be construed to prevent the adoption or enforcement by any contracting party of measures*: ...[11]

It is clear from this chapeau that the focus of the analysis under Article XX of GATT 1994 and Article XIV of GATS is on certain 'measures'. According to the Appellate Body in *EC—Seal Products*, the 'measures' to be analysed are not limited in a narrow sense to the specific aspects or elements of a law or policy that give rise to the violation in question. Rather, what must be justified are both the prohibitive and permissive components of the law or policy that, when taken together and when compared with one another, lead to a finding of inconsistency.[12] In practical terms, most aspects of emissions trading schemes necessarily affect trade in carbon units, because the very purpose and function of these schemes is to facilitate and administer such trade. It is the 'combined operation' of measures affecting trade in carbon units in emissions trading schemes—the prohibitive or trade-restrictive aspects vis-à-vis the permissive aspects—that gives rise to the prima facie violations surveyed in Chapter 8.[13] Therefore, emissions trading schemes as a 'combined operation'[14]—rather than the 'precise aspects' of a scheme that give rise to a particular violation[15]—would likely be the subject for analysis as the relevant 'measure' to be justified under these exceptions.

This is an important threshold matter, because it informs the first step of a two-tiered test for determining whether a prima facie violation can be saved by Article XX of GATT 1994 and Article XIV of GATS. This first step involves assessing whether the measure can be provisionally justified under one of the sub-paragraphs of Article XX of GATT 1994 or Article XIV of GATS.[16] The second step involves an appraisal of the measure under the introductory chapeau, extracted above, of those respective provisions. Each step is discussed in turn.

6 October 2010, entered into force June 2010) arts 2.15 and 7.50; Free Trade Agreement between the Government of the People's Republic of China and the Government of the Republic of Chile (China–Chile) (signed 18 November 2005, entered into force 1 October 2006) art 99; Free Trade Agreement Between Canada and the Republic of Peru (Canada–Peru) (signed 29 May 2008, entered into force 1 August 2009) art 2201.

[11] Italics and underlining added.

[12] Appellate Body Reports, *EC—Seal Products* [5.186]–[5.190] and [5.193].

[13] ibid [5.188]–[5.189]. [14] ibid.

[15] ibid [5.94] and [5.190]. Unless, of course, the respondent frames the 'measure' to be justified more narrowly as the particular infringing aspect in question—see eg Appellate Body Report, *India—Solar Cells* [5.126]. By contrast the respondent may frame the measure to be justified more broadly—see eg Panel Reports, *Indonesia—Import Licensing Regimes* [7.503].

[16] Appellate Body Reports, *EC—Seal Products* [5.169]. See also Appellate Body Reports, *US—Gasoline* 22; and *US—Shrimp* [119] and [120]; *US—Gambling* [292].

1 Step 1: Provisional justification

The Appellate Body has stated that, under the first step of the analysis of Article XX of GATT 1994 and Article XIV of GATS, the provisional justification of a measure under one of their sub-paragraphs requires that a challenged measure 'address the particular interest specified in that paragraph' and that 'there be a sufficient nexus between the measure and the interest protected'.[17]

With respect to emissions trading schemes in particular, Article XX of GATT 1994 and Article XIV of GATS include three sub-paragraphs that are potentially applicable:

(a) necessary to protect public morals;[18]

(b) necessary to protect human, animal or plant life or health;

...

(d) necessary to secure compliance with laws or regulations which are not inconsistent with the provisions of this Agreement ...[19]

Article XX of GATT 1994 includes an additional relevant sub-paragraph that is not available under Article XIV of GATS:

(g) relating to the conservation of exhaustible natural resources if such measures are made effective in conjunction with restrictions on domestic production or consumption;

Thus, as an initial matter, a respondent invoking Article XX of GATT 1994 or Article XIV of GATS would need to demonstrate that the measure at issue—namely, its emissions trading scheme—is adopted or enforced to: (i) 'protect public morals'; (ii) 'protect human, animal or plant life or health'; (iii) 'to secure compliance with laws or regulations which are not inconsistent with the provisions of [GATT 1994 or GATS]'; or (vi) 'the conservation of exhaustible natural resources'. This requires an assessment of the objective or objectives of the emissions trading scheme in question. Although such an assessment takes into account a respondent's articulation of the objective or the objectives that it seeks to pursue through its emissions trading scheme (through written or oral submissions in the case), such characterizations are by no means binding.[20] Rather, account must be taken of all evidence put before a panel, including 'the texts of statutes, legislative history, and other evidence regarding the structure and operation' of the emissions trading scheme in question.[21]

[17] Appellate Body Reports, *EC—Seal Products* [5.169]; *US—Gambling* [292].

[18] Article XIV(a) of GATS includes, in addition to 'public morals', measures necessary to 'maintain public order'. According to footnote 5 of GATS, the public order exception may be invoked only where a genuine and sufficiently serious threat is posed to one of the fundamental interests of society.

[19] The equivalent sub-paragraph in GATS is sub-paragraph (c). For ease of reference, sub-paragraph (d) of Article XX of GATT 1994 should be taken to also refer to sub-paragraph (c) of Article XIV of GATS.

[20] Appellate Body Reports, *EC—Seal Products* [5.144]; *US—Tuna II (Mexico)* [314] (referring to Appellate Body Report, *US—Gambling* [304]).

[21] Appellate Body Reports, *EC—Seal Products* [5.144]; *US—Tuna II (Mexico)* [314].

This is important because, if a prima facie violation cannot be justified on the basis of safeguarding or enhancing the ability of an emissions trading scheme to reduce greenhouse gas emissions, a respondent may seek to frame the objective of the scheme as an instrument to address climate change more generally. This broader framing of the objective could potentially encompass the facets of climate change that are not clearly connected to reducing greenhouse gas in particular, such as human rights, gender equality, the integrity of ecosystems, sustainable development, and poverty eradication.

A respondent would need to demonstrate the objective of its emissions trading scheme on the basis of evidence such as the text of relevant legislation, and the structure and operation of the scheme. A review of the legislative instruments of a number of schemes reveals a relatively narrow framing of their objectives. The EU scheme states that: '[t]his Directive establishes a scheme for greenhouse gas emission allowance trading within the Community ... *in order to promote reductions of greenhouse gas emissions*'.[22] The Californian scheme states that: '[t]he purpose of this article is to *reduce emissions of greenhouse gases* associated with entities identified in this article through the establishment, administration, and enforcement of the California Greenhouse Gas Cap-and-Trade Program'.[23] The Quebecois scheme states that: '[a] cap-and-trade system is established by this subdivision to contribute to the achievement of the [overall greenhouse gas reduction target] and mitigate the cost of *reducing or limiting greenhouse gas emissions*'.[24] The New Zealand scheme states that its purpose is to 'provide for the implementation, operation, and administration of a greenhouse gas emissions trading scheme in New Zealand that *supports and encourages global efforts to reduce greenhouse gas emissions* by assisting New Zealand to meet its international obligations'.[25] The Swiss scheme states that: '[t]his Act is intended to *reduce greenhouse gas emissions* and in particular CO_2 emissions'.[26]

Thus, on the simple face of these legislative instruments, it may be difficult for a respondent to make the case that its objective is broader than, or different to, reducing greenhouse gas emissions.

Of course, the legislative instrument setting out a given scheme could frame its objective more broadly than these examples, in which case it might be possible to argue that the objective encompasses other elements of climate change. Such elements could include climate adaptation, and transfers of finance and technology to developing countries to assist in addressing climate change, as well as sustainable development more generally, which in turn concerns such diverse interests as respect for human rights, indigenous communities, poverty eradication, and ecological integrity. As discussed earlier, these kinds of objectives are recognized by the Paris Agreement as part of a country's obligations in addressing climate change, and could

[22] Directive 2003/87/EC of the European Parliament and of the Council of 13 October 2003 establishing a scheme for greenhouse gas emission allowance trading within the Community and amending Council Directive 96/61/EC [2003] OJ L275/32, art 1 (emphasis added).

[23] California Cap on Greenhouse Gas Emissions and Market-based Compliance Mechanisms 17 Cal Public Health Code § 95801 (emphasis added).

[24] Environment Quality Act (Quebec) s 46.5 (emphasis added).

[25] Climate Response Act 2002 (NZ) s 3.1(b) (emphasis added).

[26] Federal Act on the Reduction of CO_2 Emissions (Switzerland) art 1 (emphasis added).

therefore potentially inform the construction of the objective of domestic emissions trading schemes—especially where these are a country's principal mechanism for addressing climate change. Indeed, recent case law suggests that a given measure can have multiple parallel objectives.[27] However, the mere accommodation of a particular interest or value in a given legislative scheme does not necessarily mean that it rises to the level of an 'objective' of that scheme, particularly if it is somewhat peripheral or tangential to its 'principal objective'.[28] For instance, in *EC—Seal Products*, although the interests of indigenous communities were accommodated in the measure at issue, they did not 'form independent policy objectives of the EU Seal Regime as a whole', whose 'principal objective' was instead to 'address the public concerns on seal welfare'.[29]

Having ascertained the objective of the emissions trading scheme in question—either as an instrument to reduce greenhouse gas emissions, or as an instrument to address climate change-related matters more generally–it would next need to be determined whether this objective addresses one of the matters in the sub-paragraphs of Article XX of GATT 1994 and Article XIV of GATS.

In respect of sub-paragraph (b) of Article XX of GATT 1994 and Article XIV of GATS—namely, measures 'necessary to protect human, animal or plant life or health'—the Appellate Body has recognized that 'measures adopted in order to attenuate global warming and climate change' could fall within its scope.[30] In respect of sub-paragraph (g) of Article XX, the Appellate Body has recognized that it encompasses 'clean air' as an 'exhaustible natural resource', and thus it too, by extension, covers measures to reduce emissions of air pollutants such as greenhouse gases.[31] Accordingly, both sub-paragraphs would cover emissions trading schemes with the objective of reducing greenhouse gas emissions (or, of addressing climate change more broadly).

In respect of sub-paragraph (a) of Article XX of GATT 1994 and Article XIV of GATS, there have been some efforts to frame mitigating climate change as a 'moral challenge' or ethical issue.[32] Indeed, the international climate regime itself incorporates a number of ethical components, such as equity and historical responsibility.[33] Further, WTO jurisprudence suggests that Members have considerable scope to define and apply for themselves the concept of public morals according to their own systems and scales of values.[34] Framing emissions trading schemes as a means to protect public morals could have the advantage of potentially encompassing value-laden considerations such as human rights and biodiversity concerns, which form the basis of some prima facie violations. However, a respondent would need to *prove*

[27] See eg Appellate Body Report, *US—Tuna II (Mexico)* [303]; Appellate Body Reports, *EC—Seal Products* [5.167] and [5.320].

[28] Appellate Body Report, *EC—Seal Products* [5.167].

[29] ibid [5.145]–[5.147].

[30] Appellate Body Report, *Brazil—Retreaded Tyres* [151].

[31] Appellate Body Report, *US—Gasoline* 14–19.

[32] See eg UNFCCC Newsroom, 'Religious Leaders Call for Effective Paris Agreement: Joint Statement Handed to Christiana Figueres in Bonn' (Media Release, 20 October 2015); Sean Kelly, 'The greatest moral challenge of our time?' *The Monthly* (19 June 2015).

[33] See above ch 2A.

[34] Appellate Body Report, *EC—Seal Products* [5.199]; Panel Report, *US—Gambling* [6.461].

this characterization of the objective of its emissions trading scheme, and certainly from the legislative instruments surveyed above, there is no indication that this is, in fact, the purpose of such schemes.

Finally, in respect of sub-paragraphs (d) of Article XX of GATT 1994 and (c) Article XIV of GATS, a respondent could argue that the impugned aspects of its emissions trading scheme are necessary to ensure compliance with laws or regulations that are not otherwise inconsistent with GATT 1994 or GATS.

In order to ground such a defence, the impugned aspects of the emissions trading scheme, such as a qualitative or quantitative restriction, would need to 'secure compliance' with the 'laws or regulations' comprising the scheme in question. This has been interpreted as meaning 'to *enforce* compliance' and 'seek[ing] to secure observance of specific rules'.[35] Whether the overall objective of an emissions trading scheme to reduce greenhouse gas emissions by a certain quantum—as reflected in the laws and regulations establishing the scheme—would be a sufficient 'law or regulation' with which an impugned aspect seeks to secure compliance remains unclear based on existing WTO jurisprudence. Instead, it may be the case that the impugned aspect would need to secure compliance with a more *specific* or *technical* element of the scheme. In other words, the degree of generality of the 'laws or regulations' for the purposes of Article XX(d) of GATT 1994 and Article XIV(c) of GATS is an unsettled area of law.

According to the Appellate Body's somewhat opaque guidance in that respect, 'the "more precisely" a respondent is able to identify specific rules, obligations, or requirements contained in the relevant "laws or regulations", the "more likely" it will be able to elucidate how and why the inconsistent measure secures compliance with such "laws or regulations"'.[36] For instance, in *India – Solar Cells*, India argued that the rule with which its impugned measures sought to secure compliance comprised 'ensur[ing] ecologically sustainable growth while addressing India's energy security challenge, and ensuring compliance with its obligations relating to climate change'.[37] The Appellate Body, however, considered that the relevant instruments did not reflect 'a sufficient degree of normativity and specificity' to establish a 'rule' as such—instead they were 'hortatory, aspirational, declaratory'.[38] The upshot seems to be that a vague objective such as 'addressing climate change' is insufficiently precise to establish a 'rule' with which a deviation from WTO law is permitted to secure compliance.[39] On the other hand, the overall objective of an emissions trading scheme to reduce greenhouse gas by a defined quantum is more specific, certain, and prescriptive than addressing climate change generally (in contrast to *India—Solar Cells*).

[35] Appellate Body Report, *India—Solar Cells* [5.108] (emphasis original).

[36] ibid [5.110]. [37] ibid [5.126]. [38] ibid [5.133].

[39] In *Argentina—Financial Services*, the Appellate Body appeared to consider that compliance with a law's 'objective' is insufficient for the purposes of this test, and instead compliance must be 'with specific rules, obligations, or requirements under such laws or regulations' (see Appellate Body Report, *Argentina—Financial Services* [6.203], [6.206], [6.210]). However, the Appellate Body indicated some role for overall objectives: 'the objectives of, or the common interests or values protected by, the relevant law or regulation may assist in elucidating the content of specific rules, obligations, or requirements in such law or regulation' (ibid, fn 495).

In any case, neither the objective of an emissions trading scheme (namely, to reduce greenhouse gas emissions) nor its more specific mechanisms for achieving the objective (namely, operating a transferable permit scheme) are inherently or 'otherwise' inconsistent with WTO law. On the contrary, the design and effectiveness of emissions trading schemes is premised on principles of non-discrimination, cost-effectiveness, and seeking the most efficient allocation of resources that similarly underpin the international economic regime.[40] Thus, the obscurity in WTO jurisprudence concerning the degree of specificity required of the 'law or regulation' in question may not ultimately matter in the context of emissions trading schemes—regardless of the level of generality at which they are framed, the 'laws or regulations' in question would be unlikely to be 'otherwise inconsistent' with WTO law.

In terms of the 'securing compliance' aspects of Article XX(d) of GATT 1994 and Article XIV(c) of GATS, it is clear that there are legitimate bases for intervening in the carbon market to secure compliance with its overall objective and practical operation. Lockie identifies a number of foreseeable and legitimate bases for laws enabling a regulator or government to intervene in carbon markets to ensure their integrity and compliance with their environmental objective, including: (i) gaming and arbitrage of markets; (ii) theft and fraud; (iii) the potential for excessive speculation by financial institutions; (iv) gaming behaviour incentivized by unfettered ownership of carbon units; and (v) the potential for monetizing carbon sequestration to not lead to emissions reductions.[41] Lockie argues persuasively that 'the essence of a fair and orderly market is that no participant in the market has an advantage and the market is free of gaming as well as theft, fraud, manipulation and excessive speculation', and that the kinds of risks identified justify the prudential regulation of the market by the government or regulator concerned.[42] Essentially, the involvement of participants in emissions trading schemes that are *not* required to acquit their own emissions with carbon units divorces their participation from the environmental objective of the scheme, thus creating potential for activities that subvert its objective. Thus, in order to secure compliance with the objective and practical operation of emissions trading schemes, certain measures or interventions might be required. It may also be the case that interventions are necessary to ensure a sufficiently stable and strong price to incentivize investment in less carbon-intensive means of production, and thus to ensure the scheme functions as intended. This could involve, for instance, restricting certain sources of carbon units with volatile prices, or sources which produce units at prices or volumes that undermine the

[40] Daniel Cole, 'Origins of emissions trading in theory and early practice' in Stefan Weishaar (ed), *Research Handbook on Emissions Trading* (2016) 12–13. See also Robyn Eckersley, 'Understanding the Interplay between the Climate and Trade Regimes' in Benjamin Simmons, Harro van Asselt, and Fariborz Zelli (eds), *Climate and Trade Policies in a Post-2012 World* (UNEP 2009) 1, 12.

[41] Damien Lockie, 'Closing Pandora's Box: The Case for Carbon Market Integrity after the Global Financial Crisis—Conditioning Ownership of the Right to Emit Greenhouse Gases in an Australian Emissions Trading Scheme' (PhD Thesis, Bond University 2011) 154.

[42] ibid 186–220.

scheme.[43] These considerations are, of course, subject to the additional 'necessity' test that will now be discussed.[44]

As an additional step, the provisional justification of measures under sub-paragraphs (a), (b), and (d) of GATT 1994 and GATS requires an assessment of whether those measures are 'necessary'. Similarly, the provisional justification of measures under sub-paragraph (g) of GATT 1994 requires an assessment of whether those measures 'relat[e] to' the conservation of natural resources.

The requirement of 'necessity' is manifestly more onerous that that of 'relating to'.[45] This is because, whereas the former requires the emissions trading scheme be the least trade-restrictive means of achieving its objective,[46] the latter simply requires that the measure be 'primarily aimed at' the conservation of clean air.[47] This means that the identification of a less trade restrictive alternative to the impugned emissions trading scheme would render the potential exceptions under sub-paragraphs (a), (b), and (d) inapplicable, whereas sub-paragraph (g) of Article XX would nonetheless apply as long as the emissions trading scheme is 'primarily aimed at' the conservation of clean air.[48]

Importantly, however, and as mentioned above, the less onerous exception under sub-paragraph (g) of Article XX of GATT 1994 is not available under GATS, and thus cannot save measures affecting offset units as services. Therefore, for prima facie violations of GATS, the emissions trading scheme in question would need to be the least trade restrictive means of achieving its objective in order to be provisionally justified under one of the sub-paragraphs of Article XIV of GATS.

The framing of the objective of an emissions trading scheme could become particularly relevant in applying the 'least trade restrictive means' test. If its objective is found to be limited to the reduction of greenhouse gas emissions—which appears to be the principal objective from the legislative instruments surveyed above—then the particular aspect of the scheme that violates GATS or GATT 1994 must contribute in some way to the reduction of greenhouse gas emissions in order to satisfy the 'necessity' test. This is because, if that particular aspect does *not* contribute to the reduction of greenhouse gas emissions, a complainant challenging that particular aspect of the scheme can simply propose the emissions trading scheme *without* that aspect as a reasonably available and less trade-restrictive alternative that contributes to the scheme's objective to the same degree.

If, however, a respondent can establish that the objective of the scheme is broader—for instance, as a measure to address climate change more generally, or to

[43] See eg New Zealand Government, *New Zealand Emissions Trading Scheme Review 2015/16* (Ministry for the Environment, November 2015) 8–9 and 21.

[44] See Appellate Body Report, *Thailand—Cigarettes (Philippines)* [174]–[181]

[45] Appellate Body Reports, *US—Gasoline* 18–19; *China—Rare Earths* [5.87].

[46] See eg Appellate Body Reports, *US—Gambling* [307]; *Korea—Various Measures on Beef* [166]; *US—Tuna II (Mexico)* [321]; *US—COOL (Article 21.5—Canada and Mexico)* [5 213]–[5.214].

[47] Appellate Body Reports, *US—Gasoline* 18–19; *China—Rare Earths* [357]–[358].

[48] The fact that the sub-paragraph (g) includes that requirement that the measures be made 'effective in conjunction with restrictions on domestic production or consumption' presents no obstacle in respect of emissions trading schemes, since emissions trading schemes satisfy this requirement by default through imposing a quantum on the domestic emission of greenhouse gas.

protect public morals—it may be more difficult for a WTO Member challenging the scheme to propose a less trade-restrictive alternative that is reasonably available. This is because objectives such as addressing climate change generally, or protecting public morals, can be multidimensional and often require a more onerous qualitative assessment of the equivalence of levels of contribution of proposed alternatives.[49]

2 Step 2: The chapeau of Article XX of GATT 1994 and Article XIV of GATS

If a measure can be provisionally justified under one of the sub-paragraphs of Article XX of GATT 1994 or Article XIV of GATS, the second 'tier' of the analysis under those provisions involves assessing conformity with their chapeau. In particular, this involves assessing whether the emissions trading scheme in question is *applied* in a manner which would constitute a means of arbitrary or unjustifiable discrimination between countries where the same conditions prevail, or a disguised restriction on international trade.

The function of the chapeau of Article XX of GATT 1994 and GATS is to prevent the abuse or misuse of a Member's right to invoke the exceptions contained in the sub-paragraphs of those provisions.[50] The Appellate Body has stated that one of the most important factors in the assessment of arbitrary or unjustifiable discrimination or disguised restrictions on international trade in the chapeau is whether the discrimination or restriction can be reconciled with, or is rationally related to, the policy objective with respect to which the measure has been provisionally justified under one of the sub-paragraphs.[51]

In this regard, the precise framing of the objective of emissions trading schemes will, once again, be particularly relevant. If the objective of an emissions trading scheme is principally found to be the reduction of greenhouse gas emissions, then aspects of emissions trading schemes that are not rationally connected to that objective—such as concerns for human rights or biodiversity—will not be likely to survive the chapeau.[52] However, if the objective of an emissions trading scheme is framed more broadly, and the impugned aspects of that scheme are rationally connected to that broader objective, then they are more likely to meet the requirements of the chapeau.

[49] See eg Appellate Body Reports, *US—COOL (Article 21.5—Canada and Mexico)* [5.268]–[5.269], [5.295]–[5.296]; *EC—Seal Products* [5.212]–[5.215], [5.221]–[5.222]; *Brazil—Retreaded Tyres* [145]–[151].

[50] Appellate Body Reports, *EC—Seal Products* [5.297]; *US—Gasoline* 22.

[51] See Appellate Body Reports, *EC—Seal Products* [5.306]; *US—Shrimp* [165]; and *Brazil—Retreaded Tyres* [227]–[228], and [232].

[52] Nevertheless, there does appear to have been a slight softening in recent jurisprudence in respect of the stringency of the required nexus between the impugned aspect of the measure at issue and the objective of that measure—the significance of this has yet to be fully played out. See Tania Voon, James Munro, and Andrew Mitchell, 'Importing WTO General Exceptions into International Investment Agreements: Proportionality, Myths and Risks' *Yearbook on International Investment Law and Policy* (forthcoming, OUP 2018).

In assessing whether certain aspects of an emissions trading scheme are 'rationally connected' to its objective, the norms and principles of the international climate regime could potentially provide some guidance. For instance, the principle of 'supplementarity' could suggest that measures privileging *domestic* carbon units in order to ensure that a minimum level of domestic emissions reduction are a legitimate and justifiable facet of mitigating climate change.[53] Similarly, the principle of 'taking into account' matters such as human rights, LDCs, and ecological concerns in addressing climate change could suggest that discrimination between carbon units on those bases is not 'arbitrary' or 'unjustifiable'.[54] As another example, the principle of common but differentiated responsibilities could suggest that, even where two countries have differing levels of ambition in their emissions trading schemes, the 'same conditions' nonetheless prevail because the international climate regime recognizes that not all countries are bound to the same level of ambition.

As discussed in Chapter 2, the clearest avenue through which these principles might affect the interpretation of the chapeau would be as evidence of the ordinary meaning of terms such as 'arbitrary', 'justifiable', and 'same conditions'. Alternatively, the reference to 'sustainable development' in the preamble of the Marrakesh Agreement Establishing the World Trade Organization (WTO Agreement)[55] could provide an opening for these principles, since sustainable development is itself described in the international climate regime as being in an 'intrinsic relationship' with addressing climate change.[56] These principles are, however, somewhat abstract in terms of practical application. Their precise meaning in the international climate regime is contested and unsettled, which would likely hinder their utility in the process of interpreting and applying the chapeau.[57] Further, the Appellate Body *rejected* the argument in *Brazil—Retreaded Tyres* that certain discrimination was not 'arbitrary' or 'unjustifiable' because it was mandated under another international agreement.[58] Rather, the Appellate Body in that case focused on whether the discrimination was rationally connected to the objective of the measure at issue, regardless of what was prescribed by the other international agreement in question.[59] In that context, it is unlikely that the principles or commitments in the international climate regime would 'apply' in any direct sense to operation of the chapeau of Article XX of GATT 1994 and Article XIV of GATS.

3 Conclusion: Applicability of exceptions under Article XX of GATT 1994 and Article XIV of GATS

Ultimately, the ability of exceptions under Article XX of GATT 1994 and Article XIV of GATS to save prima facie violations of those agreements will likely turn on the availability of evidence and the allocation of the burden of proof.

[53] See ch 2A. [54] See eg Paris Agreement (n 8) preambular recitals 8, 11, and 13.

[55] Marrakesh Agreement Establishing the World Trade Organization (n 1) (WTO Agreement) premabular recital 1.

[56] Paris Agreement (n 8) preambular recital 8. [57] See ch 2A.

[58] Appellate Body Report, *Brazil—Retreaded Tyres* [224]–[229]. [59] ibid [228].

The general principles applicable to the allocation of the burden of proof in WTO dispute settlement require that a party claiming a violation of a provision of the WTO Agreement must assert and prove its claim.[60] It is generally for the party asserting a fact to provide proof for its assertions.[61] However, the Appellate Body has stated that the burden of proof in respect of a particular provision cannot be understood in isolation from the overarching logic of that provision and the function that it is designed to serve.[62] In respect of Article XX of GATT 1994 and Article XIV of GATS, their nature as defences or exceptions means that a respondent bears, at first instance, the burden of demonstrating that its emissions trading scheme can be provisionally justified under one of the sub-paragraphs of those provisions. The Appellate Body has stated that a party will satisfy its burden when it establishes a prima facie case, namely, a case that, in the absence of effective refutation by the other party, requires a panel, as a matter of law, to rule in favour of the former party.[63] The nature and degree of evidence required for a party to establish its assertion necessarily varies from measure to measure and from case to case.[64]

If a respondent can establish a prima facie case that its emissions trading scheme is provisionally justified under one of the sub-paragraphs, the complainant would bear the burden of refuting that case by identifying, for instance, that there is a less trade-restrictive alternative means of contributing to the scheme's objective under sub-paragraphs (a), (b), and (d). As mentioned above, if the objective of an emissions trading scheme is to reduce greenhouse gas, and if the impugned aspect of the scheme does not contribute to that objective, a complainant could simply submit the emissions trading scheme *without* that impugned aspect as a less trade-restrictive alternative. The complainant would, however, bear the burden at that stage of proving that the impugned aspect does not, in fact, contribute to the scheme's objective. The burden would then shift to the respondent to rebut this assertion.[65]

Assuming that an emissions trading scheme is found to be provisionally justified under one of the sub-paragraphs, the burden would be on the respondent to make the prima facie case that the scheme is not applied in a manner inconsistent with the chapeau of Article XX of GATT 1994 and Article XIV of GATS. In practical terms, this would require the submission of evidence to demonstrate that the impugned aspect of its scheme is indeed rationally connected to the objective of the scheme, and that this aspect does not represent arbitrary or unjustifiable discrimination, or a disguised restriction on international trade. It would then be for a complainant to rebut this with sufficient argumentation and evidence.

The corollary of this is that, for impugned aspects of emissions trading that are designed to safeguard or enhance the objective of reducing greenhouse gas emissions, a respondent would need sufficient evidence to demonstrate that those aspects do indeed contribute to that objective, or are at least rationally connected to it. Such

[60] Appellate Body Report, *US—Wool Shirts and Blouses* 14. [61] ibid.

[62] Appellate Body Report, *US—Clove Cigarettes* [286].

[63] Appellate Body Report, *EC—Hormones* [104].

[64] See Appellate Body Report, *Chile—Price Band System (Article 21.5—Argentina)* [134] (referring to Appellate Body Reports, *US—Wool Shirts and Blouses* 14; and *US—Carbon Steel* [157]).

[65] Appellate Body Reports, *US—COOL (Article 21.5—Canada and Mexico)* [5.327].

evidence would be needed at two stages of the test: (i) to rebut an argument by the complainant that the same emissions trading scheme without those aspects would qualify as a less trade-restrictive alternative; and (ii) to demonstrate that, for the purposes of the chapeau, those aspects of the emissions trading scheme are 'rationally connected' to the objective of reducing greenhouse gas emissions.

The existence or sufficiency of such evidence is by no means certain. For instance, whereas the EU emissions trading scheme bars offset units generated from forestry or land-use related activities due to uncertainties over the environmental integrity of such units (ie whether those units genuinely represent one tonne of permanent reductions), the Californian, Australian, and New Zealand schemes all consider the environmental integrity of such units sufficiently capable of certainty.[66] As another example, whereas the now-repealed Australian scheme and the Korean scheme impose domestic content requirements on carbon units in order to ensure that abatement will occur domestically, the New Zealand scheme operated (at least initially) on the basis that such requirements are unnecessary to ensure domestic abatement, and an Australian Government document recommended the same. Further, a number of jurisdictions have justified qualitative restrictions on the use of offset units generated from the destruction of hydrofluorocarbon-23 or nitrous oxide (N_2O) out of a concern that those offset units did not necessarily represent any real or meaningful reductions in greenhouse gas emissions. However, those particular offset units are audited, monitored, and authorized through the Clean Development Mechanism (CDM) of the Kyoto Protocol. This is important, because the same jurisdictions that ban these units nonetheless permit the use of other classes of offset units automatically *for the very reason* that they are audited, monitored, and authorized through the CDM.[67]

For impugned aspects of emissions trading that are not specifically connected to the objective of reducing greenhouse gas emissions, a respondent would need sufficient evidence to demonstrate that the objective of the scheme itself is broad enough to encompass those aspects. Again, this evidence would be needed at two junctures for sub-paragraphs (a), (b), and (d). First, it would be needed to establish that its particular framing of the objective and the provisional justification of that framing under those sub-paragraphs. Secondly, it would be needed to show that the impugned aspect of the scheme is 'rationally connected' under the chapeau to this particular framing of the objective. For sub-paragraph (g) of GATT 1994, such evidence would only be required at this latter stage.

As surveyed above, the existing major emissions trading schemes themselves describe their objective as reducing greenhouse gas emissions. They are not described in more general terms as instruments to address climate change in all of its manifold permutations, or to address moral or ethical concerns about the environment and equitable modes of development. This diminishes the evidentiary basis for a respondent claiming that its emissions trading scheme is indeed directed at something broader than, or different to, reducing greenhouse gas emissions. As mentioned

[66] See ch 8 for further detail on these examples.

[67] See above ch 8.

above, according to WTO jurisprudence, this evidentiary basis would need to be primarily founded on 'the texts of statutes, legislative history, and other evidence regarding the structure and operation' of the emissions trading scheme in question.[68]

However, even if an impugned aspect of an emissions trading scheme cannot be justified under Article XX of GATT 1994 or Article XIV of GATS, it may nonetheless be permissible under another ad hoc exception in international economic law.

C Other Exceptions in International Economic Law

Beyond Article XX of GATT 1994 and Article XIV of GATS, a number of subject matter-specific exceptions in international economic law might save prima facie violations.

First, to the extent that trade in carbon units qualifies as a 'financial service', the GATS *Annex on Financial Services* contains an additional exception. In particular, it permits measures 'for prudential reasons, including . . . to ensure the integrity and stability of the financial system', with the good faith qualification that '[w]here such measures do not conform with the provisions of the Agreement, they shall not be used as a means of avoiding the Member's commitments or obligations under the Agreement'.[69] This exception could be invoked to the extent that otherwise impugned aspects of emissions trading schemes are designed to protect the integrity and stability of its market in carbon units. For instance, the now-repealed Australian emissions trading scheme justified recognizing the allowance units of the EU on the basis that this would improve liquidity in the market and mitigate the potential for price volatility.[70] As another example, the EU cited the risk of a flood of low-priced units undermining the integrity of its market as one reason for refusing to permit offset units generated from 'land use, land use change and forestry' for compliance with its emissions trading scheme.[71]

This exception is particularly salient insofar as emissions trading schemes are *artificial* markets in financial assets where demand and supply are not set 'naturally' by the market, but are instead heavily influenced by governmental policy settings. Protective measures such as price collars and quantitative restrictions could be viewed through the prism of ensuring stability and certainty in the market, in order to stimulate and protect long-term investments in low-carbon transitions and technology based on a particular anticipated price range for carbon units. Such measures would, however, need to be rationally related to the stability and integrity of the

[68] Appellate Body Reports, *EC—Seal Products* [5.144]; *US—Tuna II (Mexico)* [314].

[69] GATS (n 2) Annex on Financial Services art 2(a). See also Panel Report, *Argentina—Financial Services* [7.821].

[70] See eg European Commission, 'FAQ: Linking the Australian and European Union emissions trading systems' (Memo, 12/631, 28 August 2012). See also New Zealand Government, *The Framework for a New Zealand Emissions Trading Scheme* (2007) 42.

[71] Peter Kruikman and others, *Policy options for including LULUCF in the EU reduction commitment and policy instruments for increasing GHG mitigation efforts in the LULUCF and agriculture sectors: Synthesis Report* (November 2006).

market in carbon units,[72] and would not be able to stem from arbitrary distinctions that privilege domestic financial service suppliers or the financial service suppliers of particular WTO Members.

Relatedly, to the extent that trade in carbon units is regulated as trade in services or financial services, the recognition of external allowance units pursuant to mutual recognition arrangements, such as those between California and Quebec, or the EU and Switzerland, could come within the purview of Article VII of GATS and Article 3 of the Annex on Financial Services. These provisions permit Members to 'recognize prudential measures of any other country in determining how the Members measures relating to financial services shall be applied', and to 'recognize the requirements met, or licenses or certifications granted in a particular country', respectively. In practical terms, these provisions function as an exception to most-favoured-nation treatment under GATS and the Annex on Financial Services, since the obligations shift to one that merely affords 'adequate opportunity for other interested Members to negotiate their accession to such an agreement or arrangement or to negotiate comparable ones with it'.[73]

Secondly, a number of jurisdictions prohibit offset units generated from projects involving nuclear energy.[74] While this prohibition is unrelated to the reduction of greenhouse gas emissions, it could nonetheless be saved by the exception under GATS and GATT 1994 that permits Members to take any action 'it considers necessary for the protection of its essential security interests relating to fissionable materials'.[75] This provision has never been tested by a panel or the Appellate Body. However, jurisprudence of the International Court of Justice suggests that the inclusion of the language 'it considers' renders this provision non-justiciable, due to its invocation being dependent on what a given WTO Member considers to be in its 'essential security interests relating to fissionable materials'.[76] Thus, a WTO Member prohibiting the use of offset units generated from projects involving nuclear energy—which necessarily engages fissionable materials—could argue that it considers such a prohibition to be in its essential security interests.

Thirdly, the EU emissions trading scheme privileges the use of offset units generated in LDCs. Although this is a prima facie breach of most-favoured-nation treatment under GATT 1994 and GATS, it could be exempted through exceptions permitting preferential treatment to the products and services of LDCs. To the extent measures affecting trade in carbon units qualify as measures affecting trade in services or financial services, this exception is effected through a specific

[72] See eg Panel Report, *Argentina—Financial Services* [7.891]. For instance, measures to address the kinds of risks identified by Lockie might fall within the scope of this exception: (i) gaming and arbitrage of markets; (ii) theft and fraud; (iii) the potential for excessive speculation by financial institutions; (iv) gaming behaviour incentivized by unfettered ownership; and (v) the potential for monetising carbon sequestration to not lead to emissions reductions (see Damien Lockie, *Closing Pandora's Box: The Case for Carbon Market Integrity after the Global Financial Crisis—Conditioning Ownership of the Right to Emit Greenhouse Gases in an Australian Emissions Trading Scheme* (PhD Thesis, Bond University, 2011) 154).

[73] See GATS art VII.2 and Annex on Financial Services art 3(b).

[74] See ch 7A.2(b)(i).

[75] See GATT 1994 (n 1) art XXI; GATS (n 2) art XIV bis.

[76] *Military and Paramilitary Activities in and against Nicaragua (Nicaragua v US)* [1986] ICJ Rep 14 [222] and [280]–[282].

waiver agreed to in 2011.[77] However, to the extent that this measure of the EU is also a tacit import ban that constitutes a market access barrier Article XIV of GATS, it would not be saved by exceptions permitting discriminatory treatment in favour of LDCs.[78] Further, to the extent carbon units are 'goods' or 'products', the exception relating to LDCs relates only to tariffs as opposed to obligations on non-discrimination or quantitative restrictions.[79]

It should also be noted that procurements of carbon units by governments (for instance, in order to comply with their commitments under the international climate regime) could be exempt from certain provisions of the covered agreements of the WTO Agreement depending on the context and nature of the purchase, and also whether the Member in question has joined the plurilateral Agreement on Government Procurement. For instance, Article III.8(a) of GATT 1994 exempts government procurement from national treatment to the extent such procurement is for governmental purposes and not with a view to commercial resale or with a view to use in the production of goods for commercial sale. Article XIII of GATS exempts government procurement in the same circumstances from most-favoured-nation treatment, national treatment, and market access commitments.

Aside from these ad hoc exceptions, impugned aspects under emissions trading schemes that are based on justifications unrelated to the reduction of greenhouse gas emissions are unlikely to be saved by exceptions—unless, as discussed above, the objective of emissions trading schemes can be proven to be sufficiently broad to capture those justifications. For instance, the prohibition in the Swiss emissions trading scheme against any offset units that 'would contravene Swiss foreign and development policy', as well as any 'emission reductions were achieved in violation of human rights' or that were 'achieved under conditions that had significant negative social or ecological effects', would be difficult to defend unless they satisfied the legal and evidentiary requirements of Article XX of GATT and Article XIV of GATS.[80]

Further, investment-related rules are not traditionally subject to exceptions.[81] Rather, as discussed in Chapter 8, flexibility for governments or regulators to take public policy measures tends to be built into the core obligations of IIAs themselves. For instance, non-discriminatory public policy measures directed at a legitimate

[77] See World Trade Organization, 'WTO ministers adopt waiver to permit preferential treatment of LDC service suppliers' (Press Release, 17 December 2011).

[78] This is because the LDC services waiver provides exemptions only in respect of most-favoured-nation treatment obligations: see *Preferential Treatment to Services and Service Suppliers of Least-Developed Countries* (Ministerial Decision, WT/L/847, 17 December 2011) art 1.

[79] The Enabling Clause is an integral part of the GATT 1994 because it 'is one of the "other decisions of the CONTRACTING PARTIES" within the meaning of paragraph 1(b)(iv) of the language of Annex 1A incorporating the GATT 1994 into the WTO Agreement' (see Appellate Body Report, *EC—Tariff Preferences* [90] and n 192 thereto).

[80] Ordinance for the Reduction of CO_2 Emissions (2012) (Switzerland) art 4.2(b), annex 2.

[81] See eg Andrew Newcombe and Lluís Paradell, *Law and Practice of Investment Treaties* (Kluwer 2009) 483; Katia Yannaca-Small, 'Indirect Expropriation and the Right to Regulate: How to Draw the Line?' in Katia Yannaca-Small (ed), *Arbitration under International Investment Agreements: A Guide to the Key Issues* (OUP 2010) 445, 470–2; August Reinisch, 'Expropriation' in Peter Muchlinski, Federico Ortino, and Christoph Schreuer (eds), *The Oxford Handbook of International Investment Law* (OUP 2011) 407, 433; cf 437–38.

objective will not ordinarily be found, in the first instance, to constitute an indirect expropriation or a breach of the fair and equitable treatment standard.[82] Nevertheless, a small number of IIAs do contain general exceptions modelled on those contained in GATT 1994 and GATS.[83] Further, performance requirements prohibited under TRIMS are also subject to the general exceptions under GATT 1994, including those 'necessary to protect human, animal and plant life and health'.

D Conclusion

Discriminatory or trade-restrictive aspects of emissions trading schemes can be permissible under international economic law if they are genuinely required to further the environmental objective of those schemes, namely, the mitigation of climate change.

However, as this chapter demonstrates, some of the justifications for discriminatory or trade-restrictive aspects of emissions trading schemes are unrelated to the mitigation of climate change. Further, where such aspects are grounded in climate-related justifications, some seem weak, or at least open to argument. Countries maintaining these measures would need to do more than merely assert that, for instance, half of emissions reductions need to geographically occur within its territory, or that forestry activities are too difficult to measure to allow the generation and use of offset units. Rather, these assertions would need to have a firm foundation in evidence. The fact that differing countries take opposing approaches based on divergent rationales suggests that invoking climate-related exceptions could present an evidentiary challenge for respondents.

Otherwise, discriminatory or trade restrictive aspects of emissions trading schemes would need to excused by ad hoc exceptions, such as pertaining to mutual

[82] *Suez v Argentina (Decision on Liability)* (ICSID Arbitral Tribunal, Case No ARB/03/17, 30 July 2010) [128], [147]–[148]; *Fireman's Fund Insurance Company v Mexico (Award)* (ICSID Arbitral Award, Case No ARB(AF)/02/01, 17 July 2006) [176(j)]; *Saluka Investments v Czech Republic (Partial Award)* (Permanent Court of Arbitration, 17 March 2006) [254]–[255], [257]–[258], [261]–[262], [275]–[276]; *Técnicas Medioambientales Tecmed v Mexico (Award)* (ICSID Arbitral Tribunal, Case No ARB(AF)/00/2, 29 May 2003) [119], cf [121]; Cf *Patrick Mitchell v The Democratic Republic of Congo (Decision on Annulment)* (ICSID Ad Hoc Committee, Case No ARB//99/7, 1 November 2006) [53]; *Pope & Talbot v Canada (Interim Award)* (Ad hoc arbitration, UNCITRAL Rules, 26 June 2000) [99]; *Compañía del Desarrollo de Santa Elena v Costa Rica (Final Award)* (ICSID Arbitral Tribunal, Case No ARB/96/1, 17 February 2000) [71]–[72]. See further Tania Voon, James Munro, and Andrew Mitchell, 'Importing WTO General Exceptions into International Investment Agreements: Proportionality, Myths and Risks' *Yearbook on International Investment Law and Policy* (2018).

[83] Andrew Newcombe and Lluís Paradell, *Law and Practice of Investment Treaties* (Kluwer 2009) 499–505. Whether such policy space is effected through a general exception, or is embedded within the investment protection itself (as is normally the case) could have implications for how the burden of proof is allocated between a respondent and complainant. On that point, see further Caroline Henckels, 'Scope Limitation or Affirmative Defence? The Purpose and Role of Investment Treaty Exception Clauses' in Lorand Bartels and Federica Paddeu (eds), *Exceptions in International Law* (OUP forthcoming); Jorge E Viñuales, 'Seven ways of escaping a rule: Of exceptions and their avatars in international law' in Bartels and Paddeu (ibid); Joost Pauwelyn, 'Defenses and the Burden of Proof in International Law' in Bartels and Paddeu (ibid).

recognition arrangements, LDCs, or trade in fissionable material. While many of the discriminatory or trade-restrictive aspects of emissions trading schemes surveyed in Chapter 8 could be saved in this respect, this seems to be a coincidental outcome, rather than a deliberate and targeted tailoring of those measures to the policy space afforded in international economic law.

10
Conclusion

This book has sought to map out the interaction, in a direct sense, between international economic law and emissions trading schemes designed to reduce greenhouse gas emissions. With over eighty countries planning to engage in the international carbon market in fulfilment of their commitments under the Paris Agreement, and with the conversion of carbon units from domestic regulatory instruments into autonomous objects of international trade, this interaction will only become more acute in coming years.

In view of that interaction, it is obvious that emissions trading schemes are, on their face, conceptually aligned with international economic law. As market-based measures, emissions trading schemes pursue their environmental objective with a view to achieving the most efficient allocation of resources. In that regard, emissions trading schemes seek to facilitate the achievement of their environmental objective in the most cost-effective manner available. Since they are designed to achieve their objective by enabling the most cost-effective means of reducing greenhouse gas emissions, emissions trading schemes align with such principles as non-discrimination, eliminating arbitrary distortions in markets and capital flows, and securing property rights to facilitate transactions and investments that similarly underscore international economic law.

As illustrated in this book, however, this alignment of principles between emissions trading schemes and international economic law masks a deeper tension between, on the one hand, certainty, predictability, and efficiency in the market and, on the other, flexibility for governments or regulators to intervene. This tension is reflected in the fact that every emissions trading scheme surveyed in this thesis engages in some form of market intervention, such as differential treatment between carbon units based on their nature or jurisdiction of origin, quantitative restrictions that impose quotas or import bans on certain kinds of carbon units, and local content requirements prescribing the use of domestic carbon units. Further, this tension and these market interventions exist in a broader context where countries, traders, and investors have a real and substantial commercial interest in securing market access for their own carbon units in as many emissions trading schemes as possible.

Against that background, this book concludes that the objects traded within emissions trading schemes—namely, carbon units—are subject to the disciplines of international economic law in a series of complex and asymmetrical ways. Some findings are clear. Measures affecting trade in offset units are highly likely to qualify as measures affecting trade in services. Further, measures affecting trade in carbon units generally are highly likely to qualify as measures affecting the supply of financial services. Whether carbon units qualify as 'investments' under international economic law depends on their designation as 'property' under municipal law, and the degree of durability and permanence with which an investor acquires and owns the units in the host state.

As to whether carbon units qualify as 'goods'/'products', the analysis in this book concludes that tangibility is *not* a defining feature of 'goods'/'products'. This is based not only on a fresh interpretation of the terms, but also on existing WTO jurisprudence (albeit limited). How else to explain, for instance, the coverage of electricity in HS Codes and in WTO cases under GATT 1994? Rather, the ability to possess, own, store, and trade an item across borders through commercial transactions should suffice for the purposes of 'goods'/'products'. Carbon units exhibit all of those qualities. It is possible that a degree of human effort or labour must also be present in an item for it to qualify as 'goods'/'products', in which case offset units would qualify but not allowance units. If, on the other hand, the Appellate Body were to determine that tangibility is a defining feature of 'goods'/'products', it is clear that no carbon units would qualify. Such an interpretation would, however, have far-reaching consequences, leading to the wholesale exemption of major market segments, such as trade in digital products.[1] Further, it would directly contradict the existing WTO jurisprudence (albeit limited) on the coverage of intangible items such as electricity.

The significance of these conclusions is underlined by the volume and extent of prima facie inconsistencies exhibited by emissions trading schemes with international economic law. While the evidence available and justifications in respect of some of these inconsistencies suggests that they might be saved by certain public policy-related exceptions in international economic law, it is equally apparent that many would not be shielded.

Thus, as emissions trading schemes continue to proliferate as the policy instrument of choice for mitigating climate change, and as carbon units increasingly become items of international commerce through the linking of domestic emissions trading schemes, governments and regulators will need to be alert to the prospect that aspects of their schemes violate international economic law. While emissions trading schemes are certainly capable of being designed and administered in a manner consistent with international economic law, this book demonstrates that many, at present, are not.

The potential means by which jurisdictions might inoculate their emissions trading schemes from the reach of international economic law are worthy of further research. For instance, if an emissions trading scheme were to prohibit the import or export of carbon units, it may be difficult to characterize those units as objects of international trade. Rather, the insulation of that scheme from any external transactions would likely mean that its carbon units are more properly characterized as purely domestic regulatory instruments.

[1] See James Munro, 'Pushing the boundaries of "products" and "goods" under GATT 1994: An analysis of the coverage of new and unorthodox articles of commerce' (2013) 47 *Journal of World Trade* 1323.

As another example, if an emissions trading scheme were to denude its carbon units of proprietary status and expressly embed an ability for those units to be revoked or cancelled by the regulator for any reason, it may be difficult to characterize those units as items of commerce that are susceptible to exclusive ownership and use, and that have a degree of stability and permanence.

Further, if two or more jurisdictions framed the acceptance of each other's carbon units for compliance purposes as a matter of mutual recognition of each other's technical regulations or standards under international economic law, the burden of proof would likely shift to a complainant country seeking market access to prove that its carbon units meet the requisite standards in order to gain market access. Until that country could adequately demonstrate that its units meet the requisite standards, it would be permissible to discriminate against those units pursuant to a mutual recognition arrangement with other jurisdictions. In a similar vein, trade in carbon units between two jurisdictions could be framed within the rubric of a broader free trade agreement between those jurisdictions, which could also permit discrimination vis-à-vis third countries under international economic law.

Thus, carbon units themselves could be designed in such a way as to lessen the potential that they could be subject to international economic law. Similarly, their trade between jurisdictions could be structured in such a manner as to permit discrimination against the units of third countries. The feasibility of these kinds of innovations would likely be a valuable source of future research on the engagement between emissions trading schemes and international economic law—particularly as international emissions trading begins to develop and mature under the Paris Agreement.

Bibliography

Abu-Akeel, A K, 'Definition of trade in services under GATS: Legal implications' (1999) *32 The George Washington Journal of International Law & Economics* 189

Adlung, R, and Mattoo, A, 'GATS' in Mattoo, A, Stern, R, and Zanini, G (eds), *A Handbook of International Trade in Services* (OUP 2008)

Ahmad, N, and Verrinder, J, *OECD/EUROSTAT Task Force on the Treatment of Emission Allowances and Emission Permits in the National Accounts: Final Report* (Joint OECD/EUROSTAT Publication 2010)

Anderson, T, and Grewell, B, 'Property Rights Solutions for the Global Commons: Bottom-up or Top-down?' (1999) 10(13) *Duke Environmental Law & Policy Forum* 73

Anttonen, K, Mehling, M, and Upston-Hooper, K, 'Breathing Life into the Carbon Market' (2007) 16 *European Environmental Law Review* 96

Australian Government, *Carbon Pollution Reduction Scheme: Australia's Low Pollution Future* (Commonwealth of Australia, Vol 1, 2008)

Australian Government, *2017 Review of Climate Change Policies* (Department of Energy and Environment, December 2017)

Bank of England, 'Legal assessment of lacunae in the legal framework of the European Emissions Trading Scheme and the case for legislative reform' (Issue 1116, Financial Markets Law Committee, October 2009)

Barrieu, P, and Fehr, M, 'Integrated EUA and CER price modeling and application for spread option pricing' (Working Paper No 50, Centre for Climate Change Economics and Policy, March 2011)

Bartens, F, 'The Kyoto Protocol in Investor-State Arbitration: Reconciling Climate Change and Investment Protection Objectives' in Cordonnier Segger, M-C, Gehring, M, and Newcombe, A (eds), *Sustainable Development in World Investment Law* (Kluwer 2011) 681–716

Baylis, K, and Allan, T, 'Who Owns Carbon? Property Rights Issues in a Market for Green House Gasses' (2005) 7 *Current Agriculture, Food and Resource Issues* 104

Bennett, L, 'Are Tradable Carbon Emissions Credits Investments? Characterization and Ramifications under International Investment Law' (2010) 85 *New York University Law Review* 1581

Black, J, 'The Role of Risk in Regulatory Processes' in Robert Baldwin, Martin Cave, and Martin Lodge (eds), *The Oxford Handbook of Regulation* (OUP 2010) ch 14

Bloomberg New Energy Finance, *South Korea's Emissions Trading Scheme: White Paper* (Report Prepared by Ernst & Young, 10 May 2013)

Bodansky, D, 'The United Nations Framework Convention on Climate Change: A Commentary' (1993) 18 *Yale Journal of International Law* 451

Boute, A, 'Combating Climate Change through Investment Arbitration' (2012) 35 *Fordham International Law Journal* 613

Bromley, D, *Environment and Economy: Property Rights and Public Policy* (Blackwell 1991)

Brownlie, I, *Principles of Public International Law* (6th edn, OUP 2003)

Button, J, 'Carbon: Commodity or Currency? The Case for an International Carbon Market Based on the Currency Model' (2008) 32 *Harvard Environmental Law Review* 571

California Air Resources Board, 'Air Resources Board amends cap and trade program, enhances market security' (News Release, 12–27, 28 June 2012)

California Air Resources Board, 'Chapter 6: What are the requirements for offset credits and how are they issued?' in *Cap-and-Trade Regulation Instructional Guidance* (California Air Resources Board 2012)

California Air Resources Board, *Compliance Offset Protocol Capturing and Destroying Methane from Manure Management Systems* (adopted 20 October 2011)

California Air Resources Board, *Compliance Offset Protocol Urban Forest Projects* (adopted 20 October 2011)

California Air Resources Board, *Compliance Offset Protocol U.S. Forest Projects* (adopted 20 October 2011)

California Air Resources Board, 'What Are the Requirements for Offset Credits and How Are They Issued?' in *Cap-and-Trade Regulation Instructional Guidance* (2012)

Capoor, K, and Ambrosi, P, *State and Trends of the Carbon Market 2008* (World Bank 2008)

Capoor, K, and Ambrosi, P, *State and Trends of the Carbon Market 2009* (World Bank 2009)

Carbon Limits and Thomas Reuters Point Carbon, 'The Domestic Emissions Trading Scheme in Kazakhstan' (Discussion Paper, European Bank for Reconstruction and Development, 2013)

Cook, G, *A Digest of WTO Jurisprudence on Public International Law Concepts and Principles* (CUP 2015)

Charnovitz, S, 'Trade and Climate: Potential Conflicts and Synergies' in Pew Centre on Global Climate Change, *Beyond Kyoto: Advancing the International Effort Against Climate Change* (2003)

Chichilnisky, G, 'International payments for ecosystem services: Principles and practices' in Thomas Koellner (ed), *Ecosystem Services and Global Trade of Natural Resources* (2011) 204–24

Choi, W, *Like Products in International Trade Law* (OUP 2003)

Cole, D, 'Clearing the Air: Four Propositions about Property Rights and Environmental Protection' (1999) 10(13) *Duke Environmental Law & Policy Forum* 103

Cole, D, 'Origins of Emissions Trading in Theory and Early Practice' in Weishaar, S (ed), *Research Handbook on Emissions Trading* (Edward Elgar Publishing 2016) 9–26

Commission of the European Communities, *Building a Global Climate Change Alliance between the European Union and Poor Developing Countries Most Vulnerable to Climate Change* (COM(2007) 540, 18 September 2007)

Commission of the European Communities, *Green Paper on greenhouse gas emissions trading within the European Union* (COM(2000) 87 final, 8 March 2000)

Condon, B, and Sinha, T, *The Role of Climate Change in Global Economic Governance* (OUP 2013)

Conrad, C, *Processes and Production Methods (PPMs) in WTO Law* (CUP 2011)

Copeland, B, and Taylor, MS, 'Trade, Tragedy, and the Commons' (2009) 99 *American Economic Review* 725

Dales, J H, 'Land, Water, and Ownership' (1968) 1 *Canadian Journal of Economics* 791

de Cendra, J, 'Can Emissions Trading Schemes Be Coupled with Border Tax Adjustments? An Analysis vis-a-vis WTO Law' (2006) 15 *Review of European Community & International Environmental Law* 131

de Cendra de Larragan, J, 'Emissions trading schemes and WTO law: a typology of interactions' in Van Calster, G, and Prevost, D (eds), *Research Handbook on Environment, Health and the WTO* (Edward Elgar Publishing 2013) 636–69

Deane, F, *Emissions Trading and WTO Law* (Edward Elgar Publishing 2015)

Deatherage, S, *Carbon Trading Law and Practice* (OUP 2011)

Delaunay, J, and Gadrey, J, *Services in Economic Thought: Three Centuries of Debate* (Springer 1992)

Deleuil, T, 'The Common but Differentiated Responsibilities Principle: Changes in Continuity after the Durban Conference of the Parties' (2012) 21 *Review of European Community and International Environmental Law* 271

Department of Climate Change and Energy Efficiency, *Carbon Farming Initiative Handbook* (Commonwealth of Australia 2012)

Department of Climate Change and Energy Efficiency, *Implementing links to overseas emissions trading schemes—Draft legislation Explanatory Note* (31 August 2012)

Department of Climate Change and Energy Efficiency and Directorate General for Climate Action, *Registry options to facilitate linking of emissions trading systems: Consultation paper* (Joint Publication of the European Commission and Australian Government 2013)

Department of Environment, 'Australia and New Zealand advance linking of their emissions trading schemes' (Media Release, GC 333/11, 5 December 2011)

Di Benedetto, S, *International Investment Law and the Environment* (Edward Elgar Publishing 2013)

Diebold, N, *Non-Discrimination in International Trade in Services* (CUP 2010)

Dolzer, R, and Schreuer, C, *Principles of International Investment Law* (OUP 2012)

Douglas, Z, 'The Hybrid Foundation of Investment Treaty Arbitration' (2003) 74 *British Yearbook of International Law* 151

Douglas, Z, *The International Law of Investment Claims* (CUP 2009)

Dugan, C, Wallace D Jr, Rubins, N, and Sabahi, B, *Investor-State Arbitration* (OUP 2008)

EC, IMF, OECD, UN, and World Bank, *System of National Accounts 2008* (United Nations 2008)

Eckersley, R, 'Understanding the Interplay between the Climate and Trade Regimes' in Benjamin Simmons, Harro van Asselt, and Fariborz Zelli (eds), *Climate and Trade Policies in a Post-2012 World* (UNEP 2009) 11–18

Emissions Trading Scheme Review Panel, *Doing New Zealand's Fair Share. Emissions Trading Scheme Review 2011: Final Report* (Ministry for the Environment 2011)

Eni-Ibukun, TA, *International Environmental Law and Distributive Justice: The Equitable Distribution of CDM Projects under the Kyoto Protocol* (Routledge 2013)

European Commission, 'Emissions trading: Commission announces linkage EU ETS with Norway, Iceland and Liechtenstein' (Media Release, IP/07/1617, 26 October 2007)

European Commission, 'Review of the Markets in Financial Instruments Directive (MiFID) and Proposals for a Regulation on Market Abuse and for a Directive on Criminal Sanctions for Market Abuse: Frequently Asked Questions on Emission Allowances' (Memo/11/719, 20 October 2011)

European Commission, 'Report from the Commission to the European Parliament and the Council: The state of the European carbon market in 2012' (Report COM(2012) 652 final, 2012)

European Commission, 'FAQ: Linking the Australian and European Union emissions trading systems' (Memo, 12/631, 28 August 2012)

European Commission, 'Impact Assessment: Accompanying the document Communication from the Commission to the European Parliament, the Council, the European Economic and Social Committee and the Committee of the Regions A policy framework for climate and energy in the period from 2020 up to 2030' (Staff Working Document, SWD/2014/015 final)

European Commission, the Hon Greg Combet AM MP, 'Australia and European Commission Agree on Pathway Towards Fully Linking Emissions Trading Schemes' (Media Release, 28 August 2012)

European Court of Auditors, 'The Integrity and Implementation of the EU ETS' (Special Report No 6, 2015)

European Environment Agency, *Application of the Emissions Trading Directive by EU Member States—reporting year 2008* (Office for Official Publications of the European Communities 2008)

Executive Board of the Clean Development Mechanism, 'Sixty-Second Meeting Report' (15 July 2011) CDM-EB-62

Executive Board of the Clean Development Mechanism, 'Annual report of the Executive Board of the clean development mechanism to the Conference of the Parties serving as the meeting of the Parties to the Kyoto Protocol' (12 November 2015) FCCC/KP/CMP/2015/5

Executive Board of the Clean Development Mechanism, 'Annual report of the Executive Board of the clean development mechanism to the Conference of the Parties serving as the meeting of the Parties to the Kyoto Protocol' (19 October 2017) FCCC/KP/CMP/2017/5

Fernandes, D, 'Twins, Siblings or Friends: The Conceptual Case of Goods and Services, Where Do We Stand and Where Could We Be Headed To?' in Alexander, K, and Andenas, M (eds), *The World Trade Organization and Trade in Services* (Brill 2008) 119–60

Firger, D, and Gerrard, M, 'Harmonizing Climate Change Policy and International Investment Law: Threats, Challenges and Opportunities' in Sauvant, K (ed), *Yearbook on International Investment Law and Policy 2010-11* (OUP 2011) ch 13

Franck, S, 'The Legitimacy Crisis in Investment Treaty Arbitration: Privatizing Public International Law through Inconsistent Decisions' (2005) 73 *Fordham Law Review* 1521

Garnaut, R, *The Garnaut Climate Change Review* (2008)

GATT Secretariat, 'Trade in Services and the GATT: Background Paper by the Secretariat' (6 March 1981) CG.18/49

GATT Secretariat, 'Services Sectoral Classification List: Note by the Secretariat' (10 July 1991) MTN.GNS/W/120

GATT Secretariat, 'Scheduling of Initial Commitments in Trade in Services: Explanatory Note' (3 September 1993) MTN.GNS/W/164

Gayer, T, and Horowitz, J, 'Market-based Approaches to Environmental Regulation' (2006) 1(4) *Foundations and Trends in Microeconomics* 201

Gehring, M, and Streck, C, 'Emissions Trading: Lessons From SO_x and NO_x Emissions Allowance and Credit Systems Legal Nature, Title, Transfer, and Taxation of Emission Allowances and Credits' (2005) 35 *Environmental Law Reporter* 10219

Godard, O, *Domestic Transferable Permits for Environmental Management: Design and Implementation* (OECD 2001)

Godard, O, 'Domestic Transferable Permits: Summary of Lessons Learned' in *Implementing Domestic Tradeable Permits: Recent Developments and Future Challenges* (OECD 2002)

Government of Japan, *Recent Development of the Joint Crediting Mechanism (JCM)* (January 2017)

Grant, S, and Quiggin, J, 'Climate Change and the Precautionary Principle' in John Quiggin, et al (eds), *Carbon Pricing: Early Experiences and Future Prospects* (Edward Elgar Publishing 2014) 167–79

Grosz, M, *Sustainable Waste Trade under WTO Law* (Brill 2011)

Hammick, K, and Gallant, M, *State and Trends of Voluntary Carbon Markets 2017* (Ecosystem Marketplace 2017)

Hedges, A, 'The Secondary Market for Emissions Trading' in David Freestone and Charlotte Streck (eds), *Legal Aspects of Carbon Trading: Kyoto, Copenhagen, and beyond* (OUP 2009) 311–34

Higgins, R, 'The Taking of Property by the State: Recent Developments in International Law' (1982) 176 *Recueil des Cours* 263

Hill, P, 'On Goods and Services' (1977) 23(4) *Review of Income and Wealth* 315

Hill, P, 'Tangibles, intangibles and services: a new taxonomy for the classification of output' in Kariyawasam, R (ed), *The WTO, Intellectual Property, E-Commerce and the Internet* (Edward Elgar Publishing 2009)

Hindley, B, 'Principles in Factor-related Trade in Services' in Messerlin, P, and Sauvant, P (eds) *The Uruguay Round: Services in the World Economy* (World Bank 1990) 12–19

Hirsch, M, 'Investment Tribunals and Human Rights: Divergent Paths' in Dupuy, P, Petersmann, E, and Francioni, F (eds), *Human Rights in International Investment Law and Arbitration* (OUP 2009) 98–114

Howse, R, and Eliason, E, 'Carbon Trading and the CDM in WTO Law' in Stewart, R, Kingsbury, B, and Rudyk, B (eds), *Climate Finance: Regulatory and Funding Strategies for Climate Change and Global Development* (NYU Press 2009) 254–58

Howse, R, and Eliason, A, 'Domestic and international strategies to address climate change: an overview of the WTO legal issues' in Cottier, T, Nartova, O, and Bigdeli, S (eds), *International Trade Regulation and the Mitigation of Climate Change* (CUP 2010) 48–92

Intergovernmental Panel on Climate Change, *Special Report on Land Use, Land-Use Change, and Forestry* (2000) http://www.ipcc.ch/ipccreports/sres/land_use/index.php?idp=78

International Emissions Trading Association and Environment Defense Fund, *Kazakhstan* (September 2013) http://www.ieta.org/assets/Reports/EmissionsTradingAroundTheWorld/edf_ieta_kazakhstan_case_study_may_2013.pdf

International Law Commission, 'Report of the International Law Commission on its Fifty-eight Session (Fragmentation of International Law: Difficulties Arising from the Diversification and Expansion of International Law)' (13 April 2006) UN Doc A/CN.4/L.682

International Monetary Fund, *Balance of Payments and International Investment Position Manual* (6th edn, IMF 2009)

Islam, MR, *International Trade Law of the WTO* (OUP 2006)

Jegou, I, and Rubini, L, 'The Allocation of Emission Allowances Free of Charge: Legal and Economic Considerations' (ICTSD Issue Paper, No 18, August 2011)

Jeżewski, M, 'Development Considerations in Defining Investment' in Cordonnier Segger, M-C, Gehring, M, and Newcombe, A (eds), *Sustainable Development in World Investment Law* (Kluwer 2011) 211–35

Jinnah, S, 'Emissions trading under the Kyoto Protocol: NAFTA and WTO concerns' (2003) 15 *Georgetown International Environmental Law Review* 709

Joint Implementation Supervisory Committee, 'Annual report of the Joint Implementation Supervisory Committee to the Conference of the Parties serving as the meeting of the Parties to the Kyoto Protocol' (16 October 2015) FCCC/KP/CMP/2015/4

Kallbekken, S, 'Observations from the climate negotiations in Durban, South Africa' in Cherry, T, Hovi, J, and McEvoy, D (eds), *Towards a New Climate Agreement: Conflict, Resolution and Governance* (Routledge 2014)

Kariyawasam, R, 'The classification of electronic intangibles in the WTO' in Kariyawasam, R (ed), *The WTO, Intellectual Property, E-Commerce and the Internet* (Edward Elgar Publishing 2009)

Kaufmann-Kohler, G, 'Interpretation of Treaties: How Do Arbitral Tribunals Interpret Dispute Settlement Provisions Embodied in Investment Treaties?' in Mistelis, L, and Lew, J (eds), *Pervasive Problems in International Arbitration* (Kluwer 2006) 257–76

Kitamori, K, 'Domestic GHG Emissions Trading Schemes: Recent Developments and Current Status in Selected OECD Countries' in *Implementing Domestic Tradeable Permits: Recent Developments and Future Challenges* (OECD 2002)

Kossoy, A, et al, *Mapping Carbon Pricing Initiatives: Developments and Prospects* (World Bank 2013)

Kossoy, A, et al, *State and Trends of Carbon Pricing 2014* (World Bank 2014)

Kossoy, A, and Ambrosi, P, *State and Trends of the Carbon Market Report 2011* (World Bank 2011)

Kossoy, A, and Guigon, P, *State and Trends of the Carbon Market Report 2012* (World Bank 2012)

Krajewski, M, 'Public Services and the Scope of the General Agreement on Trade in Services (GATS)' (Research Paper, Center for International Environment Law 2001)

Kruikman, P, et al, *Policy options for including LULUCF in the EU reduction commitment and policy instruments for increasing GHG mitigation efforts in the LULUCF and agriculture sectors: Synthesis Report* (Report commissioned by European Commission, November 2006)

Krukowska, E, 'EU Adopts Emergency Carbon Fix Law to Curb Permit Glut' *Bloomberg* (17 December 2013)

Law, J (ed), *A Dictionary of Finance and Banking* (5th edn, OUP 2014)

Leake Quinn, E, 'The Solitary Attempt: International Trade Law and the Insulation of Domestic Greenhouse Gas Trading Schemes from Foreign Emissions Credit Markets' (2009) 80 *University of Colorado Law Review* 201

Levine, J, and Chan, K, 'Global human dependence on ecosystem services' in Koellner, T (ed), *Ecosystem Services and Global Trade of Natural Resources* (Routledge 2011) 11–29

Lin, J, 'Private Actors in International and Domestic Emissions Trading Schemes' in David Freestone and Charlotte Streck (eds), *Legal Aspects of Carbon Trading: Kyoto, Copenhagen, and beyond* (OUP 2009) 134–54

Lockie, D, 'Closing Pandora's Box: The Case for Carbon Market Integrity after the Global Financial Crisis—Conditioning Ownership of the Right to Emit Greenhouse Gases in an Australian Emissions Trading Scheme' (PhD Thesis, Bond University 2011)

Ludlow, M, 'International carbon permits may be fast-tracked' *Australian Financial Review* (23 September 2015)

Mace, M J, 'The Legal Nature of Emission Reductions and EU Allowances: Issues Addressed in an International Workshop' (2005) 2 *Journal of European Environmental and Planning Law* 123

Mace, M J, and Anderson, J, 'Legal and Design Issues Arising in Linking the EU ETS with Existing and Emerging Emissions Trading Schemes (2009) 6 *Journal of European Environment and Planning Law* 197

Martin, M, 'Trade Law Implications for Restricting Participation in The European Union Emissions Trading Scheme' (2006) *Georgetown International Environmental Law Review* 437

Matsushita, M, Schoenbaum, S, and Mavroidis, P, *The World Trade Organization: Law, Practice, and Policy* (OUP 2003)

Mavroidis, P, *Trade in Goods* (OUP 2007)

Mehling, M, 'Linking of Emissions Trading Schemes' in David Freestone and Charlotte Streck (eds), *Legal Aspects of Carbon Trading: Kyoto, Copenhagen, and beyond* (OUP 2009) 109–33

Mitchell, A, and Munro, J, 'State-State Dispute Settlement under the Trans-Pacific Partnership Agreement' in Voon, T (ed), *Trade Liberalisation and International Co-operation: A Legal Analysis of the Trans-Pacific Partnership Agreement* (Edward Elgar Publishing 2014) 156–78

Mitchell, A, and Munro, J, 'Someone Else's Deal: Interpreting International Investment Agreements in the Light of Third-Party Agreements' (2017) 28 *European Journal of International Law* 3

Mizrach, B, 'Integration of the Global Emissions Trading Markets' (Working Paper, Rutgers University, December 2009)

Munro, J, 'Pushing the boundaries of 'products' and 'goods' under GATT 1994: An analysis of the coverage of new and unorthodox articles of commerce' (2013) 47 *Journal of World Trade* 1323

Munro, J, 'Climate Change in the Trans-Pacific Partnership and Transatlantic Trade and Investment Partnership' in Delimitas, P (ed), *Research Handbook on International Trade and Climate Change* (Routledge 2017) 394–411

Nazifi, F, 'Modelling the price spread between EUA and CER carbon prices' (2013) 56 *Energy Policy* 434

New Forests, 'The California Carbon Market: Implications for Forest Carbon Offset Investments' (2012) 2; American Carbon Registry, 'Compliance Offset Supply Forecast For California's Cap-and-Trade Program (2013-2012)' (2012)

New Zealand Government, *The Framework for a New Zealand Emissions Trading Scheme* (2007)

New Zealand Government, *Consultation on proposed regulations restricting the use of certain international units in the NZ ETS* (Ministry of Environment, November 2012)

New Zealand Government, *New Zealand Emissions Trading Scheme Review 2015/16* (Ministry for the Environment, November 2015)

Newcombe, A, and Paradell, J, *Law and Practice of Investment Treaties* (Kluwer 2009)

Norwegian Ministry of the Environment, *Norwegian National Allocation Plan for the Emissions Trading System in 2008–2012* (March 2008)

Panayotou, T, *Economic Instruments for Environmental Management and Sustainable Development* (Environmental Economics Series Paper No 16, United Nations Environment Program 1994)

Partnership for Market Readiness and Forest Carbon Partnership Facility, *Emissions Trading Registries: Guidance on Regulation, Development, and Administration* (World Bank 2016)

Pauwelyn, J, *Conflict of Norms in Public International Law: How WTO Law Relates to other Rules of International Law* (CUP 2003)

Pauwelyn, J, 'The End of Differential Treatment for Developing Countries? Lessons from the Trade and Climate Change Regimes' (2013) 22 *Review of European Community and International Environmental Law* 29

Petsonk, A, 'The Kyoto Protocol and the WTO: Integrating Greenhouse Gas Emissions Allowance Trading into the Global Marketplace' (1999) 10 *Duke Environmental Law and Policy Forum* 185

Platjouw, F, 'Reducing Greenhouse Gas Emissions at Home or Abroad? The Implications of Kyoto's Supplementarity Requirement for the Present and Future Climate Change Regime' (2009) 18 *Review of European Community and International Environmental Law* 245

Rajamani, L, 'The changing fortunes of differential treatment in the evolution of international environmental law' (2012) 88 *International Affairs* 605

Reinisch, A, 'Expropriation' in Peter Muchlinski, Federico Ortino, and Christoph Schreuer (eds), *The Oxford Handbook of International Investment Law* (OUP 2011)

Reuters Point Carbon, 'Ukraine and Kazakhstan eye linkage of ETSs with EU scheme' (Press Release, 12 October 2012)

Sanehi, A, 'Market Contracts' in Watchman, P (ed), *Climate Change—A Guide to Carbon Law and Practice* (Globe Law and Business 2008)

Sasson, M, *Substantive Law in Investment Treaty Arbitration: The Unsettled Relationship between International Law and Municipal Law* (Kluwer 2010)

Schiele, S, *Evolution of International Environmental Regimes: The Case of Climate Change* (CUP 2014)

Schofield, N, *Commodity Derivatives* (John Wiley & Sons 2008)

Schreuer, C, 'The Relevance of Public International Law in International Commercial Arbitration: Investment Disputes' (Unpublished Paper, University of Vienna)

Schwartz, J, et al, 'Republic of Korea: An Emissions Trading Case Study' (IETA, EDF, SFOC, CRIK Joint Publication 2016)

Shih, W, 'Legal nature of the traded units under the emissions trading systems and its implication to the relationship between emissions trading and the WTO' (National Chengchi University 2011)

Smith, F, and Woods, L, 'A Distinction Without a Difference: Exploring the Boundary Between Goods and Services in the World Trade Organization and the European Union' (2005) 12 *Columbia Journal of European Law* 1

Snape, R, 'Principles in Trade in Services' in Messerlin, P, and Sauvant, K, *The Uruguay Round: Services in the World Economy* (World Bank 1990)

Soltau, F, *Fairness in International Climate Change Law and Policy* (CUP 2011)

Sornarajah, M, *The International Law on Foreign Investment* (3rd edn, CUP 2010)

Spoorenberg, F, and Vinuales, J, 'Conflicting Decisions in International Arbitration' (2009) 8 *The Law and Practice of International Courts and Tribunals* 91

Stern, N, *Stern Review: The Economics of Climate Change* (CUP 2007)

Tietenberg, T, 'Tradable Permits in Principle and Practice' in Jody Freedman and Charles D Kolstad (eds), *Moving to Markets in Environmental Regulation* (2007)

Trebilcock, M, Howse, R, and Eliason, A, *The Regulation of International Trade* (4th edn, Routledge 2012)

UN, IMF, OECD, WTO, UNCTAD, EuroStat, UNWTO, *Manual on Statistics of International Trade in Services 2010*, ST/ESA/M.86/Rev.1 (United Nations 2011)

UNCTAD, 'Scope and Definition' (UNCTAD Series on Issues in International Investment Agreements II, United Nations 2011)

UNFCCC Secretariat, Ad Hoc Working Group on Long-term Cooperative Action (14th sess), 'Views on the elaboration of market-based mechanisms: Submissions from Parties' (Ad Hoc Working Group on Long-term Cooperative Action, 14th sess) FCCC/AWGLCA/2011/MISC.2

UNFCCC Secretariat, 'Financing options for the full implementation of results based actions relating to the activities referred to in decision 1/CP.16, paragraph 70, including related modalities and procedures: Technical Paper' (26 July 2012) FCCC/TP/2012/3

UNFCCC Secretariat, 'Framework for various approaches: Technical Paper' (25 November 2014) FCCC/TP/2014/9

UNFCCC Secretariat, 'Ideas and proposals on the elements contained in paragraph 1 of the Bali Action Plan Submissions from Parties Addendum' (7 April 2009) FCCC/AWGLCA/2009/MISC.1/Add.4

UNFCCC Secretariat, 'Implications of the establishment of new hydrochlorofluorocarbon-22 (HCFC-22) facilities seeking to obtain certified emission reductions for the destruction of hydrofluorocarbon-23 (HFC-23): Submissions from Parties' (23 August 2006) (Subsidiary Body for Scientific and Technological Advice, 25th sess) FCCC/SBSTA/2006/MISC.11

UNFCCC Secretariat, 'Issues arising from the implementation of potential project activities under the clean development mechanism: the case of incineration of HFC-23 waste streams from HCFC-22 production: Technical paper' (26 April 2005) FCCC/TP/2005/1

UNFCCC Secretariat, 'Proposal from Papua New Guinea for amendments to the Kyoto Protocol' (17 June 2009) FCCC/KP/CMP/2009/13

UNFCCC Secretariat, 'Report on the workshop on the new market-based mechanism' (30 October 2013) FCCC/SBSTA/2013/INF.13

UNFCCC Secretariat, 'Views on a framework for various approaches' (7 May 2013) FCCC/SBSTA/2013/MISC.11

UNFCCC Secretariat, 'Views on issues relating to modalities and procedures for applying the concept of additionality' (14 October 2013) FCCC/SBSTA/2013/MISC.19

United States Environmental Protection Agency, *Acid Rain Program SO2 Allowances Fact Sheet* http://www.epa.gov/airmarkets/trading/factsheet.html

Van Asselt, H, *The Fragmentation of Global Climate Governance* (Edward Elgar Publishing 2014)

Van Damme, I, *Treaty Interpretation by the WTO Appellate Body* (OUP 2009)

Van den Bossche, P, *The Law and Policy of the World Trade Organization* (CUP 2008)

Voigt, C, 'WTO Law and International Emissions Trading: Is There Potential for Conflict?' (2008) 1 *Carbon & Climate Law Review* 54

Voigt, C, *Sustainable Development as a Principle of International Law* (Brill 2009)

Voon, T, 'Sizing Up the WTO: Trade-Environment Conflict and the Kyoto Protocol' (2000) 10(1) *Journal of Transnational Law & Policy* 71

Voon, T, James Munro, and Andrew Mitchell, 'Importing WTO General Exceptions into International Investment Agreements: Proportionality, Myths and Risks' (2018) *Yearbook on International Investment Law and Policy* (forthcoming)

Vranes, E, 'Climate Change and the WTO: EU Emission Trading and the WTO Disciplines on Trade in Goods, Services and Investment Protection' (2009) 43 *Journal of World Trade* 707

Waibel, M, 'International Investment Law and Treaty Interpretation' in Hoffman, R, and Tams, C (eds), *International Investment Law and General International Law: From Clinical Isolation to Systemic Integration?* (Nomos 2011)

Weber, R, and Burri, M, *Classification of Services in the Digital Economy* (Springer 2012)

Weeramantry, JR, *Treaty Interpretation in Investment Arbitration* (OUP 2012) 205–06

Weishaar, S, *Emissions Trading Design* (Edward Elgar Publishing 2014)

Wemaere, M, Streck, C, and Chagas, T, 'Legal Ownership and Nature of Kyoto Units and EU Allowances' in David Freestone and Charlotte Streck (eds), *Legal Aspects of Carbon Trading: Kyoto, Copenhagen and beyond* (OUP 2009) 36–58

Werksman, J, 'Greenhouse Gas Emissions Trading and the WTO' (1999) 8 *Review of European Community & International Environmental Law* 251

Werksman, J, Baumert, K, and Dubash, N, 'Will International Investment Rules Obstruct Climate Protection Policies?' (2003) 3 *International Environmental Agreements: Politics, Law & Economics* 59

Western Climate Initiative, *Recommendations for the WCI Regional Cap-and-Trade Program* (23 September 2008)

Western Climate Initiative, *Design for the WCI Regional Program: Detailed Design* (2010)

Wilder, M, 'Nature of an Allowance' in Watchman, P (ed), *Climate Change—A Guide to Carbon Law and Practice* (Global Business Publishing 2008)

Wilder, M, and Fitz-Gerald, L, 'Carbon Contracting' in David Freestone and Charlotte Streck (eds), *Legal Aspects of Carbon Trading: Kyoto, Copenhagen and beyond* (OUP 2009) 445–68

Windon, J, 'The Allocation of Free Emissions Units and the WTO Subsidies Agreement' (2010) 41 *Georgetown Journal of International Law* 189

Wiser, G, 'Frontiers in Trade: the Clean Development Mechanism and the General Agreement on Trade in Services' (2002) 2 *International Journal of Global Environmental Issues* 288

Wiser, G, 'The Clean Development Mechanism Versus the World Trade Organization: Can Free-Market Greenhouse Gas Emissions Abatement Survive Free Trade?' (1999) 11 *Georgetown International Environmental Law Review* 531

Wolfrum, R, Stoll, P, and Feinaugle, C, *WTO—Trade in Services* (Brill 2008)

World Bank, Ecofys and Vivid Economics, *State and Trends of Carbon Pricing 2017* (World Bank 2017)

World Customs Organization, *HS Nomenclature 2012 Edition* (WCO 2012)

WTO Secretariat, *Guide to GATS: An Overview of Issues for Further Liberalization of Trade in Services* (Kluwer 2001)

Yamin, F, and Depledge, J, *The International Climate Change Regime: A Guide to Rules, Institutions and Procedures* (CUP 2004)

Yannaca-Small, K (ed), *Arbitration under International Investment Agreements: A Guide to the Key Issues* (OUP 2010)

Yannaca-Small, K, *International Investment Law: Understanding Concepts and Tracking Innovations* (OECD 2008)

Young, M, 'Introduction: The Productive Friction Between Regimes' in Margaret A. Young (ed.), *Regime Interaction in International Law: Facing Fragmentation* (CUP 2012) 1–20

Young, M, 'Principle 12: The Environment and Trade' in Vinuales, J (ed), *The Rio Declaration on Environment and Development* (OUP 2015) 325–47

Zdouc, W, 'Legal Problems arising under the General Agreement on Trade in Services: Comparative analysis of GATS and GATT' (PhD Thesis, Universität St Gallen 2002)

Zhang, Z, 'Carbon Emissions Trading in China: The Evolution from Pilots to a Nationwide Scheme' (CCEP Working Paper No 1503, Australian National University April 2015)

Zhang, M, Liu, Y, and Su, Y, 'Comparison of Carbon Emission Trading Schemes in the European Union and China' (College of Management and Economics, Tianjin University, Tianjin, September 2017)

Index

The manufacturer's authorised representative in the EU for product safety is Oxford University Press España S.A. of el Parque Empresarial San Fernando de Henares, Avenida de Castilla, 2 – 28830 Madrid (www.oup.es/en or product.safety@oup.com). OUP España S.A. also acts as importer into Spain of products made by the manufacturer.

www.ingramcontent.com/pod-product-compliance
Lightning Source LLC
LaVergne TN
LVHW011801200926
848484LV00003B/755

* 9 7 8 0 1 9 8 8 2 8 7 0 9 *